ADVANCE PRAISE FOR

Smart Relationships is a welcome departure from the plethora of simplistic self-help books that line bookstore shelves and sit on page after page of online bookstores. Dr. Wish is a leading authority on the love issues of today's women and a thoughtful researcher who interviewed thousands of women over a number of years to write what will certainly be the must-have book of the decade for real women in real love relationships. This book is their story and YOUR story, and offers practical exercises, easy-to-understand charts that offer mind-blowing insights and page after page of solid, reliable content, and a much needed view of the real state of women's intimate relationships! If you only buy one book this year, make it *Smart Relationships.*

—*Jackie Black, PhD, BCC, internationally recognized relationship expert and author of* LOVE Like a BLACK BELT: Cracking the Code to Being a Happy Couple.

Even the savviest women can stumble in their desire to find true love. Just as Dr. Wish advised women about love with her charming cartoon book, *The Love Adventures of Almost Smart Cookie*, once again, with her new book, Dr. Wish proves to be an innovative and deeply informative educator about women and love. The insightful strategies she uses are spot on. Dr. Wish elaborates with ease and understanding, as well as highly sensible and usable advice. As a dating coach, I recognize the problems that her research has uncovered. All busy women can benefit from this book, which also includes some of her fun cartoons that teach with solid help and findings that will really open women's eyes to their love patterns.

—*Betty Russell, CC, BCC, Dating Expert, Coach, and Educator, www.BeFreeToLove.com*

Just as we would expect from Dr. Wish, she continues to provide women with an effective, inventive and highly informative way to reach and teach about their most common love traps. And what an extra bonus that *Smart Relationships* includes some of her wise, fun and right-on-the-mark tips about top dating and relationship issues—like falling for individuals who demand too much or give too little. Dr. Wish writes from both her research findings and her heart.

—*Jodi Rigotti, Senior Editor, www.QualityHealth.com, a Top Ten Health Site*

Advance Praise for *Smart Relationships*

Dr. Wish has hit a home run again! *Smart Relationships* offers women that missing piece in self-help—an education about how relationships function! Today's women want more than clever tips. They want something that will guide them through all their intimate relationships. As an educator, I need to make sure that my students receive material that is solid and trustworthy. Women can rest easy that Dr. Wish's book comes from sound research findings—and she offers them in a very original way that does not skimp on depth for today's women who want and expect more from relationship help.

—*Jane Roberts, PhD, Chair of the Duvall Family Studies Initiative,*
University of South Florida

Resounding support for *Smart Relationships*. As in her other work, this book offers answers to many of women's life, social and familial snafus. More hats off to LB—a writer, therapist, role model and recent recipient of the *Focus on Women* Magazine's Women of Impact Award.

—*Joslyn Wolfe, Professor and Publisher,*
Focus on Women Magazine

It's reassuring to find an expert in the field of women's issues who offers wisdom, wit and advice that has depth and ease of use. *Smart Relationships* is a very valuable guide for relationships that are truly satisfying. Again, Dr. Wish delivers on her promise to help us all learn from her research findings—and her cartoon character Cookie's mistakes—so women don't have to repeat them.

—*Jed Diamond, Ph.D, author,* MenAlive:
Stop Killer Stress with Simple Energy Healing Tools

SMART RELATIONSHIPS

SMART RELATIONSHIPS

HOW SUCCESSFUL WOMEN
CAN FIND TRUE LOVE

LeslieBeth Wish, EdD, MSS

NEW HORIZON PRESS
Far Hills, New Jersey

Requests for permission should be addressed to:
New Horizon Press
P.O. Box 669
Far Hills, NJ 07931

LeslieBeth Wish, EdD
Smart Relationships: How Successful Women Can Find True Love

Cover design: Wendy Bass
Interior design: Scribe Inc.
Author photography: Dick Dickinson

Library of Congress Control Number: 2012945211

ISBN 13: 978-0-88282-438-3

New Horizon Press

Manufactured in the U.S.A.

17   16   15   14   13   1   2   3   4   5

For Erilda Waters, one of life's angels,
and for all the brave women who told me their stories

Author's Note

This book is based on the author's research, personal experience, interviews and real life experiences. In order to protect privacy, names have been changed and identifying characteristics have been altered except for contributing experts. All of the stories and individuals represented are composites and do not represent any one person or story but many combined.

For purposes of simplifying usage, the pronouns his/her and s/he are sometimes used interchangeably. The information contained herein is not meant to be a substitute for professional evaluation and therapy with mental health professionals.

Contents

Introduction

I f you are an ambitious and capable working woman, it can be very confusing to be smart about your career but not about love. You wonder how your relationships started out one way but ended up another, why recovery from hurt takes so long and what made your affairs go wrong. You go to sleep disappointed, wake up anxious and spend the day mistrusting your judgment about men.

Being unhappy in love becomes larger than just a problem to work on. It makes you worry that something is wrong inside. And then it hits you—you may have broken through the glass ceiling at work, but you haven't broken through the love ceiling. As one of my clients, Jennifer, said about her previous relationships, "I feel that I missed out on being a full adult member of the world. I guess I don't do love, and it embarrasses me to admit it."

If those words sound like your feelings, you are not alone. This love shock has also baffled more than nine hundred women in my research about their intimate relationships and the thousands of women I've counseled over thirty years. Like them, you're used to achievement and results. You're educated, trained, responsible and respected. You're in charge of your money, lifestyle and body. Nevertheless, when it comes to men, your past mistakes in love have made you pickier but not smarter.

It's not that you haven't tried. You've likely received some counseling or read books about communicating better, recognizing abusive behavior or honoring your needs—all worthy relationship topics. Yet something was missing. You have gathered bits and pieces of information, ideas and tips that have some meaning for you, but you want more.

I am both a psychologist and a licensed clinical social worker, yet in my perspective as a therapist trying to help women who were in bad or no relationships, I was frustrated too. I ran out of books to recommend and I was baffled by the love problems of such capable women. Though I offered my clients some help, I knew I could do more. My goal was to offer women more than just tips and tools. I wanted to help them gain a bigger picture of their dilemmas, educate women and arm them with a template that would aid them regardless of the relationship problem. And when I met with women, they said that was what they were looking for too.

I had to learn more about the love issues of today's women. I asked women to tell me about their love lives. The participants spanned many ages, came from all over the world and from different backgrounds, including Hispanic, African-American, Vietnamese, Native American and Caucasian women who work as attorneys, physicians, publicists, television personalities, teachers, nurses, interior designers, accountants, business owners, managers and administrators.

These brave women offered in-depth interviews, took surveys and attended workshops, focus groups, lectures and professional meetings. I then used a combination of quantitative-qualitative analyses, semi-structured interviews and surveys to gain a deep perspective on their relationship issues. Case histories from the thousands of women and couples I've helped over the years provided additional sources. I've followed the lives of some of these women from five to more than twenty years. As a result, the information in this book provides, I believe, a reliable, current—and much needed—view of the state of women's intimate relationships today.

In my research at local and national professional meetings, I discovered that my findings prompted the "ah-ha" response in many women. Many communicated that they felt heard, less alone and more aware of how their fears of falling in love with the wrong person got in the way of finding and keeping a healthy and loving relationship.

I learned a great deal about relationships alongside my participants. In this book I focus on research, practical exercises, charts and information from the women with whom I spoke, using their own words about their disappointments and successes. I based my analysis on theories of attachment, family systems, cognitive-behavioral approaches and mindfulness.

My breakthrough findings and solutions address the unexpected and dangerous consequences from factors such as:

- Being done with men
- Being all work and no play
- Not trusting your own judgment
- Fearing you won't recover from break-ups and emotional hurts
- Being surprised at the difference in your man now from how he was in the beginning
- Secretly longing for a ticket out of your economic, love, family and career struggles
- Looking for your perfect soulmate

My goal is to provide you with tools and education about how relationships can and do work. I will help you focus on reading men better and observing the *You Who Is You* in your relationship. It's tempting to fit your man into a category such as "snake" or "charmer." It can be a beginning step, but I teach you not to let these labels distract you from the real job of studying how you relate to your man and how your behaviors with him might be contributing to your problem. After all, one woman's ex is another's good match and not all charming men, for example, make bad mates.

When you pay attention to your actions, you will learn more about your fears and needs. You will also build the ability to be your best self with your partner so you can increase the opportunity for him to be his best self, too. When you are no longer part of the problem, you can determine whether he is a healthy and wise match for you.

Getting smart about love also includes learning how you handle your fundamental needs of feeling "safe" and "warm"—words that some women whom I surveyed thought were their new four-letter curse words. Too many of the women I counseled believed that being in charge of the relationship was the best way to avoid any more unhappy endings in love.

When they became disappointed that their seemingly pliable men were not responsible in times of crisis, the women felt even more frightened that they had made unwise choices of their partners. They vowed that their next men would be much more capable of supporting them emotionally. However, some women made the mistake of over-correcting their previous relationship style of interacting by next choosing men whose air of authority turned into authoritarian—and often cruel—control.

As you become familiar with new ways to relate, you will also learn to tolerate a temporarily uncomfortable emotional zone instead of falling back on the unhealthy, automatic emotional comfort zones that you learned from your family and caregivers—or care-*takers* as many of the women said. When you understand the power of your family roles and messages in shaping your relationship choices and behaviors, you will be more able to choose wisely, date and relate by forgoing your usual style and adapting to a now more fulfilling one.

To help you learn more effectively, I've included visual cues, charts, questionnaires and the *Almost Smart Cookie*™ cartoons that I created as teaching tools. In my workshops I have found visual material proved valuable because it bypassed verbal defensiveness. The women's excellent verbal skills had become their armor and they were equipped with many "Yes, but..." responses. The visual tools helped them *experience* rather than just read or hear about their own behavior.

The book contains five parts that transport you on your journey to getting smart and brave about love. The parts begin on a path that takes an outward, whole-picture view of your relationship behavior. Next, you will arrive at confronting the unique innermost factors from your family and childhood that contribute to your love dilemmas. Then you move further inward by learning to take greater control of your feelings, fears and beliefs about women, work and career.

Part I

Recognizing the Most Dangerous Relationship Patterns

Chapter 1

Dangers of Being Done with Men

Disappointment in love can make you think that deleting men from your life and closing up your heart are the safest strategies. It makes sense. You've been hurt. You're wary. Yet, as they say in those infomercials, "But wait, there's more!" By the end of this chapter you'll see how your approach can lead to more missteps in love.

You'll learn the basics of relationship patterns and discover why focusing on *your* behavior with your partner is wiser than thinking about what *type* of man you chose. For now, I want to spark your awareness of the *You Who Is You* in your relationships, and examine why you chose to wall up your heart. Getting brave enough to observe your actions is a key tool in becoming smart about love.

Meet Cookie, professionally known as Christine Olivia O'Keefe, family law attorney. She is the cartoon character I've created, whose love adventures are based on my research findings about women and love. She is an accomplished lawyer with several close girlfriends and a divorced mother whose dream for her only child is to "settle down"—mother code for "get married to someone of whom I approve and have babies." Throughout this book you'll follow Cookie's missteps in love and learn from your own.

COOKIE SHUTS DOWN HER HEART

She had never cried in front of him before, after all this time, but there were tears streaming down her cheeks. Alex took her hand but the touch felt wrong. Cookie jerked away from him on the couch as Alex said, "I thought you'd be happy I met someone. You'd like her. She's a great girl..." He paused and the silence felt as though something had slammed Cookie in the back.

She couldn't move and she thought of the time her cat was trapped behind the dresser. Alex resumed speaking. "—you're my best friend, Cookie. The first one I wanted to tell." His voice seemed far off, not real, like the announcements at airports, and Cookie closed her eyes. This was worse than her old boyfriend Steve's text message: "we r thru" more than two years and four months ago—she was still counting—and she hadn't gone on a date since then. Cookie thought she and Alex would be like sister and brother forever, watching sports and scary movies on television—one night at her place, the next his—both building careers as attorneys with no need for another heart.

She was wrong again. How could she be so smart at work but not with men? The only solution was no more looking for love. If it was meant to be, it would just happen, probably when she wasn't looking—wasn't that what everyone said? My first cartoon shows how Cookie handles the loss of Alex.

ALMOST SMART COOKIE ™

Panel 1: I'M DONE WITH MEN! LET'S LIVE TOGETHER AND START OUR OLD LADIES' HOME NOW.

Panel 2: ?

Panel 3: OKAY-- HOW ABOUT IF I JUST GET A LOT OF CATS?

ISN'T IT A GOOD IDEA TO TAKE A BREAK FROM LOVE?

It's very confusing to be in a situation similar to Cookie's. You probably recall advice such as you're supposed to "take time off" after a break-up, spend more time with friends, jump-start that forgotten bucket list, examine what went wrong and vow not to repeat the same mistakes once you start dating again—whenever that is. If you're unhappy with your long-term partner, you heard you're supposed to lead your own life within the relationship and possibly cool your feelings for your existing partner or spouse.

Unfortunately, there aren't any rules about how long you should take your "love time out." My best answer to the question, "What's wrong with taking a break from love?" is this: Nothing—as long as you measure most of your break from love in weeks or sometimes months rather than years, and that you spend your time being emotionally brave enough to look at yourself, or get counseling when you can't figure things out.

However, taking time out is not the same as taking a *done with men* attitude where you keep your emotional shields up against getting wounded again—even as you continue dating or relating to your current partner. Most of us have been hurt—really hurt—in love, but a wiser response is to learn about the situation and get back into life and love. Cookie took more than a two-year dating hiatus after Steve broke up with her via text message.

WHAT ARE THE TOP REASONS FOR WANTING TO SWEAR OFF MEN AND BEING DONE WITH THEM?

If I ask you to explain why you took a break from love, your response might be on this list. Add your own.

MY MOST COMMON REASONS FOR FEELING DONE WITH MEN

My partner, boyfriend or spouse:

- Had an affair
- Lied about important things such as being currently married or in trouble financially
- Took off with my money
- Abused me

- Had an addiction problem such as drugs, alcohol, gambling, pornography or sexual hook-ups—and wouldn't address it
- Was unreliable—especially at key moments such as my becoming ill
- Kept me "dangling" too long without moving toward commitment
- Made me do things I didn't want to do—especially sexual activities
- Made me feel used, used up, disrespected, insecure and unappreciated
- Blindsided me because he changed from how he was in the beginning

No one would sign up for these things in relationships. Yet, as impossible as it seems, you might be able to open your heart to a new partner or triumph over these obstacles within your relationship. It's encouraging, for example, to know that about one third of the women whose partners had affairs were able to rekindle love with them. The single women who found love again with a new partner overcame horrendous situations with their previous partners. Some of those men ran off with the women's investments or harbored secret lives of relationships with call girls or other men. Yet, even though these events are terribly frightening, love with a new person can still happen. As one of the women in my study said, "I learned that in my heart, there is always room for love."

So, why can't you get over your previous hurt? Why are you now so wary? And how did you—as smart as you are—get blindsided? The items on the list seem like strong reasons to wall up your heart. The next points show you their underlying meaning.

THE UNDERLYING CORE REASONS FOR RETREATING FROM LOVE

- Not trusting your own judgment in reading men
- Not wanting to make another mistake ever again
- Not believing you can recover easily from another hurt
- Never ever risking being abandoned again

Like most of the women in my study, you probably thought that being pickier about men would save you from getting hurt or abandoned. You are smart to be more selective, but pickiness only works when you know what to be picky about. Relying on instant chemistry or being swept away by looks, excitement or lots of money are not good guides. Later you will learn how to identify your unique needs and zero in on how to spot a man who can help you with most of them. You'll also become emotionally strong enough to recover wisely from hurts and boost your judgment and people-reading skills. For now, your beginning step to breaking the love ceiling is to recognize these core factors and to learn how to kiss with your eyes open.

HOW DO I KNOW THAT I'M IN THE "DONE WITH MEN" MINDSET?

In my workshops I found many women learned better through pictures

rather than words. These images show you the most common relationship sequence of a broken heart, tears and stop signs against men. This sequence would never stand a chance of breaking that love ceiling.

If your heart has been broken and you've sworn off men, you are not alone. More than 40 percent of the women in my study felt so hurt, disappointed and confused by love that, like Cookie in the cartoon we previously viewed, they avoided dating and relating. The next chart can help you determine whether you've become *done with men*. Check the signs that describe your behaviors and feelings.

Most Common Warning Signs of Being "Done with Men"

❑ Feeling pessimistic about finding love

❑ Thinking that needing a man is a sign of weakness

❑ Believing love will happen when you're not looking for it—so why bother trying?

❑ Believing if there isn't instant chemistry then he's not the one

❑ Avoiding fix-ups, parties and other places where you might meet men

❑ Over-valuing your "me time"

❑ Withdrawing your positive feelings from your current partner

❑ Hiding at work by working long hours

❑ Restricting yourself to hanging out only in groups with the same friends or colleagues

❑ Getting overly picky about dating site matches because you are looking for "the one"

I've learned that there is no magic number or score as to how many or which one of these warning signs is most powerful. What turns one woman's heart off may not affect you. And sometimes, just one item on the list can be strong enough to make a woman give up on love.

One of my clients, Jenny, is a single engineer with her own company. She meets men every day. Her profession is filled with them, and when she goes to conferences, men flock to her. But Jenny never meets anyone she wants to date because, in her words, "None of them grab my heartstrings." She's waiting for that rush from chemistry. Truth is, her husband, whom she said she "really, really fell for," divorced her. Jenny doubted she would ever trust someone again who made her feel that way.

Another client, Martha, is a school superintendent and successful educational consultant. She was married for over twenty years to her childhood sweetheart, Ray, a division manager at a large insurance company. Life was fulfilling and happy for them until Ray lost his job when the company he worked for closed his division. He was shocked. Two years later, he was still unemployed. Martha said that at this point she "pulled her heart back from Ray." She described him as her "rock who turned into a lump." They lived apart in their home, but Martha could not get over her disappointment, anger and fear. Later she had an affair with another man. When Ray finally found a good job, Martha was caught in a whirlwind of going back and forth between the two men. But Ray was so hurt by her abandonment of him that he filed for divorce.

Focus on the warning list again. You might even have your own warning signs to add. Can you guess what the items have in common? They are all self-protective defenses and rationalizations against being disappointed, angry or blindsided. In the stories of Jenny and Martha, both women tried to guard against all these experiences because they couldn't handle the abandonment, one of our fundamental fears.

Yet, healthy, mutually-satisfying love *requires* risking those hurts and fears. When you fall in love, hopefully you feel the satisfaction of fulfilling your needs for closeness, acceptance, safety, warmth, belonging and partnership. As your commitment and connection increase, so do the emotional defenses against getting hurt, abandoned and tossed into life without a safety net. Often these defenses are on auto-pilot. They can sneak up on you. In Martha's story she began sniping at her husband. "I had never treated him like that before," she said. Too late she realized she had reprised her mother's behavior when Martha's father became ill and could no longer be the major breadwinner.

Like it or not, love doesn't work unless you are willing to get in the love ring and, paradoxically, *drop* your guard, take off your gloves and *expect* some of those recoverable, emotional hurts that even the most loving couples inflict on each other.

EVEN IF I GET OVER MY FEAR OF MAKING MISTAKES, WHAT AM I REALLY TRYING TO FIND IN MY RELATIONSHIPS?

Many of the disappointing and hurtful experiences of dating and relating are dashed hopes of feeling safe and warm. Using coping strategies that result in a *done with men* mindset is a misguided attempt to feel safe—a case of nothing ventured, nothing lost.

We human beings want the safety of knowing that our partners are not just capable but also loyal. You need to feel loved, understood, accepted and important enough to your partner that he wants to be with you and can put you first at times. All these factors produce feelings of warmth, closeness and trust that you won't be abandoned.

You might regulate your fear of abandonment by clinging to a partner or you might avoid being close so that if serious problems occur, you can leave or pull back your feelings because you really haven't risked very much in the first place. You act as though you expect to be hurt and will have such a hard time recovering that you hedge your bets way ahead of time. The next graph illustrates how your needs to feel safe and warm form the structure of relationships.

Safe and Warm Relationship Structure

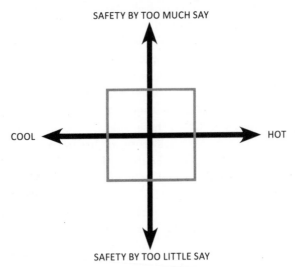

The vertical line represents your attempt to feel safe. Notice that you can be either toward the top or the bottom of the line. You might try to feel safe by taking charge and having too much say. Problems arise when you feel too burdened by carrying the relationship. Over time, you can begin to resent or disrespect your partner for not pulling his load or you might think you would feel safe if you turned over major life decisions, responsibilities and capabilities to your partner and had less say. Problems arise when you feel too controlled.

Again, there is no magic formula that is good for everyone on this range. However, your relationship flexibility with overlapping skills builds strength, partnership and capability in life. Some situations require you to alter your place on the range. Let's say you are normally the logical and practical one who makes financial and household maintenance decisions in your relationship. If you become ill, you'd feel safer if you knew that your partner could manage at least some of your areas of expertise.

The horizontal line represents the range of your competing efforts to feel warm and close but also independent. You might think that you can avoid being hurt by distancing your inner self from your partner and remaining on the cooler emotional end. You tend to be busy, travel a lot or even live in separate cities. Your time with your partner is restricted. Usually people with greater needs to be apart tend to find each other. When you feel out of touch, you somehow manage to signal to your partner that you need to reconnect.

On the other hand, you might believe that you can prevent being alone and abandoned by remaining at the hot end of the warmth spectrum by clinging, monitoring and vetoing certain decisions that keep your partner from being more independent. Some couples who are at the hot end of the range spend all their time together. They create families that do everything as a unit.

One of my clients, Lenora, told her teen children that they could only apply to colleges that had easy-access airports or short drives to their home. Lenora's father died young and so did her stepfather. Even though she was married, the thought of her children being far away terrified her. "I saw the loneliness my mother went through. I never wanted to have that in my life," she said. When Lenora's children all went off to nearby colleges, Lenora's husband wanted to travel the world, but Lenora wouldn't go anywhere. She wanted to retain her close family even though her husband felt suffocated.

The box at the center of the relationship structure shows a typical healthy range. Don't worry if you are happy with your mate or if your overall place on the scale is not in the middle range. Love comes in all kinds of varieties and surprises! For now, hopefully you can see that a *done with men* mindset puts you clearly on the cool end and near the top of having your say. You are headed for a life of living alone. This is usually the result of a misguided attempt to feel safe.

WHAT ARE THE SERIOUS DANGERS OF BEING DONE WITH MEN?

Like Sleeping Beauty, you close your eyes to dating or resolving key issues with your partner. Soon your life becomes a flat-line on a heart monitor. If only you could sleep and awaken the minute the right man appears. Closing your eyes and your heart can have serious consequences. The goal is to be open to love—while still kissing with your eyes open. Here are the top dangers:

THE FIRST DANGER: GETTING TRAPPED IN THE HURT CYCLE

Letting your love life flat-line leaves you vulnerable to the Hurt-Avoid-Lonely Cycle.

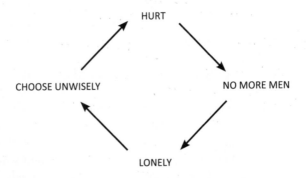

The Hurt-Avoid-Lonely Cycle

At first, you may be so hurt that you swear off men. And if you already have a partner, you may close your heart to him. You might banish men from your life for a week, a month, a season or years. Or, out of loneliness, fear, financial problems or the sake of the children you decide to stay with your man—but give up on feeling loved. Avoiding intimacy seems safer than risking what feels like such a mortal wound from love's disappointments that you don't think you could survive it again—or at least not very soon.

Your loneliness increases, but you just busy yourself. Activities become more precious, because you want so much from them. One of my clients, Nora, a pharmaceutical representative, said that she was no longer satisfied with just going out with her girlfriends for dinner. "It had to be a special place—atmosphere, great menu, a little formal," she said.

Then, almost out of the blue, things change. Some event triggers you to drop your guard with your existing partner or to look again for love. When challenging events uncover your partner's ineffectiveness, you feel lonelier, pull away or seek another partner. Here is a list of the most common events that can alter your receptivity to love and put chinks in your defenses.

TOP FACTORS THAT CAN MAKE YOU DROP YOUR LOVE SHIELD
- Trauma such as rape, robbery or surviving a crash
- Loss or illness of a loved one
- Ticking of your "biological clock"
- Serious financial difficulties such as job loss or foreclosure
- Aging
- Widowhood and fear of being alone
- Becoming the "old maid" of your family or among your friends

When these life events derail your misguided resolve to protect your-self from any more hurt, you become *more* susceptible to being duped in love. You're headed for a perfect storm of increased loneliness combined with your lack of skills in reading men and your failure to understand your missteps and the power of your triggering event.

Nora said that her loneliness got to the tipping point when both her younger sisters got engaged and married. "All of a sudden, I wasn't this successful professional woman anymore," she said. "At thirty-seven, with no partner in sight and no children, I was on my way to becoming what my mother always feared—an old maid."

The intensity of Nora's unhappiness led to meeting Hector, falling in love and moving in together. But the match was not a good one. "He just used me," she said. In less than a year, it was over. She gave up on men and she found herself once again caught in the Hurt Cycle.

THE SECOND DANGER: GETTING RUSTY

Your *done with men* mindset makes you risk becoming interperson-ally rusty and hyper-vigilant without knowing what to look out for or how to spot it. Understandably, you feel burned—and burned out—so you set a goal to avoid liars, cheats, sponges and losers. But deep down inside, you're not sure you would catch the signs soon enough with new men or with the one in your current relationship. Many of the women in my study were shocked that they ended up in the same soup but with different ingredients.

Nora thought she'd never again be with a man who didn't respect her or couldn't make a commitment. After she kicked her previous boy-friend out of her place for loafing, she threw her energies into work. Then, shortly after her sisters' weddings, she met Hector at a charity event. He said he was looking for a long-term relationship. Hector was kind, even courtly, holding open doors and pulling out her chair for her when they dined. But when Nora's professional contacts turned down Hector's artwork, he bolted. "I invested time and money in him. I let him move in with me, bought him clothes. I loved his work. It showed his sweetness. He had *promise*. But the timing wasn't right for his kind of work from an unknown. I couldn't believe I ended up with another lopsided love. Hector seemed so *different*," she said.

It's easy to miss what's in front of you, to get lost in the details and false differences between your men. You need to step back and think about whether you are reproducing similar *relationship patterns* such as Nora's recreating an imbalance of giving and taking.

Do a relationship reality check by referring to the Safe and Warm Relationship Structure on page 14. Where would you put yourself on the Too Much/Too Little Say continuum? See if you and your partner have *swapped* positions and did a relationship flip where you are now in the opposite place on that vertical line from where you were in your previous relationship. Look at your horizontal Cool and Hot line. Have you over-corrected and now find yourself too close to the style opposite from the one you had before? Remember, flexibility and mid-point ranges on the graph can be signs of strength and wise choices. Your responsibility is to educate yourself about relationship functioning, to maintain your ability to read men and to detect signs of danger by continuing to date and relate.

THE THIRD DANGER: BEING SWEPT AWAY BY LOVE

How easy it is to go from *done with men* to a big, bad event to being overwhelmed by the fireworks of sudden love. Few of us are immune to the force of these occurrences. Don't underestimate their power. Many of the women who closed their hearts to love got caught off guard by major life events and then fell head over heels for new men. If you fall into this trap, you raise the odds of turning into a Sleeping Beauty or Cinderella who is waiting for Prince Charming to come rescue you from your life situation.

It may not *feel* as though you've been rescued—or that you even wanted to be. Get mindful. The combination of experiencing fireworks while you feel lonely and hurt should sound the warning bells. Yes, healthy love can sneak up on you, and there are women who knew instantly that a man was for them, but these meetings of the mind and heart are not so common. There's a reason they call it "falling" in love.

Go ahead, see the man, but be wary of over-valuing him. When you are in the midst of a storm, almost any haven can seem imperative. You feel alive, special and capable of a renewed—or new—self. Love does have the power to do that, but after the turmoil subsides, you don't want to see that you have given up too much of yourself, or that you really don't have much in common with your partner. Believing that you *owe* someone too much can make you tolerate—and accommodate to—things you normally wouldn't accept. Gratitude should never become the glue in your intimate relationship.

Clarissa's Story

While one of my clients, Clarissa, was mourning the death of her teenaged daughter, she walled herself off from men. She was afraid that she had too much emotional baggage for anyone to value her. Besides, just before her daughter became ill, she broke up with her long-term boyfriend who had never really established a relationship with her daughter.

Despite her good job as a regional manager of a major retail chain, Clarissa's medical bills ate away her savings. It seemed that overnight she met and fell for Tom, a politician. She jumped into his life and Tom seemed to respect her. He asked Clarissa to organize all his political events. And then one morning she woke with a sickening churning in her stomach. She was supposed to call the caterer, order flowers, count the RSVPs, steam press his jacket, write thank-you notes, buy linen napkins that matched the new plates from London and provide a massage with benefits for Tom, because he was a very important man who was having a fundraiser at his new apartment and he didn't want a woman who had too many needs of her own.

She felt overwhelmed, but Clarissa knew not to tell Tom about her feelings. He needed a woman who was happy to be an old-style politician's wife and that wasn't for Clarissa. After the event, she packed her things and told Tom goodbye. Clarissa was appalled at how close she came to disappearing in a relationship. "He made me feel swept away from my pain. For the first time I didn't feel *under* life." Clarissa said. "But all I did was get run over by him."

Marlene's Story

Calamities can really open your eyes to the limitations in your existing relationship, especially if it began with a perceived rescue. One evening, Marlene had a bitter fight with her husband Mason about his lack of attention during her cancer treatments. She knew that the early death of both his parents made him avoid anything to do with illness. She protected his fears by not discussing the results of her frequent medical tests. She kept up a cheery attitude, and she cried alone at night in another room.

She was lucky, she told herself. When she met Mason, a high school principal, she was on her thirteenth month of unemployment from a good job as a sales manager, and the third month of her divorce from her going-nowhere husband. After she and Mason married, she hid every little hurt or disappointment from him, but on the night of their big fight her fears and loneliness reached the tipping point and she exploded in anger.

Eventually, Marlene and Mason went to counseling and learned to communicate as soon as an incident bothered them. She stopped protecting him from her emotional and physical pain.

THE FOURTH DANGER:
FALLING FOR THE LAST MAN STANDING

It is easy to go from *done with men* to a big, bad event to falling for the last man standing. Sometimes, you do get lucky in love and meet a great man, or discover that the man you are with has really come through for you. Other times, though, you end up in an affair or with the last man standing.

Romantic happiness seems so remote, and life feels as bleak and weak as a bare tree. Without being aware of it you lower your love expectations. You think you are being rational—more *realistic*—about it, and then you pick a relationship that requires you to settle.

WHAT IS THE DIFFERENCE BETWEEN
SETTLING AND COMPROMISING?

A crisis can make a warm body seem better than none at all. It can also make you excuse previously unacceptable behaviors in your existing partner. No relationship is perfect. So how do you know if you are settling or compromising?

You must recognize your bottom-line needs. You probably fantasized about what kind of man or life you wanted. However, fantasies are not the same as needs. Your needs are unique to you. Your disposition and experiences in your family background and adult life shape your choice of partner and your interactions with him.

These needs are neutral—and you don't have as much say about them as you think. So there's nothing wrong with you if you need an easy-going person or a decision-maker, for example. Settling is when you give up your bottom-line needs such as having family values, working hard, saving money, living within your means, obeying laws, being respected and forming a team with your partner. Compromising is when you tweak, postpone or even give up some of your wishes and choices that do *not* erode your bottom-line needs or your sense of self-worth, overall contentment and peace of mind.

HOW DO I KNOW MY BOTTOM-LINE NEEDS?

One of the tasks of adulthood is to be aware of your unique needs. Here are some ways to begin your search to identify them and determine whether you have given them up in your new or existing relationship. Ask yourself the questions on the following list and discuss your answers with your partner and a counselor. You might even want to write them down in a journal so you can review your responses. You will have a chance to refine your list as we discuss your needs in other chapters.

Learning about My Needs

What was missing in my past relationship—or in my present one?

Which values and behaviors that I learned from my family do I want to maintain?

How happy would I be if my sibling, parent or child chose someone like my partner?

What issues eat at me that I haven't expressed to my partner for fear of rocking the boat?

Am I tolerating my partner's abuse and hurtful insensitivities because of my current circumstances?

If life were more normal, would I be choosing this person?

If life were more normal, would I be making this decision, such as moving in together, getting married or deciding whether to have children or not?

Crises can compel you to do things that you will later regret. The best way to take charge of your life is to trust your decisions. Peace of mind comes from knowing that you thought things through *after* the intensity and sense of urgency have subsided. For example, don't rush into marriage, divorce or other legal arrangements such as buying a home together while you are in the grip of the incident.

If you have met a new person, don't make any hasty decisions. Observe the relationship during both good and bad times. The partner you felt you needed during your crisis might not feel like such a good match when you get your life back on course. You might see that your existing partner has either surprised you by being there for you—or not.

THE FIFTH DANGER: BECOMING A PESSIMIST

Turning off your heart to love is a sure way to become a pessimist. Pessimists always have their critic button set to "on." They can't go to a movie or concert without offering a running commentary. They are likely to reject a man after an initial meeting, or to have an impossible checklist for finding or loving a good man. They look with a critical eye at their friends' partners and feel lucky that they don't have one with whom to deal. If they do have a partner, they dialed down their expectations and efforts long ago. Most of all, they are down on love.

This negativity is a contagious poison. It turns the sky gray, and curbs hope, joy and generosity. Being pessimistic is a very economical defense because as it sours love for you, it simultaneously shields you from going on a path that could very well lead to your getting hurt and disappointed again.

Your pessimism blunts your ability to reckon honestly with yourself—which is the point. When you blame others, you don't look into yourself and you take wrong turns instead of staying on the path that could just as well lead you to love. The greater relationship fall-out from pessimism is that you rob yourself of a chance to be your best self. You end up far under that ceiling of love for a man and for yourself, too.

Pessimism also allows you to avoid the risk-taking necessary for overall personal growth in your career, family, interests, values and wellness. Think of pessimism as a powerful vacuum cleaner that sucks up all the hope, happiness and health. In other words, pessimism handicaps you at every turn in life.

I know psychological examination is a rough journey, but if you want to be your best self, you have to go through the woods before you can find your destination. Self-knowledge is painful because we have excuses, rationalizations and blinders for a reason: Truth hurts! But if you've come this far you have already learned about relationship structure and focused on your role. You have definitely increased your bravery—a key ingredient for finding and sustaining happiness in love.

Here's a quick review to use when you think you might be slipping into the *done with men* mindset.

Review Tips for Avoiding Being *Done with Men*

Keep in mind your tendency to fall into the pattern of being *done with men.* Ask yourself questions such as: Am I angry at the world or men? Do I try to fool myself by saying a little too forcefully that I don't need a man? Don't wall up your heart to love with a new or existing partner. Stay positive.

Rely on the Safe and Warm Relationship Structure (page 14). Keep a visual image in your mind of the chart that shows you the continuum of your human needs to feel safe and warm. Keep a copy in your handbag when you go on dates—or when you have disagreements with your partner.

Focus on what you *need emotionally* in a relationship so that you can avoid settling. Be willing to compromise on issues that do not cause you to give up your values.

Don't let yourself get rusty. Hang out with friends and colleagues and practice observing others and your reactions to them. Life is people—and endless opportunities for learning about how you interact with them.

Become aware of increased loneliness or tumultuous life events that you might be experiencing. Respect the power of disappointment in love, and losses of homes, jobs or health to make you fall for a man or grab the last man standing. Stay mindful of your life situation when making relationship decisions.

Chapter 2

Damaged Self from Roller Coaster Love

Excitement is a powerful chemical process in the brain. It floods you with feelings of invincibility and exceptionality. When you mix excitement with romance, you get an even more potent brew. Romance makes you feel valued and alive. You aren't weak if you want to have these feelings with your partner. All the women in my study liked romantic evenings and getaways. But there is a difference between feeling romantic and being swept away.

Edgy men are often very good at courtship, particularly in the beginning, and they know just how to make you feel special—and how to blind you to their serious problems. The danger lies in wanting a thrilling man to take you away from it all. These men have radar for women who secretly long for this rescue.

The exhilaration of being swept away by a man of fame, fortune or danger can be so intoxicating that you overlook his mistreatment, temper or insensitivity. However, one day that thrill will be gone and your emotions will range from elation to fear—a perfect description of the ups and downs of roller coaster love.

At the amusement park, if you don't like the thrill of the ride you are on, you can calm yourself by knowing that it will soon be over and that you don't have to go on the ride again. Not so true if you feel stuck with a man whose promise of adventure and delight has turned into incidents of abuse and control. Let's see the dangers of this kind of relationship and learn how they can happen to smart and successful women like Cookie and you.

COOKIE LOSES HER MIND BY FALLING HEAD OVER HEELS

Cookie was out of tissues. She looked down at the crumpled ones that were scattered on the floor in front of her couch and picked up the biggest wad. She dabbed at her tears and tossed the tissues back onto the floor. It took every ounce of her to break it off with the new man in her life, Tim. She felt really guilty about it. He was so sweet and she could tell him anything.

In the beginning, Cookie felt so peaceful with him. Now she was exhausted. Cookie never realized how much energy she spent propping up Tim. She was his cheerleader, best friend—and bank. In her heart of hearts, she knew that it would take years for Tim to find himself and a good job. It felt cruel to her to be the one to leave. It was like saying, "I don't believe in you anymore." That wasn't true. She did think that one day he'd get going on his dreams. It just wouldn't be with her.

She had no choice, really. Cookie knew it. Her work as an attorney was suffering. She came home exhausted. All she wanted to do was snuggle with Tim on the couch and watch a movie together—her favorite thing to do. Yet, there was Tim, waving a folder in his hand about another exciting project that he wanted her to finance.

At those moments all the air seemed to leave the room. She was choking. Tim—her loving, kind, sweet Tim who rubbed her neck and aching feet, who made her feel so warm and cared for—now made her feel suffocated, drained and, yes, in a strange way, scared. It was tough having all the responsibility. But if leaving was the right thing to do, then why was she crying herself to sleep every night? Guilt, she thought, and fear of not finding anyone else and ending up alone.

Then along came Nick Saint. Handsome, rich, successful, charismatic, exciting—did she mention successful?—Nick. Suddenly, the air came back into the room. She could breathe, had energy, hope and safety. What a relief.

Do you recognize this love sequence? Look at the next cartoon that shows how just one factor—Nick's wealth—can turn Cookie's head and heart.

WHAT'S WRONG WITH BEING ATTRACTED TO MEN WHO ARE "MOVERS AND SHAKERS"?

It's not wrong to be attracted to powerful, successful and dynamic partners. Many high-octane men are fascinating and caring people, and some of the capable women in my study developed special skills in dealing with the high maintenance personalities of these movers and shakers. In fact, successful women often discover that these resourceful men are great matches since the men's savvy makes them strong team players who know how to cope alongside their partners with life's ups and downs. Kara, one of the women in my study, described a healthy version of a relationship with a highly-able man by saying: "We both like a partner you can rely on. It's like each of us goes about our separate high-flying lives during the day in our own jet in the clouds, looking out the window, waiting for the end of the day when we can be together and being at peace from having a 'wing-person' you trust and respect right there in view in the clouds nearby."

If you are drawn to charismatic men, you are not alone. More than 40 percent of the women in my study said they liked lots of excitement in their relationships. The only danger is that these men's personalities and promises of excitement and luxury can tempt you to fall for them quickly—and make you close your eyes to everything about them *and* you long before your first kiss. You love that high of losing yourself to what feels like love, especially when you have sex within the first three dates—an experience that almost 40 percent of the women in my study said they tended to do.

That high can land you in a relationship where your partner's commanding personality turns into a demanding force that requires you to go along with things you don't want to do. Many of the women were terribly shocked and frightened that they had given up so much—including quitting their jobs and no longer having control of their own money. To keep their men and peace, they tolerated violent fits of alcoholism, philandering or verbal, emotional, physical and sexual abuse.

We've all been fooled in love, but it's still terribly upsetting to find that you put up with denigration for the sake of a relationship-with-bonuses. It's horrible to wake up one morning and feel that you've had enough—and don't know how things went so badly.

Some of these dynamic men remind me of the mating behavior of birds. The actions of the male birds amuse me. They strut about, fluff their feathers and plumes, puff out their chests, change colors and build unbelievably elaborate nests out of twigs, ribbons and shiny scraps of metal.

The winners are always the birds that do this mating ritual well. And there's good reason for female birds to choose them. The females sense that the males' outrageous displays demonstrate abilities to be resourceful, brave and formidable providers.

Of course, we are not birds, but this female attraction to the most competent male shapes most animals' choice of partners—including human beings. Yet, I was still surprised to discover that women's second most common dating and mating mistake is choosing movers and shakers who eventually minimize and deny the women's needs. Typically, you start your relationship by believing that you found an exciting man of authority. You are shocked that you ended up with a man with authoritarian control.

Almost 50 percent of the women who took my survey said that these men abused them physically, emotionally or sexually. The men intimidated, hit, stalked, threatened violence and some ran off with the women's money. Many of the women said that these men "sucked out their souls."

WHAT ARE THE TOP REASONS THAT I WOULD ALLOW A POWERFUL MAN TO MAKE ME FALL HEAD OVER HEELS?

If I asked you, "What made you fall so hard and fast for such a forceful man?" your response might be on the next list. Check the items that most describe your situation and add your own. As I said previously, it often does not matter how many of the items apply to you. Sometimes, just one reason is powerful enough to have made you fall hard for a man.

Emotional Triggers for Falling Head over Heels with a Successful, Exciting Man

❑ I have work burn-out and I am disillusioned with my profession.

❑ I work and work until I almost drop and I need some excitement in my life.

❑ I don't laugh a lot or feel really enthusiastic about my life in general. I like getting a life by being dropped into his.

❑ I feel inner death in my life. I don't have a lot of non-work-related interests and his lifestyle or bad boy personality has the power to break through my shell and make me feel alive again.

❑ I am tired of dating basket-case men who need me to take care of them all the time.

❑ I've never been the popular girl and now I feel chosen and appreciated.

❑ I love the goodies that this lifestyle gives me.

❑ I come from a background of wealth and I am expected to choose a mover and shaker.

❑ I've been dead sexually and these men really revive me.

❑ I like the ticket out of the rat race that these men offer.

❑ My accomplishments make me a woman who deserves a powerful man and I am willing to put up with things I shouldn't.

❑ I have children with this man and I am afraid he will become an abusive or deadbeat dad.

What ideas did this list of reasons spark? Jot down a few of your thoughts. Knowing how and why you were susceptible to an unloving relationship is one of the key tools in breaking through your love ceiling and keeping your eyes open.

If you are dissatisfied with your life, you are more likely to grab a man who can whisk you into excitement, luxury and even danger. There is nothing wrong with enjoying luxury or excitement. The problem, however, lies in the potential hidden cost of what you have agreed to give up or endure in order to keep your man and the goodies and highs that he offers.

Many of the women in my study said that the beginning of the relationship with these forceful men was filled with charm, expensive gifts and the magic of a lifestyle that included temptations such as lavish homes, famous people and jet-away weekends.

Some of these relationships worked out well, because the man did not abuse his power. As Lara, one woman said, "My husband actually likes being nice. I don't think he'd respect himself for acting any other way or accepting any woman who didn't have a self."

However, the relationships that went wrong went really wrong. Women revealed horrible incidents of physical and sexual abuse. They told how they were asked to participate in demeaning sexual activities, often involving group sex or being filmed for others to see. Other women experienced broken jaws or wrists and bruises from slaps and pushes.

The women who were brave enough to speak out about the under-side of their lives with abusive men said that they were terrified of leaving or defying their partners. They feared escalating abuse and the lies about them that their man would tell their friends and family. These men would cut off the women financially and restrict access to the children.

Keeping up appearances to obscure the horrid life at home was important to the men. "I couldn't even talk on the phone with a girl-friend unless my boyfriend was in the room. He was afraid I'd tell the truth," several women said. The women felt trapped and ashamed. "How could this happen to me—to *me*—and why didn't I see the signs?" was a common refrain.

If you feel trapped in an abusive and unloving relationship, you are probably wondering how you—as smart or accomplished as you are—got stuck in this terrible situation. The next list addresses key factors in your psyche that may have contributed to the dilemma.

THE UNDERLYING CORE REASONS FOR PUTTING UP WITH DISRESPECT OR ABUSE

- Not believing you have the inner strength to leave him
- Not believing that you can forge an exciting life on your own
- Not believing you can recover easily from the shame
- Not believing that you deserve better
- Not wanting to give up the goodies
- Not believing you can really take care of yourself

For most of the women who were unhappy with their powerful men, it was the gray area of disrespectful behavior from the men that created the most anguish and a disturbing blindness to the relationship. The men expected their partners to be a mix of courtesan, maid and trophy. "I exercised and dieted incessantly to please him. I could never be thin or beautiful enough for my husband," Susan confessed. Her words resonated with many of the other women. Because these demands from the men did not rise to the level of being beaten, most of the women struggled to identify what really constituted behavior bad enough to make them leave and sacrifice their exciting and easy life.

Men's domineering actions such as criticism, picking out the women's clothes or even insisting that the women quit, their jobs did not surface from what the women called the "gray soup" of unacceptable behavior. Most often, the women denied their feelings of unhappiness. Rocking the relationship, they feared, might end up with them living on the street.

Like most of the women who stayed in relationships and lived with varying degrees of dissatisfaction, fear and self-loathing, you might have rationalized that you had good reasons, such as the items on the last list, for remaining with them. But all these reasons end up being a bad bargain where you have exchanged self-respect and personal responsibility for economic safety and an instant—and seemingly fuller—life.

Because the danger of over-accommodating to a successful or exciting man is the second most common dating and mating pattern, here is a Cookie cartoon to use as a reminder about how even exciting dates can lure you into an abusive and disrespectful relationship with a charismatic man of wealth, fame and power.

AlmostSMART COOKIE ™

Exciting times together in your relationship—especially within the first few dates—can become a skyrocket to mistakes. Cookie is impressed that Joe got hard-to-find tickets to the hottest concert in town. Experiences that are intense or dangerous arouse your brain. Your neurochemicals of pleasure increase. When your dates and time together include scary activities such as sky diving or the intoxication of jetting away somewhere, the attachment hormone oxytocin also increases. Teenagers, for example, love to go on dates to scary movies. The anticipation of danger arouses the fight-or-flight hormones. This emotional state also increases your bonding to the person you are with because you feel safer when you are not alone. Imagine the potency of pounding music and the exciting fear of love from a new person. Now add to that mix a hefty dose of not liking your current life. In the last cartoon, notice how Cookie's mindfulness and self-control are no longer reliable.

HOW DO I KNOW I'M IN THE "SEDUCED BY EXCITEMENT AND GOODIES" MINDSET?

The most common relationship sequence begins with either being sad about your limited life or being disappointed that you allowed yourself to take command of a relationship with a cuddly, teddy bear man who then turned into a needy and ineffective man. We'll learn more about that pattern in the next chapter. For now, wherever you start in this sequence, you long for fireworks. You feel dulled and disappointed by love.

Then one day a man whose wealth makes him seem like Santa Claus comes along. You envision a life of ease, luxury and perhaps even kindness of spirit. In another variation, you fall for a man who reminds you of a lion. He's an undisputed leader with charisma and a sense of danger. You imagine a life of excitement and meeting people with status, power and wealth.

Over time the truth in some of these relationships creeps up on you. Your Santa is a false St. Nick whom you allow to take more than he gives and your lion of a man abuses, denigrates and controls you. Then you really open your eyes and see that the behavior of your Santa or lion has turned him into a pig.

If you go back and forth between men whom you regard as teddy bears and men whom you see as Santas or lions, then you are *over-correcting* your previous relationship pattern. This attempt to remedy your past missteps snares you in the relationship flip cycle.

Even worse, your seemingly wise new choice of partner fools you into thinking that changing your type of man will make you happy. But it usually doesn't. It's far better to focus on how you interact in a relationship and to keep your eye on the *You Who Is You*. Make sure you like the version of you whom you are seeing. Are you your best self?

If you want to preserve your mental and physical safety, as well as your chances at healthy love with a powerful man, become mindful about jumping so soon into love—and bed—and giving up so much for excitement and riches. Here are two stories of women who experienced the sequence just described.

Anita's Story

At night as a child, Anita heard her mother's sobs. Another man had come and gone. Anita would tiptoe into the kitchen and pat the top of her mother's head. Her mother's shoulders would heave in sorrow and Anita would stare at the kitchen with its chipped yellow cabinets and tiny refrigerator. She felt like Cinderella, appreciated only for sweeping, cooking and cleaning. Anita was glad she was smart in math. It would be her ticket out of this miserable existence.

Anita grew up, went to college on a scholarship and became an investment banker. She worked long hours, yet she was secretly ashamed that she felt her life was dull and demanding. She did nothing but go to work, the gym and then home for dinner in front of the television. So much for a ticket out, she thought. Anita fantasized about Prince Charming coming to her rescue, but all the men who liked her were men who over-relied on her. She regarded them as babies and leeches.

When she met Cal, she fell hard and she had sex with him the first night. It was the best sex ever. Cal was handsome and rich and Anita literally rode off with him into the sunset on the back of his motorcycle. Soon, though, his possessiveness and temper were out of control. She had the bruises to prove it. She couldn't believe how completely he had changed. Later, when he stormed into her workplace and screamed at everyone, she finally had the courage to leave him. Her secret unhappiness was out in the open. She had stayed with him too long. It wasn't easy giving up a life of excitement and amazing sex.

Anita cried for weeks, although she knew she had done the right thing by leaving. He had been so tender, so courtly in the beginning of their relationship. But there were no signs of the Prince Charming in him any longer.

Many of the women in my study expressed aspects of Anita's problems. 13 percent said that they stayed in abusive relationships for the great sex. More disturbing is the almost 40 percent who said they still did not feel good enough for their dashing man—even after he became abusive.

Anita's shock at how different her man was from how he acted in the beginning was a very common awakening. Over 46 percent of the women said that they didn't know how such a dramatic change had happened. The transformation can sneak up on you like a slow-dripping faucet of cruelty that one day fills the sink. If you have similar feelings and thoughts, it must be very frightening and confusing to think that your education, training, success and responsibility have not helped you avoid such a serious relationship mistake.

Virtually all the women in my study who ended up with physically abusive men said that they felt they had not only fallen in love in the dark but that they had flunked love. Their need for a powerful love with a powerful man was so strong that they dimmed the lights on their awareness. One woman, Charlotte, captured these feelings by saying, "I thought God or the president of my university should take away my degrees for being so stupid in the love department."

This underlying core of feeling undeserving ran through the comments of many of the women. They were ashamed that they allowed themselves to be so mistreated. "I stopped being kind to myself," Charlotte said.

Melody's Story

Melody's experience exhibits another version of the potential dangers of giving up too much to keep a man of authority. Melody ran as tight a ship in her heart as she did at her law firm. She was holding out for the kind of man who could give her the lavish lifestyle of her parents. They were divorced and her father rarely saw her, so Melody had learned to settle for his generous gifts and money.

She decided to date only men who had income and status, who weren't intimidated by her take-charge personality. These men came with swagger and edge—and arguments that usually ended with her apologizing or feeling confused. After she received a promotion and a raise, she met Leon and married him right away. "I felt like I finally got the man I deserved," Melody said. "I was at the top in my life, so why shouldn't I get a top man, too. At least that was my thinking at the time. Boy—was that ever wrong."

The extended honeymoon lasted less than six months. For a while, their adventure vacations to private islands with famous people made her feel alive—and right about her choice of husband. And even when it was bad, it was excitingly bad. "Looking back," Melody said, "I was in chase mode—for the father I never had. I couldn't believe how many times I apologized to Leon for absolutely nothing."

When Leon asked—well, almost insisted—that she cut back her work hours so she could be home to "take better care of the house," she agreed. Then she became depressed. To get out of the blues, she accepted an offer to tutor a few law students for the bar exam. When Leon saw the deposit slips from the students' checks, he went ballistic. They yelled and screamed at each other for hours. He accused her of breaking their agreement. She felt she had no choice except to stay because she was three months pregnant.

After the birth of their daughter, Leon lost interest in the relationship. He worked longer hours and Melody was sure he was cheating on her. After a few more years, she left him. "By then, my eyes were open," she said.

She found another position at a new law firm. She wasn't making as much money as she did before, but Melody said that she had flexible hours so she could take care of her daughter. "I did two relationship flips by dating sweet but passive guys and realized that wasn't the solution either. I can't say that I have earned my A in love yet, but at least I'm more aware of not tolerating controlling men."

Did you find any themes or situations in these stories that felt familiar? Both Anita and Melody accepted emotional crumbs in exchange for what seemed like a great match. Perhaps the next chart will help you see the relationship shift from exciting and dangerous love to crumbs.

Roller Coaster Love: Emotional Highs and Lows

At First	Later
I feel alive and special	I feel unloved, exhausted, scared
I love our hot sex	But mostly we have it on his terms or after fighting
I love always being together	I have no life or say of my own
He's a difficult but special man	He's secretly not so great

Long after the lure of the benefits of jet-away vacations, fancy homes and access to people in high places wears off, you are often left with disillusionment, injuries and the astonishment and shame that you have read these men—and yourself—so inaccurately. You feel numb; your soul seems lost. A strange kind of loneliness and self-loathing takes over and you realize you've given up and tolerated too much.

Hollywood movie moguls of the 1940s knew the appeal of this kind of man very well. The sly, street-smart, slightly dangerous man sensed that just below the surface of the buttoned-up suit of the career woman was a secret self screaming to get out and feel alive. The films show the woman succumbing to his ardent kisses, which were movie language for having hot sex. The sex became the gateway for the woman to feel loved, special and appreciated.

Then one day the vixen in the film woke up to find that she was with a man who cheated, absconded with her money or controlled her. She realized her previous life and a huge part of her identity and self-worth had almost disappeared. She was left with crumbs because that was what she was willing to accept almost at the very beginning from her man. Losing the *You Who Is You* is too big a sacrifice.

Here is a review chart about the warning signs of the potential dangers of being with a powerful man. Refer to it often and check the items that apply to you in both your present and past love situations. Don't concentrate on how many things you select. We all have unique differences within the same problem. So there is no specific number as to how many or which one of these warning signs is most powerful. What is dangerous to one woman may not be to another. Often, only one item, such as violence, can be a serious warning sign.

Warning Signs that You Might be Headed for Danger with a Powerful Man

❑ Feeling you've won the brass ring—or are living life to the fullest—with this man and have been given a ticket out of the rat race

❑ Believing a high-powered man is the only kind of person you should select

❑ Believing that even if you don't feel comfortable with this man, you will choose him

❑ Under-valuing yourself and your current life

❑ Restricting yourself to his activities and his choices

❑ Holding back on speaking up about things that make you feel diminished, hurt and afraid

❑ Accepting emotional crumbs from him—and rationalizing that it's okay

❑ Being willing to put up with a lot, including demeaning sex, abuse and drugs, to stay with him

---

EVEN IF I GET OVER MY ATTRACTION TO AN UNHEALTHY VERSION OF SANTA OR A LION—AND EVEN IF I VOW TO CHANGE MY INTERACTIONS WITH THESE MEN— WHAT AM I REALLY TRYING TO FIND IN LOVE?

It seems unfair, then, that even though you feel you've toughened your hide and heart to life's disappointments, you secretly long for closeness. And then an exciting and successful man comes into your life. You have sex too soon, fall too hard and discover too late that your safety net of confidence has holes in it.

Slowly, like water coming to a boil, there is a moment when you realize you've over-accommodated to your partner, accepted emotional crumbs and ended up losing yourself to keep him. But take your eyes off him. It's too easy for you to become distracted and lost in figuring out what's wrong with your man or which type your man might be.

Instead, a better way for you to burst through your love ceiling is to stay focused on the *You Who Is You* in the relationship. Read the next sentences carefully:

The *You Who Is You*

It's not the type of man that is important—it's what you give up, what crumbs you accept and how you allow these men to make you feel, act and think about yourself in the relationship. Yes, learn about your man—but always keep one eye open on yourself!

Just what are you trying to find in relationships with movers and shakers? You might not like the answer, but you are trying to feel safe. Despite your accomplishments, income or fame, you don't really want to be the lone pilot in the sky. The idea of a trusted and competent "wingman" sounds good—if you can only let it happen.

The next diagram shows you the structure of relationships. If you recognize this chart, that's because it was also in the first chapter. This time you will be learning about being in a relationship with a powerful and exciting man. Let's review the chart: think about where you'd place yourself on the lines for safety and warmth.

The vertical line represents your attempts to feel safe. You can be either on the top or the bottom of the line—or anywhere in between. Let's say for the moment that in your previous relationship, you took too much control and had most of the say on important things. You discovered early about yourself that being in control made you happier and calmer—more or less. You generally don't like delegating too much responsibility to others, especially in intimate relationships. What if the man makes a big mistake? What if he does something wrong?

You've learned not to trust that others can get it right. Problems arise when you feel too burdened by carrying the relationship. Over time, you began to resent or disrespect your partner for not pulling his load. Now you think perhaps you would feel safer after all if you choose relationships where your man is more capable.

Safe and Warm Relationship Structure

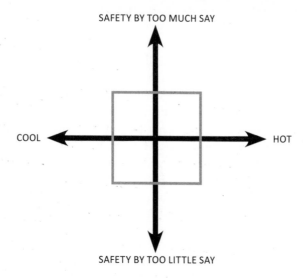

Or, in a second scenario, you believe that your personality and accomplishments have earned you a dashing, highly successful man. Perhaps you are secretly tired from being in charge all the time. You work long and hard hours and your life seems to have shrunk or limited you to work-related activities. When you come home at night, the peace of your home seems great at first, but then the emptiness and silence aren't so great. You talk to yourself out loud just to make sure you can still talk. Maybe a crisis occurred such as an illness, and now your feelings of being alone terrify you.

Regardless of where and how you place yourself on the graph, something sparks you to choose a charismatic man. The hope is that he is your equal and that you have strong and complementary skills. It can be quite a comfort to know that your partner can manage the investments or repair your home. You trust this man and you like turning over varying degrees of the reins of control in certain areas to him. This arrangement can be very satisfying. Complementary styles and areas of expertise are usually vital to mutually happy, long-term relationships.

If your buried need to be taken care of—and taken away from the pressures of life—is too high, you might turn over too many major life decisions, responsibilities and capabilities to your partner. One day it hits you—you have less and less say and feel too controlled. If you saw yourself as a highly capable woman, it may shock you to see how much you turned over to your charismatic and exciting man. At first, you thought you were in good hands. And then you found out that those hands did not act so lovingly after all.

The horizontal line in the graph represents the range of your competing efforts to feel warm and close but also independent. You might think that you can avoid being hurt by distancing your inner self from your partner. Demanding men typically either want you at their beck and call or they want you to leave them alone and let them go off on fishing trips and business meetings whenever they feel like it. So, you end up feeling either suffocated or stranded.

As I discussed in the previous chapter, there is no magic formula on any of the ranges that is good for everyone. The box in the graph represents an optimal area of relating. But that can change, depending on circumstances. Relationship flexibility with overlapping skills builds a strong team with your partner. After all, some situations require you to alter your usual responsibilities with your man. If you are normally the logical and practical one who makes financial and household maintenance decisions in your relationship, when you become ill you would feel safer if you knew that your mate could manage at least some of your responsibilities. Complementary styles and abilities also allow you to learn from each other.

Most of the women surveyed who gave up too much of themselves were brave enough to face their contradictory needs to be in charge but also to be swept away. One common pattern was to choose a man of wealth, fame and accomplishment. Sometimes, he was an older man who either agreed to have children or who didn't want to have a family—or at least another one.

All these variations were highly appealing. The common core was that they all satisfied the woman's needs to grab the brass ring of life and feel relieved from having to face the road ahead all alone. The more unstable the economic times, the more intensely the women felt the need to seize back-up men. And if the men were highly eligible, the women tended to rely on the hook of providing amazing sex as soon as possible.

There is nothing wrong with choosing movers and shakers, as long as they are not physically and sexually abusive. Unfortunately, there are lots of gradations of not being treated well, and too many women allowed themselves to be diminished because they lost sight of the fact that a fundamental building block of love was to make sure that they acted lovingly toward themselves. Believing that you deserve kindness from your partner is a potent defense against hurtful love.

However, even if your eyes are open, it's still easy to be blinded to your partner's insensitivities. Often, the most emotionally lethal hurts from the man are the total of the small ones—those numerous cuts that contribute to the death of a thousand accommodations. Because no single emotional cut feels painful enough to make you leave your man, you put up with a lot. Juanita's story is an example of how giving in and giving up too many important things can create heart-wrenching sadness.

Juanita's Story

Juanita had a great job in marketing. She made good money and met all the top people in town. She attended black-tie charity events and frequently had her picture in the newspaper. At one of the season's premiere events she met Jorge—a handsome former athlete and now a successful entrepreneur. They made a very photogenic couple and were always in demand. Juanita loved the attention because she never had it as a child. Her mother always treated her as the ugly duckling. Juanita's mother was a former beauty queen, and Juanita's two other sisters had her beauty. "I got the brains," Juanita said.

She and Jorge soon became an item. They spent weekends at all the luxury resorts. At first, life was exciting. Juanita thought that she had met her match. So what if Jorge told her she wasn't good at small talk, or that she wasn't up to speed on politics and the arts? Soon he was voicing his frustration with her social limitations while they were with other people. Juanita responded with silence.

Then Jorge began making excuses for not being with her during the holiday season. His holiday gifts were either very inexpensive or the kind of lingerie that had holes cut in them for sexual pleasure. When he was with her, he was on his phone with women—whom he called business associates.

The day after New Year's, in a burst of courage, she checked his cell phone messages. There were too many messages from too many women about how much they enjoyed their private times together with him. Several thanked him for the gorgeous earrings and anklets. Jorge signed these messages with the word "Amor." That was how he signed his messages to her! *Anklets*, Juanita thought. That was so personal.

Then the whole cascade of her accommodations to him and her acceptance of mistreatment came crashing down on her. When she got up the nerve to confront him, he proposed marriage. "The whole scene felt wrong," Juanita said. She couldn't explain why, but she envisioned years of subtle but painful slights from him. Still, she said yes.

But there was never any ring. He was busy traveling. "When I get back, we'll go ring-shopping," he'd say. Then his mother became ill. Then he got a cold. And soon she felt like a nag whenever she mentioned the ring. He accused her of being materialistic, of not trusting him. She apologized.

It took her a while to break up with Jorge, but eventually she was able to pull all those gray areas of disrespect together into one big picture of unhappiness. "It wasn't easy," Juanita said. "I always felt I was wrong or being too emotional. If there was a way for me to see myself in the wrong, I used it."

WHAT CAN I DO TO AVOID THE POTENTIALLY SERIOUS DANGERS OF BEING WITH A MAN OF POWER, WEALTH AND EXCITEMENT?

Stay mindful of all your interactions, especially in the beginning when you are most likely to be swept away by his charms and excitement. One of the biggest shocks for almost 50 percent of the women in my study was realizing how much their men had changed from the first several dates. "I was so fooled," was a common reaction.

Keep a question mark in your head during your dates with these charismatic men. Pay special attention to the "wow factor" on dates that seduces you into shutting your eyes to the man's shortcomings or dominant nature. Some women, for example, flew in their men's helicopters to the rooftops and runways of hideaway places.

Also pay attention to his tendency to court you by acting overly gallant. For example, when Elena went out with James, she liked that he always walked nearer to the street. "I felt like I was in one of those movies that take place in Victorian England." His gestures made Elena feel special and cared for. "But then it got to be ridiculous. He went through all these gyrations when we came to a ladder or a fork in the road. It began to feel like a performance rather than real concern."

Elena was smart—and right. James was performing for her. He had turned into a fisherman who had all the right hooks. Kindness is certainly a quality you want from your man, but you want it to be genuine. James' gallantry was a clue to his demanding nature. We will learn more about reading men's behavior later. For now, keep that observant eye open.

However, you're not going to make much headway in breaking the love ceiling if you don't look out for yourself. The more you can accept who you are, and the more you stay focused on being your best self, the less likely you will tolerate mistreatment in an intimate relationship. Your next exercise is to start a success journal.

REMAINING MINDFUL ABOUT YOUR ACHIEVEMENTS: THE SUCCESS JOURNAL

The women in my study learned that keeping a success journal was a great way to sustain their sense of self-worth and become their own cheerleaders. They referred to it whenever they needed a boost and a course correction in self-evaluation.

Your success journal is a record of your effective ways of getting through difficult times. Through reviewing it you can see yourself again as a person with inner strength and good coping skills. Regulating your positive self-view protects against tolerating mistreatment and gives you a powerful tool to change your relationship mistakes.

Qualities • Achievements • Victories
Skills • Forgiveness • Remedies • Awareness

Complete the following sentences. In parentheses are examples of what some of the women I've surveyed wrote.

Qualities. My best qualities are (smart, helpful, caring).

Achievements. I've accomplished or am on track toward my goals of (getting an education or job).

Victories. I overcame (unhappy childhood or relationship, illness, loss of a job or money).

Skills. The skills, efforts and self-talk I used to get through hard times include (never giving up, becoming more realistic, gaining a perspective, getting help).

Forgiveness. I forgive myself for (taking wrong turns, making mistakes, saying yes when I should say no, being too hard on myself).

Remedies. I will fix the current problem by (speaking up, asking for things I need, keeping my friends).

Awareness. I know my shortcomings and will work on (being aware of my feelings, not putting up with maltreatment, remembering my successes and how I achieved them).

STAYING MINDFUL:
CREATING YOUR OWN FLASH CARDS

Sometimes, though, re-reading your journal is too time-consuming. I suggest making your own flash cards to use as reminders. The most powerful flash cards reflect your responses to the first three items on the list above. Look at your answers again. Write down some quick reminders that you can place in key locations such as your bathroom, your nightstand, your handbag or a drawer in your desk at work. The next exercise will help you organize your thoughts.

My Self-Love Flash Cards

Good Qualities. Write down your top good qualities on separate flash cards. Select between three and five so you don't get overwhelmed with too many cards.

Progress. Now write down, one per card, your actions or plans that are in progress. To paraphrase one of the lessons of the Buddha, it is a blessing to die in progress. Reminding yourself that you are in the process of moving forward makes you feel more in charge of your life. An ongoing effort of mastery is the best medicine to combat depression, low self-worth and denigrating relationships and interactions.

Triumphs. I once read somewhere that it is not just what you've accomplished but what you've overcome. Write down on individual flash cards reminders of how far you've come—and what you've overcome. This set of cards is especially powerful in re-invigorating your sense of advancement and inner strength. You might write something such as "recovered from a serious illness" or "got out of a very bad marriage."

Now you will be more fortified to become brave enough to take action so you can put some chinks in that love ceiling. But I don't want you to end this chapter by thinking you should avoid exciting or powerful men. There were plenty of women participants who married strong men and did not feel unhappy or diminished. It's good to have your antenna up, but not all relationships with powerful and charismatic men become abusive or negative.

The women in my study who were happy with dynamic men said that they still had to be vigilant about voicing their preferences and discussing things that bothered them. "It's too easy to give in and even let important things go," many women said.

Here are some review tips that happy women used to avoid disappearing into their partner's world or being unkind to themselves by over-accommodating.

Tips on How to Avoid Relationship Dangers of Exciting Men

Become aware of your feelings of inner death. Do you dislike your work or life? Do you have a life? Don't look to an exciting man to give you one. Develop interests in multiple areas of your life so, in case one area of your life is not going well, you have other areas to be your buffer zone and your joy. Strengthen ties with loving friends and family members. Be wary of your fantasies of wanting a man to give you a ticket out of the rat race.

Don't get into the mindset that you are "Little Orphan Annie." Sometimes, your inner identity of fearing you are not good enough for your man can make you feel grateful that such a seemingly wonderful man chose you. Gratefulness can lead you to accepting emotional crumbs from a man.

Pay attention to your enthusiasm level. Sometimes, being too excited about a man is a set-up for losing your ability to see and think clearly about him. Why are you so excited? Be mindful of the seduction of exciting dates.

Be wary of the relationship flip cycle. Over-correcting your previous love disappointments can leave you in the dark to your next disaster. Become vigilant about your needs to be whisked away from life's problems.

Hold off on sex. Don't let feeling high blind you. Don't seal the deal by having sex too early in the relationship. Set your goal to know the man. Tough out your fears of not getting him

Make sure you like the *You Who Is You* in the relationship. Are you proud of yourself and your interactions? Observe your behavior. What are you agreeing to that might diminish your self-regard?

Chapter 3

The False Calm of Two Peas in a Pod

Nice guys are hard to pass up. And why should you? Almost everyone likes being treated with kindness and empathy. You feel as though you can tell him anything. His tenderness and emotional support make you feel valued. This sense of specialness increases if your man is unusual, quirky, out of the mainstream and just somehow different from your typical choice of partner. He might, for example, have less education or income than you, or unique career aspirations.

Those issues don't necessarily make him a bad choice. Love and life are often unpredictable. There are always exceptions and wild-cards. So don't worry if you are happy with a man whose warmth and attentiveness attracted you. However, let's look at what often occurs if your happiness goes away and what to do about it.

COOKIE IS CONFUSED AND PUZZLED
ABOUT HER KIND MAN

What right did she have to be so unhappy with Tim? Tim was amazing. He helped out with the household—something none of her boyfriends ever did. They were too busy with important phone calls—and all of them were important.

Tim was so sweet in every way. He ran errands for her, sometimes searching all over downtown for the right tomatoes or special shampoo. And sex—well, truthfully, Tim was the most amazing lover she'd ever had. There was no afterwards—he didn't get up, check his phone or channel surf for the latest sports event. With Tim, it was like the affection just kept going on and on. He'd rub her feet if she'd been standing up in court all day or he'd rub her head and neck if she had one of her sinus headaches. It was like having a human teddy bear. When her mom called, Tim just knew to pretend that dinner was ready and call out that it was time to eat so Cookie could get off the phone.

She loved that he had wonderful projects. Who cared if they didn't generate income? She believed they would one day and besides, she made enough for both of them. His job as a permanent substitute teacher in the public schools paid for his health benefits and it didn't zap the energy he needed when he came home to focus on his true calling. He had great ideas for marketing art to young people.

His enthusiasm rubbed off on her. She learned so much from him about art history and improvements in perspective and paint application. He made her world bigger—which she needed badly. Before she met him, Cookie had no idea how narrow her life had become. It seemed that all she ever knew before was about being an attorney.

She thought of the first time they met. She was with her good friend Rae at a neighborhood pub. Cookie was about to leave when she spotted Tim at the end of the bar. He had on a T-shirt and jeans and his hair was rumpled. He looked so—approachable—compared to all the men still in their suits from the courthouse.

Months later, she was asking herself why her good feelings for Tim were fading. Why did his rumpled hair now bother her? Why was she so impatient with him about his projects? And—strangely—why did his constant affections that once made her so happy now make her feel crowded and irritated?

Maybe it was because her friends were getting married, having babies and buying homes and condos? Was it a case of her "biological clock" ticking or maybe, now that she was promoted at her law firm, she found herself over-explaining—almost apologizing—for Tim's appearance and lack of ambition whenever he came with her to one of her law firm's parties. The only thing she knew for sure at this point was that she was unhappy.

Do you recognize this love pattern? Look at the next cartoon. It shows Cookie's life with Tim.

AlmostSMART COOKIE ™

THE PROJECT WITH KEN WENT GREAT!

YOU MEAN YOUR BOOK?

NO--A FILM. LEND ME $1,000 AGAIN?

UH...SURE.

SO, WHAT'S WRONG WITH BEING ATTRACTED TO NICE GUYS?

It's never wrong to be attracted to partners who care about you and treat you with respect. If the compassionate nature of a man drew you to him, you share that appeal with more than 50 percent of the women in my study. Many nice guys truly are good matches.

Sometimes, though, when the going gets tough (such as financial, emotional or family crises), these men show their inability to face difficult issues. Their kindheartedness soon dissolves into ineffectiveness.

Many of the women who chose men for their warmth and tenderness were surprised to see this other side of their partners. The man's sweetness seemed to morph into passivity, avoidance of conflict and inability to be decisive. It's very puzzling that a man who seemed like such a great match eventually feels like a burden.

The cartoon you just looked at shows Cookie's change of mood. Cookie has been Tim's main cheerleader and money supply. Tim brought out her empathy and generosity—qualities that she didn't experience from her self-centered mother and absent father. Now Cookie's benevolence is beginning to crumble.

If I asked you, "What drew you to your man?" your response might be on the next list. Add your own reasons and check the ones that most describe your situation. As I mentioned previously, it often does not matter how many of the items apply to you. Sometimes, just one reason is powerful enough to put you in a relationship where you give too much to prop up your man.

Most Common Reasons for Choosing a Kind and Gentle Man

❑ I work and work until I almost drop, and I need some love and care in my life.

❑ I don't ever again want to put up with the abuse I endured from powerful men.

❑ My family has not really made me feel loved, and I thrive on how my man appreciates me.

❑ I've been dead sexually, and this man really makes me feel warm and wanted.

❑ I feel more relaxed with him because he lets me be in charge.

❑ I like an agreeable and sweet man who enjoys doing everything together.

❑ I don't feel so lonely anymore.

What ideas did this list of reasons spark? Jot down a few responses. Knowing why you tend to fall for an easy-going man who later takes too much out of you is a necessary step in understanding your needs and fears.

Let's look at a common path of love with pliable and sweet men. Frequently, these men are drawn to your steadfast qualities. Many of the successful women in my study—most notably teachers, nurses, attorneys and business owners—didn't mind carrying the responsibility for finances or decisions. If that description sounds like you, it's possible that you feel more comfortable taking the reins in the relationship. You enjoy coming home, nestling, cooking together and living as a happy, cuddly, warm, peaceful couple.

You build a private world and you feel safe and warm in the beginning. Almost a third of the women in my study preferred a relationship where they did everything together. He makes you laugh and feel less lonely—if you are like 20 percent of the women surveyed, you haven't had a good laugh in months.

Your friends, however, are actually surprised at your choice of man. Perhaps they are a little jealous or just don't understand. Your man is so different from theirs. Your friends may never have felt the specialness of being the only one who's ever loved and understood. They probably haven't experienced the joy of being with a partner who likes doing what you want, and doing everything together.

Your happiness lasts as long as you like this arrangement. Trouble begins, however, when you feel too burdened or tired of always having to be the leader. Those cuddly times turn into feelings of annoyance, suffocation and disappointment.

You begin to think that your man is actually needier than you are. His mildness masks a fear of confrontation, criticism and rejection—the other side of the same coin of your fears. His cuddling was not just about being loving *to* you—it was about what he needed *from* you.

In healthy relationships, a shared need for affection is normal. It turns into a problem when you allow your man to over-rely on you. It feels as though he's drained out your lifeblood. Sadly and slowly, you see that your warm and affable man is secretly a mild and initially painless version of a vampire.

Then you begin to wonder if there is any truth to your friends and family's reasons for being surprised about your choice. Breaking up frightens you. It's not easy to pass up a personal cheerleader and a ready companion. Could there really be something fundamentally wrong?

In one of my workshops, women nodded their heads in agreement when Theresa, a brave woman, stood up and said: "It comes to this about me and my relationships—I thought that control was the way to happiness. I didn't want any more unhappy endings. I wanted to throw up when I realized that being in charge of everything for so many years almost ruined my chances at love."

If you feel exhausted and lonelier from being with a man who ended up draining you, then you are probably puzzled about how your nice man turned into a noose. The next list illustrates key factors that may have contributed to your dissatisfaction.

THE UNDERLYING CORE REASONS FOR BEING A TAKE-CHARGE WOMAN IN RELATIONSHIPS

- Not believing that you can get over the guilt of leaving
- Not believing that you can ever give up control
- Not believing that you are allowed to make mistakes
- Not believing that you can recover easily from hurt
- Not believing that you deserve better

- Not believing that you should drop your guard
- Not believing that you can really take care of yourself

When I asked women in my workshops what would happen if they didn't call the shots in their relationships, many women said, essentially, "All hell would break loose."

Think about that comment for a moment. It's no surprise that you are tired and disillusioned with your man. It's not easy being a female version of the mythic figure of Atlas who has to hold the world on his shoulders. After a while, you have to decide what's worse—resenting your man for not being able to hold up his side, or continuing to fool yourself into thinking control will protect you from emotional hurt.

You probably set your goals to get things right in just about all your endeavors. See if this description sounds like you: At work you are very reliable—maybe a bit of a perfectionist. You hate delegating because people get it wrong so much of the time. At home you want things to run just as smoothly. You'd rather do it yourself than risk your partner messing things up.

Even though you've let your man into your life, your way-deep-inside emotional guard is always up. You don't want to reveal or experience your doubts and fears, especially your barely-realized feeling that for some reason you don't deserve good things.

Maybe your family background has bred in you a fierce fear of chaos, unpredictability, tension, lack of approval, affection and any other versions of unhappy endings that unsettle you. You tend to push away those thoughts because you believe you've already come a long way from your family's culture. It does seem logical to think that being in charge would take care of all these fears anyway. "It's just a bunch of psycho-babble," many of the women said. They all felt that they had already faced their past.

Breaking up doesn't seem to be an option. You've been in emotional turmoil before, and it took far too long to get over it. You never want to feel that emotional turmoil again.

HOW DO I KNOW I AM IN THE MINDSET OF BELIEVING CONTROL IS THE WAY TO HAPPINESS?

A typical progression of your unhappiness in this situation usually begins with a man who at first seems warm and caring. You create a private world of living like two peas in a pod. Without having to spell it out, you and your partner have agreed that in exchange for your taking command of most things, he will act lovingly toward you.

You are happy enough until one day you need to rely on him to help you get through some rough times. Maybe you or a family member is ill or perhaps your house was destroyed by a tornado. You are a little concerned that he won't be there for you. He's great at consoling you, but he has a history of not being so great at taking charge and managing life's large issues.

This time he really lets you down. His problems with conflict and decision making have broken your heart. You don't feel warm and safe with him any longer. When you stand back to get a perspective on your relationship, you see that your sweet man is more like a snail with an outer shell that protects him from life's ups and downs.

Changing the relationship is a long shot at this point. In the past, when you've tried to change him, you've used criticism, sarcasm and negative comments in the hopes of jolting him into taking more effective action. But that didn't work.

There's a break in the dark clouds in your heart, and for a moment you think that you have contributed to the problem. Maybe you helped turn your teddy bear of a man into a snail by not allowing him to have a more active role in the relationship.

Even though you are aware of the signs, ending the relationship feels very frightening. You feel the pang of loss. It had been so calming to be able to call the shots and be placed on that pedestal. Now you know that you've exchanged being loved for being worshipped and being in charge. And even though you are going to be the one to break it off, you feel abandoned.

In your mind you unroll the carpet of the rest of your life and it feels very lonely and scary. Who will care about you? Perhaps, like the 20 percent of the women in my study, you sometimes think you should stay with him anyway just to avoid feeling such loneliness.

You also feel horribly guilty for leaving a good man. What if once again you are likely to get caught in the flip cycle and allow your needs for safety to lead you to an exciting man who seems competent at first but then turns into a man whom you permit to run or ruin your life? The choices seem horrible.

But if you are getting smarter about assessing your relationship issues and if you are willing to kiss with one eye open, then you'll see that you've lost sight of being the best *You Who Is You* in the relationship. You might not have been so critical. If you had given up some control and your fears of being hurt, you might also have seen more quickly whether your kind man was a true teammate. You might have discovered that your man could learn from you.

For now, it's best to concentrate on understanding your relationship shifts from happiness to disappointment in your agreeable man. Look at this next chart:

Changes in "Peas in a Pod" Love

At First	Later
I feel warm and special	I feel drained and alone
I love our fun and tender sex	I wish he'd stop clinging
I love always being together	I have no life of my own
He's a sweet, special man	He's a frightened and limited man

We'll look next at a list of the top warning signs of the potential dangers of taking too much control. Check the items that describe you. There is no specific number as to how many or which one of these warning signs is most powerful. What is dangerous to one woman may not be to another. Often, only one item, such as resenting your partner's lack of being there for you, can be a serious warning sign.

Warning Signs of Taking Too Much Control or Living Too Closely

❑ Believing that you cannot trust others—and especially your partner—to do things right

❑ Believing there is one right way to do things

❑ Not delegating responsibilities to your partner

❑ Not including your partner as much in important decisions

❑ Using criticism or sarcasm with your partner—especially when you are unhappy with him

❑ Becoming a martyr and doing everything yourself

❑ Feeling exhausted from responding to his needs

❑ Feeling resentful that your partner isn't more helpful

- ❑ Not discussing your innermost feelings with him
- ❑ Restricting your world to cling to your partner
- ❑ Rationalizing your partner's serious shortcomings
- ❑ Feeling embarrassed sometimes when others spend time with you and your partner
- ❑ Feeling guilty for your unhappiness and being unable to leave because of fears of loneliness and not feeling alive again.

Talia's Story

Talia's experience with her husband Stephen is a sad illustration of how easy it is for your sense of control to trap you in an unhappy relationship. Her struggles express many of the fears and behaviors that you might be experiencing.

It was the second time that Stephen threatened to break up, but he really meant it this time. His biggest complaint was that Talia's position in the family's lucrative jewelry and gemstone business took up too much of her time. Stephen was a retired college professor and enjoyed outdoor activities.

The day that Stephen threatened to leave again, Talia reminded him that he knew that her family's business meant traveling to trade shows around the world. They were sitting on their deck, and Stephen was upset that her trade show travels took her away from gardening with him. He didn't understand why Talia just didn't quit and let her brothers run the show. He knew her father didn't really approve of women working. "The house gets too quiet when you aren't here," Stephen said. Talia knew that was what she called Stephen-code for "I'm lonely and want sex."

The thought of Stephen leaving and filing for divorce felt like a mixed blessing to Talia. She would definitely have more freedom to attend the gem shows. But then she'd also feel so terribly lonely. Stephen was the one who told her she was pretty and smart—something her parents never said. There was no question that Talia was smarter than her three brothers, but her father didn't believe in women running the business. Talia spent every business trip trying to show her father that she had better ideas and abilities than her brothers. And she did—but that didn't seem to impress him.

Her mother's only achievement was holding onto her beauty. Talia's mother was obsessed with working out and restricting her food intake. "A girl can never be too thin or too rich," was her motto. Talia was built like her father—more athletic and muscular. Talia disliked her mother for disliking her.

Talia also didn't approve of her mother giving up so much of herself just to snag and keep Talia's father, who had established one of the largest gemstone businesses in the world. Years before when her mother had laid eyes on Talia's father, she dropped out of college and put on high heels and tight dresses with plunging necklines. She continually criticized Talia's appearance.

As soon as Talia turned twenty-one, she married the first decent-enough man who came along. He was a surgeon, slightly cruel and demanding, and after Talia gave birth to their daughter, he became physically and verbally abusive. Talia left him and spent all her time working for her father in the family business. She didn't have time to feel lonely. Besides, she promised herself she would never put up with abuse again.

One afternoon she met Stephen at the dry cleaners when he was upset that his shirt came back wrinkled. Before he walked away, she took the shirt from him and held it up to the store clerk. "I think you can fix this," she said to the clerk.

From that day, Talia and Stephen became a couple. He moved into her house. She loved his easy-going nature and he thought she was beautiful and fun. He loved her athleticism, and they went on long excursions on bikes and kayaks, followed by great sex that lasted for hours, with Stephen bringing strawberries to the bedroom and giving her massages while they listened to entire symphonies.

Over time, though, the hours of sex and outings were too long and boring. Even worse, he never wanted to include other people in their outings. She even sent her daughter off to boarding school so they could be alone.

When she went away on family business, he'd call her at least five times a day to see when she was coming home. When she returned, she saw that the house was a wreck, with an unmade bed, crumbs on the counter, the laundry piling up, bills not sorted and phone messages that he didn't handle. It was just as well, Talia thought. He always made things worse.

They were both unhappy. And it almost all blew up when Stephen said that he couldn't take her being away so much. He pointed to the overgrown garden,

"We haven't weeded together in months." She quit working for the family business and stayed with Stephen and her unhappiness.

Can you see what's wrong here? It's not so easy to spot the trouble. The fall-out and disappointment from living like two peas in a pod and always being in charge do not appear in big print. Talia's core issues are an unseen mix of wanting control so she wouldn't get hurt and yearning to feel loved—at almost any cost.

She discovered too late that there was no flexibility in their partnership. Talia's relationship with Stephen started out with his being a man who catered to her and made her feel warm. But it ended up with Stephen not being able to be alone. Talia couldn't believe that her happiness had disappeared and that her view of her partner had changed.

WHAT AM I REALLY TRYING TO FIND
IN MY LOVE RELATIONSHIPS?

Become more familiar with our chart about managing your needs to feel safe and warm in relationships. As a quick review, the vertical line illustrates your attempt to feel safe. Women who like to be in charge tend to feel safe by calling all the shots and having too much say.

As you've learned in this chapter, problems can crop up when you feel too burdened by carrying the relationship. You begin to resent or disrespect your partner for having limitations that prevent him from being a team player. You are exhausted from his indecisiveness, ineptness in dealing with life and needs for lots of exclusive time with you.

You are actually surprised that you've had enough of his warmth. All that time together has turned the two of you into a small, suffocating clump that does everything as a unit. It's so ironic—in the beginning you were the one who basked in the long hours of attention, approval and sex.

Now, it's lonely and exhausting at the top. His needs and his agreeability no longer make you feel safe and warm. You wonder if you were in the way of your partner being more independent. In our *Safe and Warm Relationship Structure* chart (see page 14), the box outlines a possible healthy range that allows for flexibility for you to choose a strong team player who brings his own brand of competent skills. You might be brave enough to give up some control.

Where would you place yourself on the chart? If you've been in charge, place yourself higher up on the vertical line. And if you initially liked the warmth from cocooning or feeling so highly loved, appreciated and respected, place yourself closer to the hot end of the horizontal line. The key word in that sentence is highly. Your partner should have similar feelings for you, but be careful of the potential rigidity that extreme versions of these feelings create. Their intensity can make you feel trapped and struggling to breathe your own air.

What can you do to avoid living at the extreme ends of these continuums and killing love? Even if your man tends to be on the easygoing side, it certainly doesn't mean that you should break up with him. Let's review his good qualities in the next exercise. Think back on your excitement when you met.

GOOD AND BAD EXERCISE

The highly competent women in my study liked this exercise, because it offered them hope and techniques to manage their dissatisfaction with their loving—but often too passive—men. These women described themselves as living with an underground spring of disappointment that could well up when they felt let down by their men. Let's assume that when you fell crazily in love that you weren't totally crazy, and that you found someone who has positive aspects.

This exercise will help you sort out your feelings and better understand your situation. It does *not* give you the answer as to whether to stay or go. If you use it several times, the actual process of writing your responses can yield new insights that can help you evaluate your relationship more clearly.

I highly recommend that you seek counseling before making a decision about staying or leaving in this kind of relationship. Love is personal and what you can't accept in a relationship, someone else can. In the next chart, write out your responses.

1. In the "Beginning Good" section of "The Good" column, write down what attracted you to your man at first. Write whatever comes into your mind. There is no right or wrong answer. In the "Now Good" section of "The Good" column write down things that are still good.

2. In "The Annoying" column write down things that irritate you about your partner.

3. In the "Not so Great" section in "The Bad" column write down the things that are not so great. In the "Not Tolerable" section of "The Bad" column write down the things that are not tolerable.

The Good	The Annoying	The Bad
Beginning Good:		**Not so Great:**
Now Good:		**Not Tolerable:**

4. Review both sections in "The Bad" column. Put an X over the items that you think are totally unacceptable. Put a circle around those items that you can commit to improving if your partner will also commit to the same things. Now show this chart to your partner and ask him to help you make your relationship better. Usually, things that are not tolerable are best addressed in counseling.

5. As your relationship improves, your reactions to the items in "The Annoying" column lessen. They will most likely never go away. However, intensified reactions to the behaviors are warning signals that your stress and unhappiness have increased. Heed the warning, think about what could be troubling you and explain it to your partner. Focus on a new solution instead of blaming or repeating past failed efforts.

6. Take a look at your items in the "Beginning Good" column. Circle the ones that are *not* in the "Now Good" column. Show them to your partner. Come up with solutions about how to restore these good things.

Now that you are perhaps feeling a bit calmer and more optimistic, let's focus on how you can like the *You Who Is You* in the relationship.

The more you respect your own behavior, the more room you give your partner to develop strengths. You certainly didn't like being controlled, so why would you want to control or take charge of someone else? As I mentioned earlier, you will learn more about your man when you allow him to reveal his effectiveness levels. Here's that tip in a reminder box.

The Danger of Remaining in Charge

The more you take charge of the relationship, the more you obscure the view of your man's strengths and weaknesses. You risk making your love so rigid and brittle that you can't be each other's wing-person and face life's ups and downs together.

This next exercise will help you address your comfort zone around needing to be in charge.

TAKE CHARGE OF NOT BEING IN CHARGE ALL THE TIME EXERCISE

1. Think about what it would be like to give up so much control. Quickly write down the words that come to you.

2. Then think about one or two things that make you feel exhausted or resentful of your partner.

3. Show these items to your partner.

4. Get solution-oriented about how to remedy the situation. Do not play "history" where you say things such as, "Well, you did..." Or "You didn't..." Only work toward a solution. Play it forward. Pick one or two problems to solve.

5. He promises to ask for help if he needs it. You promise not to micromanage. You also promise that even if it is not done exactly as you want, you will not criticize.

6. After you arrive at a solution, put it into action. Evaluate the outcome and discuss with your partner how you both could improve it. Keep your eye on an acceptable range of outcomes, not just the one you have in your head.

7. Describe to each other what it is like for him to take more responsibility, and for you to delegate it.

Now that you are braver and kinder, here is a quick review.

Tips for Becoming More Mindful about Taking Control

Pay attention to your interactions. If you take charge too much, you won't leave room for your man to contribute effectively. Remember, the problem can lie in your interaction and not necessarily in your choice of man. Maintain respect for how both you and your partner act in this relationship. Aim to approve of your own interaction, tone and words.

Develop mindfulness about your feelings of disappointment in your man. It's very possible that you made a wise choice of mate by selecting a kind man. The next time you are frustrated or disappointed, think of words that describe your feelings and actions. Ask yourself questions such as: Am I contributing to my partner's ineffectiveness by taking over or being critical? If you develop a best self approach, you will be less likely to use criticism and control as coping reactions.

Keep your friends, family obligations and interests. Don't give them up in order to protect your man and yourself from being anxious— even if your partner doesn't like being with these people. Don't turn into two peas in a pod. Maintain your activities and interests outside the relationship. You will be less susceptible to allowing your man's need for too much togetherness to strangle you.

Keep an eye on your needs to be special and loved. We all have these needs, but take-charge women often allow these needs to run away from them. Soon, you find yourself in a relationship where the closeness of having sex or being worshipped take the place of other key aspects of healthy partnerships such as being able to rely on each other.

Don't become a bank or a nursemaid. Yes, partners help each other in times of need, but make sure your bank doesn't get drained. When you begin to feel "empty and spent," sit down, close your eyes and think about your behavior in the situation. What feelings and sensations are you experiencing? Now imagine yourself acting differently.

Part II

Family Roles

Chapter 4

Family Roles and Their Impact on Chemistry

You may be wondering: *How did I get this way?* When I give a talk or workshop, women often ask me: "Do I have to talk forever about my parents? When do I talk about what's happening now?"

We human beings are all "emotional time travelers." Whether we like it or not, we bring to our current situation the memories of past hurts as well as successes. This emotional travel bag includes many of our thoughts, feelings, happiness and life lessons from our childhood, family and previous love partners.

Melding the there-and-then with the here-and-now is actually a survival mechanism against getting harmed or abandoned. Animals such as dogs, primates, horses and elephants also have memory banks about their environment. They learn which trees yield fruit or which predators or people to avoid, how to band together as a group for safety or how to use tools. The animals make their decisions based on trial and error and on parental instruction. If you didn't allow your past to inform your present, then you would be starting over from the beginning every time.

Your family experience becomes the environment where you learn about things such as trust, love, men, women, closeness, risk-taking, education, money, personal growth, anger management and sex. Problems develop, however, when parents don't teach smart lessons or serve as role models for life, love, work and joy.

Children and adults will test or modify these parental lessons by learning from their experiences. But, if your family has not given you healthy role models and emotional permission to build the flexibility necessary for forging your own values, life path and self-awareness, then you grow up without full freedom to know yourself and be your best self. Luckily, if you are willing to withstand the anxiety of change and self-examination, you can surpass or differentiate yourself from your family. You first have to know a lot about the family environment in which you grew up.

Focusing on your present problem *automatically* includes information about your past intimate relationships and family. As a result, talking about the now always engages the then. For example, if you are in love with a man who is insensitive or abusive, but you are not sure whether to leave him, then if I was counseling you I would ask you to answer certain questions. Become your own therapist for a moment and write down your answers to the next questions. These questions are part of your beginning inquiry into a deeper understanding of what makes you tick.

My Own Therapist

1. When have I been in this situation before? Am I surprised that I am in this situation?
2. Looking back, could I have predicted that I might end up in a relationship like this?
3. Why do I have such a hard time breaking up?
4. Why do I act this way in relationships?
5. Where did these thoughts and feelings come from? Whose relationship pattern does mine resemble?

Good-enough families provide a foundation of trust, care and closeness. However, certain experiences such as abuse, poverty, abandonment, divorce or critical and negligent parents can put chinks, cracks and sometimes breaks in that foundation. All the women in my study listed many negative elements in their families. The next box lists the women's most frequent descriptions of their family environment. Check the ones that sound like you and add your own.

> ## Family Environment Descriptions
>
> ❑ Intense fights between my parents
> ❑ Atmosphere of criticism, negativity and perfectionism
> ❑ Neglect or emotional or physical abandonment of me
> ❑ Anxiety or sadness from parental divorce
> ❑ Anxiety or sadness from impairment in a parent such as depression or alcoholism
> ❑ Physical or sexual abuse of me

None of us would sign up to have these problems in our family. But no matter how much stress, fear or damage occurred in your family, there are almost always enough stones and pebbles to form a new foundation. Horrible childhoods do *not* doom you to unhappiness.

Healthy families, on the other hand, work like well-enough-run cruise ships. No ship, for instance, could run if everyone were a cook or navigator. Almost all family members eventually take on unique roles which are highly determined by birth order. A good resource on the subject is Kenneth Leman's *The Birth Order Book*. Birth order can help explain someone's personality and overall orientation to life about issues such as leadership, decision making, peace keeping, risk taking and being a rebel.

Firstborn children can become carbon copies of their parents. Older brothers and sisters tend to be highly responsible, and even a bit bossy, difficult and competitive. Many leaders are often an only or first-born child.

Middle daughters between sisters close in age are often peace-keepers who seem a little lost since they are not really sure how to be both an older and younger sibling at the same time. Yet, this ability to juggle things from multiple perspectives also makes them good entrepreneurs.

Babies of the family can be sociable, rebellious or favored—coddled children in need of guidance. Last-born children are often outgoing and fun, so it is not surprising that they become comedians, actors, salespeople or social directors. They also need help staying focused.

The descriptions of birth order are a general guide to the most common—but not the only—profiles. If we go back to the cruise ship that families form, oldest children might be officers, middle children could become staff with fewer decisions to make and youngest children could be the social directors, the entertainers, the salespeople—or the ones to jump ship and go to another one.

Think about your birth order and personality. What words would you use to describe yourself? Here are a few choices. Circle the ones that sound like you. Add your own.

First Glance at My Birth Order and Personality

My Birth Order: only, oldest with next-born sister, oldest with next-born brother, middle between two sisters, middle between two brothers, middle with older brother and younger sister, middle with older sister and younger brother, youngest with sister just above you, youngest with brother just above you

My Personality: outgoing, quiet, thinker, emotional, intuitive, analyzer, leader, rebel, teammate, challenger, optimist, pessimist, joiner, loner, problem solver, reader, sociable, decider, perfectionist, maverick, questioner

---

WHAT DOES MY BIRTH ORDER HAVE TO DO WITH MY CHEMISTRY AND MY CHOICE OF PARTNER?

Your birth order in relation to your siblings is one of the major factors that establishes feelings of familiarity and comfort in your attraction to and chemistry with a man. Chemistry can happen when you and your man have what researchers and therapists call "compatible birth orders." It's unlikely that one of your top questions on the first date is going to be about his birth order, but it is likely you are attracted to men whose behavior fits a particular profile that mimics your relationship with your family, because you feel safe and very much at home with the mesh of your two different styles. Here is a list of typical pairings:

BIRTH ORDER AND THE MOST TYPICAL AND COMPATIBLE COUPLES

An oldest sister of brothers knows a boy's world, and tends to feel more comfortable with a younger brother of sisters who also knows a girl's world.

An oldest sister of sisters often feels chemistry with an oldest brother so that she can share equally in being in charge because the only man she trusts is one who is most like her. On the other hand, she might be attracted to a man whose younger sibling position makes him a man who likes a woman in charge.

A middle child might feel more comfortable with a man who is an older sibling because he tends to be decisive. Or, she might choose a quieter, less outgoing man who thrives on her social and creative skills.

An only child could be attracted to either a man who needs guidance or a man who is reliable and decisive.

It all seems so simple and logical. But these pairings are *not* a recipe for happiness because the familiarity and comfort from your birth order could lead you to make either good or bad choices in men. If you are the oldest of sisters, you could just as easily fall in love with a man who is also an oldest but who dominates or abuses rather than acts as a co-equal. If you are the youngest who is a rebel, you could choose a caring man who understands you because he has younger sisters—or a man who, at first, liked your sense of fun but who now becomes remote, demanding and critical.

SO, AM I STUCK WITH MY SIBLING PROFILE?

Here's the good news—you are not stuck! Birth order is *not* a fixed, static rule. Many things affect birth order profiles and attractions, including disposition, intelligence, age and nature of the other siblings, birth order of the parents, impact of step- and half-siblings and events in the family. The death of a sibling, for example, can dramatically affect behavior, life choices and sense of responsibility of surviving siblings. Former United States presidents John F. Kennedy and Richard Nixon had siblings who died. Each of these men felt a responsibility to become the one to carry on the family values, wishes and dreams.

Similarly, the death of a parent can be instrumental in affecting a person's life course. Overnight, it can spur a child into taking over the deceased parent's role. Charlotte and Emily Brontë, the famous nineteenth century authors of *Jane Eyre* and *Wuthering Heights*, lost their mother. Unlike many sisters—especially siblings who share the same career—they became collaborative rather than competitive. Along with another sister, who was also a writer, they took parental responsibility for their drunken and wayward brother.

Other factors can influence your attraction to a man, such as your unique life experiences outside your family and your emotional role within your family.

WHY EMOTIONAL FAMILY ROLES ARE IMPORTANT

When I was doing post-graduate training in marriage and family systems, I learned that your role in your childhood family was more predictive of your attraction and interactions with future intimate partners than your actual birth order. There is hope about the flexibility in your family role and birth order and its impact on your feelings of chemistry with a man. Keep these thoughts in mind:

MAIN FACTORS THAT ARE MORE IMPORTANT THAN BIRTH ORDER

- How you *actually function* in your family will affect your attraction to a man more than the traditional profiles of oldest, middle or youngest.

- Your emotional importance in the family will also strongly influence your experience of feeling chemistry with a man.

- You might still get some of the benefits of your actual birth order.

- Your unique combinations of all these factors contribute to making you feel more comfortable with certain men. You may experience chemistry and feel as though you and he "fit" together.

- These feelings of chemistry and comfort can lead you to choose men who are either good or not good for you.

Let's see how that works. For instance, on my father's side of the family, his mother—my paternal grandmother—was the third child. Her oldest firstborn sibling was a brother, followed by a second-born sister. My grandmother was third. The fourth and fifth children were a boy and girl who were born very close in age.

Traditional birth order theory would say that the firstborn boy was a kind, attentive caretaker of his two younger sisters. The theory would also predict that the firstborn girl—the second child—would become like a mother hen to her younger sibling. This mother hen would become very important to the parents, especially the mother who would rely on this firstborn daughter to serve as her extra eyes, ears and arms.

But that is not what happened in my grandmother's family. Her older brother and sister were not as intelligent as she. They also lacked discipline. When my grandmother was born, she was calm, quiet, shy and very responsible. She became the mother figure who helped raise the children. Her *function* in the family changed from being the baby to being like the oldest child.

As more children were born, her function as the "oldest" increased the importance of her emotional family role. My grandmother often said to me: "I don't think my sisters could have tied their shoes without me."

When my grandmother married, she was very attracted to my paternal grandfather—who had brothers who were far more dominant and independent than he. My grandfather was a peacekeeper who was risk-adverse. He needed my grandmother's guidance, but also had an outgoing personality that coaxed my grandmother from her shyness. Their opposite styles complemented each other. My grandmother recreated her emotional childhood role as leader and caregiver, and my grandfather recreated his role as the more agreeable one.

HOW TO CONNECT THIS INFORMATION ABOUT YOUR FUNCTIONAL BIRTH ORDER AND EMOTIONAL FAMILY ROLE TO YOUR EXPERIENCES OF CHEMISTRY AND ATTRACTION TO A MAN

Let's take a more mindful look at your actual function in your family and how it might differ from the traditional description of your birth order. Complete the sentences in the next exercise.

You, Your Family and Your Attraction to Men

1. Even though in my family I am (fill in the blank with descriptions such as: the responsible or perfectionist oldest, the maverick or sociable baby, the agreeable or creative middle, etc.)

   _____

   _____ ,

2. I act more like (fill in the blank with descriptions such as: the responsible or bossy oldest, the maverick or sociable baby, the agreeable or creative middle, etc.)

   _____

   _____ .

3. If it weren't for me, my family could have (fill in the blank with descriptions such as: fallen apart, become cold and uncaring, argued more, divorced, ignored me and my siblings, abandoned me and my siblings, gone nuts, failed to thrive, failed to be responsible, etc.)

   _____

   _____ .

4. I tend to feel comfortable with and be more attracted to men who are (fill in the blank with words such as: take-charge men, agreeable men, controlling men, insecure men, distant men, teammates, empathic men, calm men, professorial men, successful men, exciting men, etc.)

   _____

   _____ .

What are you now learning about the power of your family situation over your attraction to certain men?

This recreation of your emotional childhood role lays the foundation for your emotional comfort zone in your family. In relationships, you tend to fall back on familiar behaviors that repeat your unique combination of your actual and your functional birth order profile in your family. It's as though you have an emotional default setting that leads you by the heart whether you like it or not.

When you date, you tend to be attracted to and feel chemistry with someone whose style allows you to reproduce your emotional comfort zone. You and your partner become opposite sides of the same coin. Often this arrangement works well.

Sometimes, though, your differences can backfire. For example, if you are the oldest, you might be drawn to taking responsibility—a great quality as long as you avoid taking on so much that you feel lonely and disappointed by your partner's lack of effectiveness.

When you try to change your attraction to this less-capable man, you tend to feel uncomfortable. You don't feel like yourself. You might be tempted to try a course correction by choosing a man who is more competent, but usually this change lands you in a relationship with a mean and controlling man because you *over*-corrected. At that point, your emotional comfort zone activates your emotional default setting for choosing more pliable men and round and round you go.

You can see how easily you can feel chemistry with a man who is *not* good for you! Look at this recipe to get a richer understanding of the links between your family emotional situation and your attraction to a man:

Your Sum in Your Family and Its Effect on Chemistry and Attraction

Add these ingredients:

- One cup of the strengths from your birth order (for example: leader, peacekeeper, fun, etc.)
- Two cups of your emotional childhood role, which grew from your functional birth order (for example: truth-teller, rebel, independent, leader, peacekeeper, caring, fun, important, etc.)
- Three cups of the importance of your emotional childhood role

Subtotal: Your emotional comfort zone

Now add:

- Four cups of how you act in your relationships, which is your emotional default setting

- Four more cups of your comfort and feelings of "being you" when you act in certain ways in your relationships with certain men

---

Final Total: Your attraction for and chemistry with certain men

Let's see how Cookie handles all these factors.

COOKIE LEARNS ABOUT LOVE FROM MOM

Cookie's birth order is only child. Like many children who do not have any siblings, Cookie is a mix of rebel, independence and dependence. She has the qualities of a first born such as intelligence, leadership and responsibility, but she has some of the qualities of a youngest child such as feeling insecure and being a bit dependent on the approval of her parent. She also has a touch of the rebel in her. This description might sound like you because being a rebel or maverick was, by far, the most common self-description by the women in my study.

Cookie's functional birth order rests on her emotional importance in the family. Cookie's mother is divorced. Her mother dated lots of men, and Cookie grew up with a parade of different men in her mother's life. Cookie's mother is now in a long-term relationship with Sam, a man whom she can boss.

Yet Cookie's mother is still very unhappy. She worries that she has been a bad mother in some way. She fears so intensely that Cookie is making too many serious mistakes with men that she can't avoid giving constant advice to her daughter about men and love.

Cookie's mother is overly emotionally invested in Cookie's life. She is no longer just a mother, and Cookie is no longer just a daughter. She has put Cookie in the emotional slot of being a recreation of her second chance at life and love. Cookie's mom has crossed that invisible but necessary boundary between parent and child.

Her mother needs Cookie to find love and be happy because it will make Cookie's mother feel less guilty about divorcing Cookie's deadbeat dad, and less anxious about not being a good role model for Cookie. Oldest and only children especially end up in this predicament of high parental emotional involvement when a parent needs the child to provide the parent with a happy version of the mother or father's not-so-happy life.

As you saw in the last cartoon, Cookie's mother is more than willing to forgive her daughter for bringing the wrong Christmas gift. Her mother is thrilled that her daughter is dating an attorney because she can feel redeemed for her past love decisions.

Unfortunately, Cookie's burden of having to be the person who can make her mother happy creates lots of turmoil and insecurity in Cookie. Living to make her mother happy is doomed to fail because no child can make up for a parent's choices. Adult children often take ownership of the difficulty and failure of fulfilling this emotional task. If you are in this impossible situation of making your parent happy, you could end up carrying around a deep-seated sense of being flawed. Like Cookie, you could be unsure of what kind of man is the right one to please your over-invested parent.

Many of the women in my study said they were "too important" to their family. They often had to serve as the buffer zone between fighting parents and children. Other women said they were the only thing that held their parents together.

Cookie's dating history shows she feels comfortable either with men who need too much guidance or with men who like to take too much control. Should Cookie choose a man like her father who was mean and selfish and who abandoned his family? Should she choose a man who is pliable, just like her mother's current boyfriend Sam? What should Cookie do about that rebellious streak in her that says she should instead focus on pleasing herself?

Do these problems sound familiar to you? What thoughts have Cookie's dilemma sparked? Write down a few of the ideas running around in your head.

HOW DO I APPLY WHAT I AM LEARNING ABOUT FUNCTIONAL BIRTH ORDER AND MY IMPORTANCE IN MY FAMILY TO MY LOVE HISTORY?

The value of understanding how the impact of birth order factors in your attraction to men not only helps you learn about you, but it also gives you a powerful tool in making preliminary assessments of men.

One of your best skills in selecting men is being able to *predict* their behaviors. Knowing both your man's birth order and information about his family life gives you a potent base for testing your observations about *his* emotional comfort zone and his potential behavior with you. Is your man a rebel, an insecure middle child or a bossy brother of brothers? Does his traditional birth order contrast with how he really is in relationships?

On your dates, you can make a game of guessing things about each other. Since you may not know a man's actual birth order, explain to him that you are on a learning mission where you are testing your understanding about yourself and others. Tell him about birth order and find out whether he thinks he fits his profile or not and why.

Get creative so that you don't seem to be interrogating him. For example, ask about first impressions. You could also tell the man what attracted you to him. You might say, "I'm so glad we're getting together. You seem like a very caring and responsible person. By any chance, do you have a younger sister? You seem to feel comfortable around women. Am I right?"

You could also explain what you are learning about the danger of relying on chemistry and feeling emotionally comfortable with a man. Give him an example about how you learned to be a bit skeptical of your sense of comfort. Ask him if he's had a relationship that backfired. It might take a few false starts to get used to asking these questions.

Now let's apply what you are learning about emotional family roles and birth order to your observations about all of your love preferences, including your attraction to a certain style and behavior in your men. This next exercise will help you see the influence of your birth order, emotional comfort zone and emotional default setting in being attracted repeatedly to the same kinds of relationship patterns.

In the exercise, write the names of the men who were your main love relationships. If you know their birth orders, include them. Describe both the men's and your behavior in the relationship. Then give the relationship a happiness grade from A+ to F. Put your grade below the happy face. If your grade is in between two letters, you can use a plus or minus. Look for the common denominator. I've provided you with an overview of traditional birth order descriptions to help with the exercise.

BASIC BIRTH ORDER REVIEW

Oldest/Only: leader, tends to micro-manage or need respect, might be insensitive if she/he is an only child or has younger same-sex siblings or might be kind if she/he has younger opposite-sex siblings, reliable, sometimes risk-avoider

Youngest/Only: maverick or rebel, might need discipline or guidance—even though she/he fights it, can be either very successful or lost, fun, sometimes takes too many risks if she/he is a rebel

Middle: negotiator, sometimes too tuned in to emotions of self and others, kind, difficulty making decisions, could be resentful or competitive with close in age, same-sex siblings

Now you're ready to examine your love history. The goals are to see how your attraction to and chemistry with a man can just as easily be good or bad for you.

Birth Order and Behavior Chart of My Past and Current Intimate Relationships

His Name	His Birth Order	My Birth Order	His Behavior	My Behavior	🙂 Grade

What patterns do you see, if any? If the low happiness grade and the birth order behavior of your men form a pattern of dissatisfaction, it might be time to try to change your attraction to these types of men.

HOW DO I CHANGE MY ATTRACTION TO MEN?

In order to change the emotional default setting of your automatic chemistry, first review the last list often. Read it out loud and tell yourself that you will pay more attention to men's behavior.

Begin by dating men who are different from your usual pattern or by dating men for whom you don't feel an instant attraction. Don't turn down a man because he doesn't seem like your type. As I've mentioned before, dating a different kind of man is an excellent way to learn more about your needs and hone your skills in reading men, especially if you've been dating the same type and haven't been successful. It's not smart to do more of the same thing when that thing isn't working. Make sure you give the man at least one more chance before you end the relationship.

You may feel uncomfortable, at first, with this new man because you are now acting outside your emotional comfort zone. But there is another reason why you might feel uncomfortable: You might be experiencing the discomfort of going against your family's wishes and needs. Think about Cookie's dilemma in the last cartoon. She wants to please her mother by dating someone who will make her mother happy, such as a rich attorney. So, it would not be surprising if Cookie felt extremely uncomfortable dating someone who was good for her but who did not satisfy her mother's needs. If that dilemma sounds like one you have or are facing, then you need to learn more about the stumbling blocks of going against the feeling of chemistry that comes from pleasing your parents.

To understand more fully why this concept of comfort zones and uncomfortable zones is so important here are some stories of the women in my study:

Doreen's Story

When Doreen discovered she needed to be more mindful of her feelings of chemistry and comfort with a man, she was better able to take her time with men and choose more wisely. On Doreen's first date with Phil, she felt an instant sense of comfort. "A warning light went off," Doreen said. "I always tended to seek out men who ended up disappointing me." She broke it off with Phil to avoid falling into the same comfort zone trap.

Doreen was an older sister of two younger brothers. She fit the traditional birth order profile of being responsible, reliable and level-headed. Her mother worked all day as an interior decorator. Doreen described her mother as having big dreams of decorating the homes of the rich and famous. As a result, Doreen's mother often resented having to come home to motherhood.

Doreen's father was a younger brother of brothers and he, too, fit his traditional birth order profile of being an outgoing and charming youngest child. He was a salesman of expensive homes, but the downturn in the market reduced his income. His lack of resourcefulness in making a living shocked Doreen. For the first time she saw serious shortcomings in her father. She realized how dependent he was on a ready-made job.

Now Doreen understood better why her mother always harped on him to start his own agency—and why her father could never do it. Her dad did not have the risk-taking ability to strike out on his own. Doreen realized that her emotional role in the family was more than mother hen to her brothers. She was also supposed to provide the warmth, acceptance and cheerleading for a man with limitations and fears. Repeatedly in her intimate relationships Doreen chose kind and decent but frightened men whom she nurtured. "I was used to it," Doreen said. "It felt natural."

When Doreen decided to date more effective men, however, she said she didn't feel comfortable. The men she dated felt like bad matches to her. Doreen said she felt lost without her role as caregiver. When she went out with these successful men, anxious thoughts went through her head. "I began wondering what they saw in me. Here I am this successful, elected county official and I didn't feel good enough. What did these men *need* me for?" After a few dates, she'd tell these men goodbye.

After a few more disappointing experiences with men, Doreen made a pact with herself.

DOREEN'S COMFORT ZONE PACT

- Date *against* her comfort zone.
- Take time to know the man.
- Tough out the uncomfortable feeling of being outside her emotional comfort zone and don't bolt so quickly.

- Become skeptical of chemistry too early in a relationship.
- Build automatic *discomfort* for her usual unhealthy version of her comfort zone.

On her next few dates, Doreen put her pact into action. She forced herself to accept a date with Charlie, one of the city planners. She had never been attracted to him. "He had an edge to him that I didn't like. I thought maybe he'd be mean." Yet, after working with him on a few projects and learning about his bad divorce, she decided to date him.

On their first few dates they went to local restaurants and took walks on the beach. She asked him about his divorce and childhood. Doreen had a personality that made people feel comfortable and so Charlie talked openly. At first, she adopted her familiar role of nurturer. She learned that Charlie was an older brother of sisters, and she asked him if he fit the profile of being a sensitive and empathic man.

Dating actually began to be fun. She and Charlie started a guessing game about each other. "And then my discomfort set in," Doreen said. The more she saw Charlie as a competent, entrepreneurial and caring man, the more *uncomfortable* she felt. She knew, by now, not to bolt. She had a feeling that her discomfort was coming from the newness of her choice of man, and from the unfamiliarity of not playing the role of caretaker or woman in charge.

One night she asked Charlie what he found attractive about her. He was shocked at her insecurity. Charlie told her it was a pleasure to be with a competent woman who was also caring. His first wife needed him too much, and she called him several times a day to talk about every little problem. Doreen responded that she felt *more* comfortable as a team player than solely as a nurturer. "I loved being a coequal. It was new to me, but I just blossomed."

Here are some more illustrations about the struggles of women who needed to defy the roles and comfort zones of their birth families.

Jean's Story

Jean was an only child raised by a caretaker whom she called Nana. Jean's famous and wealthy parents traveled all over the world as professional dancers. When Jean started dating while in college, her first boyfriend, Mario, was from a family that struggled economically just as Nana did. Jean felt chemistry with Mario because of her emotional comfort zone with others who were less fortunate.

However, Mario's jealousy of Jean's wealth led to bitterness and squabbles. He felt inadequate that he could not afford gifts or dinner at even moderately priced restaurants. Soon they broke up. Yet Jean continued to date men whom, in her words, she "could rescue."

After college, when she was working as a buyer for a major department store, she found herself attracted to a man, Frederick, whom she thought was "only one of the salesmen." She really liked him, and when she learned he was actually a vice president, she felt happy. Wasn't he exactly the kind of man her parents wanted her to marry? Wasn't her family role to make her parents proud?

But Frederick turned out to be cold and remote. Jean often found herself apologizing repeatedly for the smallest infractions such as being five minutes late or for not buying enough clothes in his favorite color, green.

Then Frederick broke up with her, and Jean went back and forth between men whom she rescued and men who were distant. "I felt comfortable with both extremes," she said. Mostly, Jean was addicted to trying to fix her past emotional pain from her family by seeking men who mistreated her. She especially felt chemistry with mean men.

Jean's thirtieth birthday was her wake-up call to change. She decided to consider other dating factors such as reliability and empathy, two things that her parents didn't provide. "It took a lot of courage and patience to finally date men who didn't give me that instant chemistry feeling," she said. Jean eventually found a man who didn't have her parents' problems with expressing love. "He wasn't as wealthy as my parents hoped. But I realized that I had the strength to find happiness on *my* terms," she said.

$$\equiv$$

Like Jean, what usually determines the relationship pattern that you like is a combination of comfort, familiarity and importance in your family. You experience the total sum of all these preferences as chemistry—that relationship "click" and rush of feelings that make you believe you've found *Mr. Right*.

That click is so powerful that it can fool you into staying too long in a relationship that is not good for you. It's no wonder that chemistry is hard to change, but sometimes that is exactly what you need to do. If you don't try, then you'll fall into the same pattern over and over.

Flora's Story

Flora was so used to dealing with negativity that she couldn't see how often she accepted it in a man. She attributed her father's rejecting nature to his hard life in Hungary. One day, while at a luncheon meeting for city planners, Flora was seated next to a planner from another town. As she listened to him describe an incident with his children, she saw for the first time how a loving man would treat his family.

A memory from her childhood flashed across Flora's mind of a time she wanted to please her father. Flora spent all day painting the soiled walls of the foyer of their home with the end of a rolled-up rag. The color was warm as sunshine and she loved how it made her home seem happy. She waited all through dinner for her father to comment on her excellent paint job, but he didn't say a single word for hours. Then, suddenly, he said: "So you think you're an expert painter?"

Flora recalled the incident while listening to the man talk, and this time the pain of not getting her father's approval that night helped her make a startling discovery: Her comfort with mistreatment made her uncomfortable with kindness. She realized her emotional family role was to be the scapegoat for all her family's unhappiness. She was the middle child between two sisters who had gotten married early and left home.

In Flora's family, to be criticized was to be loved, because it was better than being ignored. Flora knew she didn't want a mean man any longer, yet her mistrust of nice men made her view them as weak.

For a while, Flora overcorrected her tendency to date mean men and dated indecisive men instead. Eventually, she was able to discern meek men from effective and kind ones. When she attended another city planning meeting, she sought out the man who had sat next to her months ago. The relationship click hit her and she smiled. She was proud that she had changed her chemistry.

Olivia's Story

Olivia saw her boyfriend Alan fitting in well with her underemployed brothers and parents around the Thanksgiving dinner table. Olivia was the only daughter, and her family expected her to bring home a man who would be just like her brothers and father. When Alan came over to her house, her brothers and father would laugh, watch football, eat a little too much and swap fantasies about playing pro ball. But the situation made Olivia uncomfortable. Alan fit in too well. He was just like her family members, willing to accept too little in life and dream impossible dreams instead. When Alan bought a new motorcycle with the money that Olivia gave him for his business, she broke up with him.

Soon Olivia met George at work. They were assigned to work together for almost a year on the same industrial design project. Over time, she began to know George better and they fell in love.

But Olivia was nervous just thinking about her family meeting George. He wasn't anything like her brothers, father and grandfathers. George was successful, ambitious and risk-taking. Her family members had been content to stay in the same routine jobs and to spend their lives counting the days until they would receive their pensions.

Even though Olivia knew George was a good match for her, she still had to fight feelings of anxiety about George not fitting into her family. She knew her family would dislike him.

And they did. Her parents and brothers took her aside and asked her whether George was from New York. When Olivia said that he was from Seattle, they all nodded their heads in unison. "Well, we knew he was from some big city. A little ambitious, isn't he? What—he doesn't put his shoes on one foot at a time like we do?"

Olivia said she spent the next month doubting her attraction and being anxious and nauseous about making her family feel uncomfortable or unhappy. Yet, the more time she spent with George the more she loved him. She eventually married George and her brothers and father were forever jealous of her prosperity and happiness. Olivia learned just in time that her previous feeling of chemistry with ineffective men was not healthy for her.

You can change your usual attraction and feeling of chemistry. But it will take time, bravery and mindfulness.

Tips for Family Roles and Chemistry

Learn about the power of birth order. Birth order gives you a style along the continuums of factors such as risk, leadership, assertiveness, optimism and compromise.

Identify your emotional role in your family. What is your importance in your family? What would happen if you were not there?

Become mindful of how you enact your emotional family role in your relationships. Do you end up in love patterns that recreate this family role? Observe your interactions with your partner.

Don't trust your feelings of chemistry too quickly. It is easy to feel an attraction to a person who is not good for you. Date men who are different from your usual type. Know that chemistry often takes time—especially if you need to modify or even go against your family's expectations of you.

Tough out feeling anxious about changing your usual relationship patterns. It takes time to build the courage to be different from your family and your emotional role in it. Continue to date and relate to many different men while you are feeling anxious. Use this time to learn about yourself and your family.

Chapter 5

Your Parents' Relationship

One of the most burning questions women in my groups asked was "Am I really doomed to repeat my parents' relationship?" Few women understood what drew their parents to each other. Understanding the emotional glue of attraction that brought your parents together is critical to knowing the forces that shaped your values, struggles, attractions to certain men and love successes.

Usually, people come together with a shared core of values, life lessons, problem-solving styles and fears that they handle differently. This core travels through family generations. The exercises in this chapter will make this core visible and help you understand how it affects your intimate relationships.

One of the core lessons from a family environment is how to handle disagreements and their impact on family members' experiences of feeling safe and cared for. In volatile family environments, usually one person learns to rely on yelling, screaming, banging doors and breaking things in order to be heard and feel safe by insisting that the other people do things the way he or she wants.

If the other partner learns to remain passive, the family also transmits the opposite life lesson of enduring the arguing and violence so that he or she can feel safe by going along and not rocking the boat. Both partners brought the same problem of needing to feel safe, but they managed it in different ways. It's no surprise that their adult daughters were attracted to men who either avoided or provoked confrontations.

This chapter will help you see the links between your family of origin and the life lessons that you enact in your love relationships. You will also learn that you have the power to alter them.

Let's see how Cookie copes with the way her mother handles her core issues and transmits them to Cookie.

COOKIE'S LOVE LESSONS FROM HER MOTHER

Cookie is struggling to follow her instincts about Ron. He lied about having another girlfriend. Cookie's gut reaction is to break up with him. Yet, she must be feeling ambivalent about her decision because she tells her mother details about Ron. Cookie knows her divorced mother is desperate to find love. Over the years Cookie has seen a revolving cast play the leading man role in her mother's life.

Cookie knows deep down that Ron is not a good choice for her. She even bucks her mother's advice to ignore Ron's indiscretion because Ron is rich. After all, her mother teaches her daughter that all men are liars, so why not hang onto a rich one? At the end of the conversation both Cookie and her mom modify the lesson. Mother assures Cookie that she'll probably find another wealthy man and Cookie holds on to the view that her mother is right.

Why didn't Cookie reject with clarity and strength the idea that it is okay to put up with unacceptable things for the sake of keeping a man? Without realizing it, Cookie has absorbed both her mother's fear of being alone as well as her mother's life lesson that it is okay to tolerate just about any unwanted behavior from a man who seems to be a good catch.

We all absorb the life lessons, problems and ways of handling them from our parents and caregivers. Sometimes we recreate them in our intimate relationships. Other times, these problems and reactions remain as dormant behaviors that activate in certain situations.

Molly's Story

Molly's mother was a screamer while Molly inherited her father's calm and kind personality. She grew up witnessing her mother yell at her father for not being more proactive and risk taking in building his business.

Molly's calm manner made her an outstanding special education teacher. In her intimate relationships she was attracted to exciting men who drew Molly out. She learned from her father that feeling safe was one of the most important factors in a relationship.

Molly felt safe with her boyfriend Maxim because of his skills in decision-making and risk-taking. "He balanced me and taught me," Molly said.

When Molly discovered that Maxim was arranging online hook-ups with prostitutes, she screamed at him. "I couldn't believe my reaction," Molly said. "I have never had that happen before."

Molly screamed because of two things. First, she had her mother's behavior coded in her brain, but the neural connections were genetically weaker and sparser than her brain wiring for her father's calmness and risk avoidance. Second, her discovery of Maxim's hook-ups destroyed her feelings of trust and safety—fundamental factors for loving attachments. Automatically, Molly's brain fired up her less potent brain wirings when she felt unsafe with Maxim. Both Molly and Maxim wanted to feel safe in life, but they had opposite styles and values about how to achieve it.

Let's see how you have incorporated the problems, life lessons and style of your family into your attractions. We'll begin by examining what you know about a key concept in attraction.

WHAT ELSE ATTRACTS PEOPLE IN ADDITION TO BIRTH ORDER COMPATIBILITY?

People, as mentioned earlier, tend to come together with a shared core of values, life views, problems and fears that they handle in opposite or different ways. Trouble happens when these differing life views and ways are handled so differently from each other that they end up on opposite ends of a continuum.

A good way to understand this process is to imagine that your parents are walking hand-in-hand up a hill like Jack and Jill. At the top of this hill is a magic well filled with special water. Your parents want to get something from this magic well such as feeling loved, safe, warm, respected, understood and accepted. Each of your parents, however, has a different method of getting these things from the well.

For instance, your mother may carry a huge open bucket with her up the hill. She plans to plunge her bucket deep into the well to scoop up as much as she can. She came from a family where her parents divorced when she was a teenager, which surprised her because she always thought that her parents were happy. Now it seemed that she didn't understand anything, and she believed that the best way to protect herself against an upset like her parents was to demand as much as she could from a man.

Your father may carry a smaller bucket with a long spout on it. He doesn't trust the well. He doesn't really know what's in it, so he feels safer if he begins by taking less and by using the spout to control how much he will pour from the special water. He came from a family that was very cautious in life. His father lost all his money in a bad scheme and he has toiled the rest of his life at a factory job that he hates to assure the family of his health and retirement benefits.

All down the hill, like Jack and Jill, your parents are spilling the special water from the well because they are arguing so intensely about the right kind of bucket to use for carrying the water. Your father insists that it is wiser to play it safe and see what happens when you drink the water. He tugs at your mother's bucket and he spills her water on the grass. Your mother is so fed up with her husband's cautiousness that she yells at her husband and tells him she needs as much water from the well as possible to feel happy, safe and loved in life.

Now, if this Jack and Jill couple is smart, they will learn from their partner's opposite style, see the benefits of their partner's viewpoint and move closer to the middle in their behaviors. This Jack and Jill would now form a stronger and more capable team because of their ability to temper their needs for safety and to build flexibility in their different problem-solving techniques. They agree to put a long spout that they can control onto the big open bucket. If your mother and father have become more flexible, you will learn the importance of flexibility and empathy for your partner's style, needs and values and his views about risk. These factors will help you and your partner become a good problem-solving team.

However, if this Jack and Jill couple cannot work together, they will spend the rest of their lives arguing about their different styles and views of the world. They will struggle to feel safe, loved or valued. You will likely have difficulties being a good problem-solver, because you will recreate these competing styles in your intimate relationships. Now it's time to apply this model of shared needs and opposite styles to your specific situation.

WHY DID MY PARENTS CHOOSE EACH OTHER?

Here is a list of some major questions for you to answer about your parents' marriage. If you don't know the answers, ask your parents or the history-keepers in your family. Often, there is someone from each side of the family who knows about the backgrounds of your parents. As you get more information and insight, you might need to amend your answers.

QUESTIONS ABOUT YOUR PARENTS

1. What were the parents of your mother and father like? How would you describe each parent of your mother and father?

2. What are the functional birth orders of your mother and father?

3. In what ways were they each important or not important in the family?

4. Describe the personalities, fears, needs and strengths of each of your parents. Which of their parents does each seem the most like?

5. How did your parents meet and fall in love? How did their personalities, fears, needs and strengths work well or not so well with each other?

These questions are not so easy to answer. I'm asking you to think about connections that you might not have seen. One of the women in my study, Angela, learned the importance of this knowledge and its impact on her relationships.

Angela's Story

Angela didn't see her parents' divorce coming. She was just thirteen when her parents Nina and Douglas split up. Angela was too busy with friends and boys to notice the pattern of distance and fighting between her parents.

As an only child, Angela had the leadership characteristics of a firstborn or only child, and she also had some of the dependency needs of an only child. She was confused by her simultaneous needs to be decisive and directed. Angela was a lonely child and her parents' divorce made her wonder if her parents had known not to have any more children.

Angela was thinking of her family relationships as she faced her own divorce from Bill. Angela had met Bill at a party ten years before. She liked him right away. He was mild and sweet. After nine months of dating, one night she mentioned to Bill that if nine months was enough time to make a baby, then it certainly was enough time to know if you loved someone enough to make a marriage. She said the perfect proposal would be in the botanical gardens, a celebration of nature and growth (Angela was the director of a botanical garden).

Two weeks later, on a Sunday afternoon after Bill finished his weekly sermon at the church where he was the pastor, he proposed to Angela in the botanical garden where she worked.

Over the next ten years, they had two boys. Angela's job expanded to include the directorship of a newly-formed coalition of international botanical gardens. Bill was still the pastor of the same church, whose congregation had shrunk dramatically. He liked his parishioners, he said, and that was why he never bothered applying for more lucrative and higher-profile positions with other churches.

Angela knew exactly when she fell out of love with Bill. Their marriage had consisted of Angela prodding Bill to push himself. She thought she was helping him realize his potential. Bill always countered her suggestions with a "Yes, but."

One night, when the boys' school had parent night, Angela learned that all the teachers said her boys were doing okay in school but that they held back from participating in school activities. The teachers said they were more anxious than shy. Angela's heart dropped. That description could have been about Bill. And that was when she fell out of love with Bill.

They divorced, against Bill's wishes. When Angela started dating, she either fell for men just like Bill or men who were too dictatorial. She was so frustrated and lonely that she decided to seek counseling.

ANGELA'S FAMILY BACKGROUNDS AND NEEDS

Angela first focused on her mother, Nina. Nina was the middle child between two sisters. She never felt as pretty, smart or loved as her siblings. Nina's mother became cold, judgmental and critical just like Nina's grandmother. She pushed Angela to pay attention to her studies and her appearance. Nina often said to Angela, "If you're going to be a smart girl, then you'd also better be pretty, thin and have a good personality. And marry rich. It's the only way to have a stable life."

Angela wasn't pretty or thin and even though she could be outgoing, she was, at heart, a studious introvert. Angela grew up believing that she'd never be happy or feel really secure in life because she lacked what her mother taught her were the essentials for a female's fulfilling future.

Nina's father was a highly successful businessman with an outgoing personality that others found charming and fun. At home, he retreated from his wife and family. He was the oldest brother of brothers and was very bossy and remote. He was orphaned at a young age and had to raise himself. He started his gardening business at age seven. He sensed early that no one would look out for him and his brothers, so later he took his brothers into his finance business. He was so bossy that behind his back everyone called him *The King*. He believed that if you wanted something done, you had to do it yourself.

Angela realized that both her parents came from emotionally cold backgrounds that taught them different views and values about life.

Angela understood how her parents each had gone to that magic well looking for the same security, safety and love.

Her mother passed messages on to Angela that said security in life rested on being perfect enough to gain love from a mother and a man. Angela also learned from her mother that safety in marriage required putting up with all kinds of bad behavior from a man as long as he was successful and aggressive. According to Angela's mother, proof of being a good mother and having a good marriage relied on her daughter marrying a rich man.

ANGELA'S REVISED MESSAGE ABOUT MARRIAGE, SECURITY AND SAFETY

Angela certainly learned the value of being aggressive and ambitious from her parents' marriage. But instead of marrying someone with these skills, Angela became the one to provide them. "Looking back, I can see that I had the same needs for security that my parents did, but I learned that it was safer to be the one in charge. I thought strong men would be mean and controlling like my dad," Angela said.

When Angela's mother remarried, however, she chose a mild man with a good salary as a research chemist for a pharmaceutical firm. He would never be the head of the department, but his salary was solid with good benefits. Angela saw that her mother seemed happier.

Angela now vowed never to choose a controlling and cold man. When she met Bill, Angela was sure she had found someone as sweet and agreeable as her mother's second husband. She was right. They seemed a good match in the beginning. Angela, as the take-charge version of her birth order profile of the only child, fit well with Bill's mild style. Bill had an older and younger brother. He never could find his place between his older brother, who was a successful corporate executive, and his younger brother, who was a successful television writer. Bill liked that Angela steered the relationship.

TROUBLE IN ANGELA'S MARRIAGE

What Angela didn't realize was how much she and Bill shared similar needs to be loved and to feel safe. At first, Bill's pliable and caring manner did make her feel loved. She didn't see that Bill's fear of life and risk made him less effective. The result was that Angela did not feel safe with Bill, and they argued constantly about Bill's passivity. She didn't regard him as an equal partner. Angela observed how her choice of spouse may have matched the style of her mother's second husband, but it didn't make Angela happy. She had reversed her parents' roles in their marriage by becoming the tough one in her relationship.

After Angela's divorce, she dated lots of men. She was more frightened of life than she thought, and she wanted to find a man quickly. She said she "couldn't stop the engine of fear" that pushed her to find someone. She knew not to choose a man who was unreliable and frightened, but she feared choosing a man whose strong character could also make him cruel.

WHAT ANGELA LEARNED

Angela now understood that she had radar for meek men with high needs for safety and predictability and she made sure her time with a man included situations that required decisions such as which seats to select for an event. She went with her dates to look at automobiles and on shopping trips to observe their bargaining styles.

Over time, she began to trust her ability to read men. She also began to feel more comfortable with stronger men. She had feared that her dependent side—that needed to please in order to feel safe—would kick in and make her susceptible to tolerating insensitive behavior from her partner.

Yet, as she focused on becoming more comfortable with able men, Angela discovered that her attraction to them was happening more readily. Eventually, Angela married a man who was secure, successful, outgoing, reliable and caring. "But it wasn't easy," Angela said. "I had to work hard not to fall in love with a man who coped by either hiding out or lording over people."

Angela's happiness also rested on her ability to challenge the fears and life lessons of her parents. She no longer saw life as a scary experience that required either cruelty or risk avoidance.

What have you learned about recreating your parents' love bond? In what way, if any, do Angela's struggles and successes apply to you?

What are you carrying around with you in your family backpack? If you don't know what's inside the load you are toting, you may not understand what it signals.

YOUR FAMILY BACKPACK: THINKING ABOUT EMOTIONAL BONDS, FEARS AND LIFE VIEW

- Have I found myself in a relationship pattern just like my parents? How were decisions made in my parents' marriage? What did they fear in life? What was their view of the world? How do my partner and I handle decisions?

- Like Angela's first marriage to mild Bill, have I reversed the roles in my parents' marriage to avoid my parents' problems— but ended up being unhappy about the same core issue in a different form?

- How do my partner and I reflect different family backgrounds that resulted in different ways of handling the core issues of feeling loved, safe and valued?

- Do I have radar for choosing men with the same styles or core problems?

- What are the functional birth order styles of my partner and myself? Are we compatible or are we so different that we've become rigid and locked into certain behaviors?

Your answer to the last question about opposites is very important in understanding how relationships such as your parents' function. It's likely that you and your partner have at least somewhat opposite styles of handling the core issues of worldview, risk, safety, security, approval and love.

Personality styles tend to incorporate compatible values. For example, optimistic people tend to trust in their ability to cope with life. They might see life as unpredictable but also filled with opportunities for happiness. They are risk takers who know that whatever happens, they will land on their feet.

Passive people avoid risk. They believe life can be unfair and scary. Even if they are unhappy, they reason that it's better not to change because the devil you know is preferable to the devil you don't know.

Think about what your family taught you about their values and worldview. How did your parents differ in their approach to life? Did they help each other grow and change and become more competent?

There is no magical formula for the perfect balance of differing styles, values or compatible birth orders and family history. Think about what your family taught you about their views and comfort with the following key issues.

My Family's Management of Important Life Issues

How did your mother and father handle each of these topics? Describe their styles.

Issues	Mother	Father
Spending and saving money		
Illness		
Anger		
Success and failure		
Positive or negative life views		
Sex		
Closeness and distance		
Decision making		
Risk taking		
Views of men and women		

Look at the list again. How do you and your partner handle these issues? Are you attracted to someone whose views help or hinder your happiness?

MAKING THE CHEMISTRY OF OPPOSITE STYLES AND VIEWS IN LIFE WORK

If we go back to the metaphor of a family or relationship as a cruise ship, it certainly seems better to choose a partner whose differences in personality and coping styles add to the relationship. You don't want to narrow your range of problem-solving ability. So, it is no wonder that you feel chemistry for someone who complements you. For example, a man with a calm demeanor might reduce your anxiety. Marital researchers such as John M. Gottman, who has done extensive observations of couples' interactions, found that couples' ability to problem solve without criticizing or avoiding are keys to happy, healthy marriages.[1]

The differences in style can increase problem-solving skills and allow you and your partner to become a ship that sails smoothly. You learn from each other and develop flexibility and depth in managing decisions, life views, values and the issues in the last exercise. This depth provides stability if one of you becomes ill or is absent. Respect for your differences replaces criticism or rejection of each other's styles. Here is an exercise to help you learn how you and your partner can better handle your differences.

GUIDE FOR SMART CHEMISTRY AND DIFFERENCES

- Each partner can more or less meet the other partner near the middle when life circumstances demand new behaviors.
- The differences help create a newer, stronger team.
- Each partner values the other's style, and sees it as a tool to enrich the relationship.
- These differences add balance and flexibility to each other and the relationship. The resulting flexibility builds the strength needed to face unexpected life events, such as the loss of a child.
- The differences also allow partners to learn from the other to develop new coping skills.
- Partners are aware of what they learned from their parents' style and bond.
- Partners are able to make course corrections when they each fall back on old learned patterns that once made them feel comfortable but are now ineffective and unhealthy.

Next we'll look at a list of the most common opposite pairings. When you read them, think about you and your partner. How flexible are you two? How much do you squabble over your differences? What can you do to regard your differences as assets? Keep in mind what you learned from your parents' marriage, varying styles and coping methods.

On the next scale, the zero marks the midpoint. Rate yourself and your current or prospective partner for each personality characteristic.

Different Style Pairs Continuum

1. Introversion										
You:										Him:
5	4	3	2	1	0	1	2	3	4	5
High										High

2. Risk Taking										
You:										Him:
5	4	3	2	1	0	1	2	3	4	5
High										High

3. Thinker										
You:										Him:
5	4	3	2	1	0	1	2	3	4	5
High										High

4. Non-Defensive										
You:										Him:
5	4	3	2	1	0	1	2	3	4	5
High										High

5. Non-Critical										
You:										Him:
5	4	3	2	1	0	1	2	3	4	5
High										High

6. Optimism and Low Fear of Life										
You:										Him:
5	4	3	2	1	0	1	2	3	4	5
High										High

7. Ability to Manage Unpleasant Feelings (sadness, anger, etc.)										
You:										Him:
5	4	3	2	1	0	1	2	3	4	5
High										High

8. Dominance										
You:										Him:
5	4	3	2	1	0	1	2	3	4	5
High										High

9. Healthy Self-Esteem										
You:										Him:
5	4	3	2	1	0	1	2	3	4	5
High										High

Different Style Pairs Continuum (continued)

10. Empathy										
You:										Him:
5	4	3	2	1	0	1	2	3	4	5
High										High
11. Ability to Apologize Readily										
You:										Him:
5	4	3	2	1	0	1	2	3	4	5
High										High
12. [Add your own items]										
You:										Him:
5	4	3	2	1	0	1	2	3	4	5
High										High

Trouble with chemistry often occurs when you find yourself attracted to someone whose differences are at the extreme edges of the range. For example, a person whose introversion prevents him from talking about problems might match up with someone whose volatility makes her seek a crisis in order to force the quiet person to burst out of his shell.

Life in this kind of relationship would be exhausting. The comfort range of each of you would be so small that flexibility would be sacrificed. Soon, you probably would find yourself in arguments where someone has to win while another loses.

Darlene and Rick's Story

Darlene and Rick argued for so long about whether to buy a contemporary home or one with Victorian features that they did nothing for years. They each came from families where the parents addressed problems through intense arguing. Darlene usually hid behind the couch in the living room whenever her father became angry. Soon, her mother would join her and hold her tightly.

Rick's father was also volatile, but when Rick became a teenager, he towered over his father so he felt comfortable arguing and pushing back whenever his father became violent. Rick was not violent with Darlene, but he reenacted the screaming and shouting matches from his family environment. He had learned that he who shouts the loudest wins. Darlene had learned that the person who remains calm can also win. Both Rick and Darlene longed for peace, but they tried to achieve it in different ways. Winning and the safety of being right were so powerful in each of them that they only bought a home when a tornado destroyed their apartment. An architect helped them meld their two styles of home into one.

I'm not recommending that you always reject a man because your styles are too opposite, but I am attaching a warning message to remember to avoid relationships with men of extremely opposite personalities or styles that recreate your childhood in unhealthy ways.

Tricia's Story

Tricia and Leo fought all the time about everything. She liked to go out to fancy restaurants. He liked diners because he didn't believe there was any reason to spend lots of money on food that you could cook at home. She liked to take several shorter vacations within a year while he liked to take three weeks off at once. He couldn't see any sense in paying for so many flights when you could pay for just one round trip.

Their fights ended with each saying cruel things to the other. When they tried to compromise, they each kept score of whose turn was next. There was no harmony or genuine willingness to give up control.

Yet, when they first met, their bickering was fun. They each came from verbally expressive families and Tricia felt comfortable with their disagreements. She didn't see that Leo's hyper-logical approach to life would clash so painfully with her devil-may-care attitude.

Unhappiness occurs when one partner no longer wants or needs the limitations of his or her position on the continuum but the relationship is so rigid that it cannot tolerate the change. Tricia realized she wanted someone who didn't examine every factor in a decision. The chemistry was gone and she broke off the relationship.

Then she had a brainstorm—she was using arguing to avoid being close. Her family's volatility frightened her, but it also taught her that fighting was less frightening than allowing someone to get close. She recalled many nights when her father would kiss her mother on the cheek, and her mother would pull back.

Many months later, Tricia met a man who was calm but not inexpressive. At first, she was so unaccustomed to peace that she picked fights, but his calm and strong personality helped her to be braver and less defensive.

What works for one couple may not work for another. There is always that element of surprise, and we all know couples about whom we say, "I can't believe they stayed together all these years."

Flexibility, without forfeiting who you are, is central to healthy relationships. There is no magical formula for which opposites are better. The only trick is to watch out for the rigidity that can arise when the opposites are too far apart on the scale.

If you and your partner fight often, you might be arguing about the different coping styles that result when opposites attract. The next exercise might help you learn from each other, rekindle your chemistry and gain more flexibility:

Flexibility Exercise

1. Each partner should list and rank the couple's top three disagreements or issues. Let's look to Sandra and Graham for an example. Sandra listed two things: Graham's kinder approach to life versus her tougher nature and his introversion versus her extroversion. Graham also listed the difficulties between his softer and her tougher approach.

2. Compare your lists to see if you selected the same problems. Agree to discuss each other's first item.

3. Each person should jot down a few notes on a piece of paper about what he or she thinks makes his or her partner tick. Toss a coin to see who will go first. Whoever is first does the following:

    Pretend that you are your partner. Imagine how he thinks and why. Now talk to your partner as though you are him. Use the word I, not you. As you talk from his viewpoint, explain the problem, decision, fears, feelings, doubts and anything else that might be important. Now switch roles. Your partner now talks as though he is you.

4. What have you learned about each other? What would you correct about what he said? What would he correct? This process usually results in a plan of action or decision because your mutual empathy has automatically led you to a new and less defensive position.

Another couple, Rebecca and Justin, argued about whether to accept a free vacation to the Caribbean. The only hitch was that, in order to get the free vacation, as soon as they arrived they would have to attend an hour-and-a-half lecture on buying a timeshare property.

Rebecca realized Justin's approach of rejecting the vacation opportunity was possibly better because he knew the sales pitch would be annoying—and last throughout their entire stay. The sales people would be so relentless that he and Rebecca wouldn't enjoy the vacation.

Justin discovered that Rebecca's initial decision to accept the offer and attend the sales pitch was better because she knew they needed a vacation. However, her guilt of knowing that they weren't going to buy would gnaw away at the fun.

Even though their approaches differed, they ended up at the same conclusion—not to go. Look for any similarities in your conclusions. This exercise may not always work, but it helps you develop empathy for the other person's point of view. Sometimes, just seeing your viewpoint through another person's eyes can help you become more flexible.

Always remain mindful of what you carry within you from your parents' views, values and different coping styles. Some qualities may actually be good to keep. On the other hand, be wary of that unhealthy type of chemistry that attracts you to someone who reproduces your family's dysfunctional patterns. It can be very unwise—but all too easy—to feel chemistry and emotionally comfortable with someone who matches your family's environment.

Ask yourself this question: Is it a good idea for you and your partner to fit into your parents' style of family? Imagine you are with your parents during your family's holiday celebration, a vacation or other event. Think of the rituals, good times, inevitable squabbles and your unhappy feelings of being with them. The next chart provides key questions that will help you assess your attraction to a man and your ties to your family.

Testing Your Feeling of Chemistry: How Would He Fit into Your Family—In a Good Way or a Bad Way?

Would my family like him because he's just like them? Would that be a good thing or bad thing?

Would my family dislike him because he's not like them? Would that be a good thing or bad thing?

Are you trying to be just like or please your family (or a particular family member)? Is that a good thing or bad thing?

Are you trying not to be just like your family (or a particular family member)? Is that a good thing or bad thing?

Can you withstand the discomfort of being different from your family?

Focus on saying: I can be my own person and choose an effective partner—even if my choices go against my family's ways, and even if I feel anxious.

You might have anxiety attacks or bouts of sadness at the thought of going against your emotional family role. These feelings might make you revert to relying on chemistry that is not good for you. Give yourself permission to be your best self. Like the little duckling that doesn't fit into his family in *The Ugly Duckling*, you, too, can later turn out to be a beautiful swan if you postpone or change your feelings about chemistry and if you take the time to learn about your family's views, values, rules and fears.

Tips for Chemistry, Differences and Your Parents' Relationship

Understand your parents' attraction. Realize that couples often come together with shared problems that they handle in opposite ways.

Learn about the impact of your parents' styles on you. You absorb some of your family's strengths, weaknesses and ideas about things such as risk, trust, optimism and defensiveness.

Observe how you recreate your parents' differences in your intimate relationships. Become wary of feeling chemistry with a man whose style and values contribute to your recreating your family environment and approach to life. Ask yourself if your relationship is healthy for you.

Take charge of modifying your emotional comfort zone with healthy attractions. If your parents' relationship is not one that you want to replicate, then focus on training yourself to become more comfortable with a different relationship pattern or a man whose style can enrich and strengthen you.

Respect your partner's differences. Build empathy, value and flexibility about your partner's different ways. Realize that strong teams are composed of various skills and viewpoints.

Chapter 6

Mothers, Fathers and Family Loyalty

One of the unexpected findings in my research is that a daughter's respect for her mother can *impair* a woman's romantic relationships. Many of the women who said their mothers were role models experienced a mix of admiration, empathy and anger at their mothers for not creating a more loving family environment. They especially felt they were left with this weed and wisteria bouquet of feelings toward their single mothers who struggled to raise their children alone and earn an income after a divorce or break-up.

Fathers didn't fare too well either. Even though many of the women whom I surveyed held their fathers' career accomplishments in high esteem, the women struggled to untangle similarly mixed feelings toward them when fathers didn't applaud their successes or were absent. Women were left longing for approval and love from an unattainable father. Chasing after unrequited love from emotionally remote or mean men became one of the women's common relationship patterns.

The winning parents were the ones who served as role models for combining strong career interests with caring and supportive childrearing.

Women who harbored the most conflicting—and often unknown—feelings toward their mothers had the most problems in love. I wondered if a daughter could love and respect her mother *too much.* More than just empathy sent these daughters down the wrong romantic path. Few of them connected their poor choices in partners and relationship patterns with their mothers' love histories. So you are not alone if you are surprised to learn that mixed feelings about your mother can seriously imperil your happiness with men.

This chapter will strengthen your ability to understand your feelings and connection to your mother, father and family so you can choose more appropriate men or relate more effectively to your existing partner.

COOKIE IS SHOCKED TO SEE HERSELF IN HER MOTHER

Just why was Cookie so nervous about having her mom and her mom's boyfriend meet Tim? Cookie thought for a moment—approval—that was it. Cookie was afraid her mom wouldn't approve of him.

Who would dislike Tim? He was so sweet, so easy-going and creative. Okay—he didn't have a traditional job, but didn't her mom teach her to be tolerant? The moment Cookie's parents got divorced, didn't her mother date tons of different kinds of men? Cookie remembered the men bringing her stuffed animals or lollipops.

Maybe Cookie was nervous because she had some doubts about Tim. Could that be it? Lately, she'd given him lots of money for one of his projects. But *somebody* had to believe in him. Cookie knew too well what it was like not to be number one in a person's life. It seemed that her mother was always pushing her aside whenever a new man came along.

The latest man in her mother's life was Sam—sweet, easy-going, creative Sam, with more dreams than money in his pocket or sense in his head. Oh well, Cookie thought, at least he's not mean to her mother.

And then after dinner, when Tim reached for the check, a light bulb went off in Cookie's head. The words she used to describe Sam were the same ones she used to describe Tim. And when her mother yanked on Sam's tie to get his attention, she did the same thing to Tim's tie. Cookie wanted to remind Tim that he couldn't afford to pay for dinner.

"Gulp!" was the right response. Cookie realized why she was so anxious about going to dinner—she didn't want to see the similarity between herself and her mom. Doomed to unhappiness again, Cookie thought. Maybe she and her mom should just stop looking for love and move in together.

The similarities between Cookie and her mother are seemingly subtle. Your connection to your mother might be, too. But could your mother really be at the center of your unhappiness in love? You might be thinking something like, "I am aware of my mother's issues. Besides, aren't absent or dismissive fathers a more important factor?"

I learned repeatedly in my research and counseling of women that empowering women to separate from their parents' intimate relationship patterns and family loyalty is part of the foundation of claiming success in love.

In my workshops, women asked lots of questions about the impact of their childhoods on their current lives. A terrible childhood does *not* mean you will have a terrible life. Think about these family statistics from my study:

- 47 percent described their family environment as consisting of frequent and intense arguments.
- 45 percent said their parents were critical, negative and perfectionists.
- 64 percent said their parents were depressed or had other forms of mental illness.
- 50 percent said that at least one parent had addiction problems.
- 33 percent said that their parents were verbally abusive.
- 25 percent said there was physical violence, while 12 percent said there was sexual abuse.

Yet, slightly more than 30 percent said they were successful in spite of their parents and were among the most well-adjusted people in the family!

Rather than stumble around and get hurt in too many trial-and-error attempts at love, use the questions and discussions below as your guide to getting off the rocky pathway of your family's influence.

FAMILY LOYALTY AND MY UNHAPPINESS

At first, when I mentioned at one of my focus groups that emotional family loyalty is like having an enormous, stretchy tether that can hold you back from happiness without your knowing it, the women were ready to run me out of the room. "But I'm not like my family," they said. As proof, they offered things such as being politically different from their parents or more educated, wealthier or more worldly.

Those differences are important, but they are the petal of the flower, not the root. And it's that root that can get you in trouble if you can't dig it up and see what it's like. So, here is how loyalty has a profound effect on your romantic choices and relationship patterns.

Begin with the idea that I've mentioned before—abandonment. Fear of being abandoned is the chief threat for mammals. Good parents protect their young from predators, they hunt or gather food and they teach their cubs or calves survival skills.

Humans have the longest childhood and they can need parental care for an extended time, especially since the human brain does not reach full maturity until around age twenty-six. Your parents may not have to hunt and gather for you, but you probably still like to know they are there for you if you need them. Being alone and abandoned and forced to live without the safety net of parental or family support is one of our primary fears.

FEAR OF ABANDONMENT

Because we all fear abandonment, it makes sense that it is *natural and normal* to fear the loss of your family's help, love and approval—even if they weren't so great. After all, who is really going to care for you? Can you rely on distant relatives, friends or your community? There certainly are good Samaritans in the world, but they may not be a lasting source of financial and emotional support. No wonder we still look to our family and long for their endorsement and assistance.

Anthropologists and other scientists discovered that even though altruism exists in humans and animals such as elephants, the most likely persons to offer the support you need are the ones who share the same genes. Animals protect their most-closely related. It makes perfect sense then that the idea of "leaving" your family by going against their wishes, scripts and values can be emotionally terrifying and paralyzing. You feel truly alone and abandoned.

Fears of Family Turning Their Backs on You

Make a list of things—big and small—that you think might make your family abandon you. Examples from the women whom I surveyed include marrying outside the family religion or race or revealing the truth that one of the parents was an addict or child abuser.

How would you handle their turning away from you if you violated these family loyalty rules? Some of the women said they'd have a nervous breakdown. Others said that they'd pack their bags, leave town, never speak to them again and *try* to feel strong. Many hoped that their inner torture wouldn't somehow get in the way of feeling lovable or finding an understanding man.

HOW CAN RESPECT FOR MY MOTHER INTERFERE WITH MY SUCCESS IN LOVE AND LIFE?

Here is a typical path of how your respect for and loyalty to your mother seeps into your life and makes you unhappy. Your course of events and feelings will undoubtedly vary, but the key issues are still there.

YOU DEVELOP EMPATHY FOR YOUR MOTHER.

If you are like almost a third of the women in my study, you have extra respect for your mother. More than likely, you witnessed terrible arguments between your mother and father. Tempers flared, doors slammed, the words got nastier, the fists more fierce.

Perhaps, like almost 30 percent of women in my research, your parents got divorced. Your single mother raised you, and you saw your mother struggle to keep the family afloat financially and emotionally. Maybe your mother was single due to the death of a spouse or a break-up with a live-in partner. Life after divorce, break-up or the death of a parent was not easy. It's possible that your dad remarried, but your mother did not. Perhaps there seemed to be an endless parade of your mother's new partners.

Regardless of their situations, the mothers had to juggle caring for children and working long hours in multiple jobs or stretching unemployment or welfare checks just to make ends meet. You admire your mother greatly for her ability to compromise, adapt, juggle tasks and often put her needs last. You feel your mother's loneliness and pessimism.

Even if your mother did not have a hard-knocks life, you respect her ability to manage a demanding household. She cooked, cleaned, car-pooled and, if your parents were married, catered to your father. You sense your mother's frustration at having to put aside her personal goals and you felt a little sorry for her. Sometimes, it was only after you were on your own that your empathy and admiration for her emerged.

Patti, one woman with whom I spoke, had to work full-time as a stock analyst and raise her twin sons at once. She realized there were barely enough hours in the day to wash her face, let alone shop for groceries and prepare dinner. The next exercise will help you discover your admiration for your mother.

I Respect My Mother for:

Make a list of the things that you like or admire about your mother. You don't have to list just big things such as finishing college.

YOU FEAR BECOMING LIKE HER—
AND YOU VOW NEVER TO LIVE LIKE THAT.

Like many women in my study, you may have believed that you learned from your mother's love choices and mistakes. Perhaps you promised yourself that you wouldn't become vulnerable to your mother's style of intimate relationships.

You seek education, training and good jobs. You vow never to be in the same predicament of multiple jobs, reliance on child support, alimony or the reduced standards of living that your mother experienced. You're going to be capable, independent and strong enough to be in charge and insulated against getting as hurt by love as your mother. Do the exercise below to learn about your vow and success.

My Family Triumphs

Complete these sentences:

When I thought about my family experiences, I promised myself that I would never:

I have truly come a long way from my family by doing the following things in love and work:

YOU STILL ADMIRE YOUR MOTHER, BUT YOU BEGIN TO FEEL
DISTANT FROM HER—OR EVEN A LITTLE ANGRY AT HER
FOR HER REACTIONS TO YOU.

As you succeeded at financial independence and your career, you began to experience conflicting feelings of admiration, empathy, pity and resentment toward your mother for giving you a painful childhood and for not cheering who you are now.

Your mother hints and questions about when you are going to settle down or when you and your spouse are going to have children. "Are you planning on working full time?" she asks. She senses her intrusion and hastily adds that "you've made me proud," but you bristle at her judgment of you. You feel an angry gulf growing between yourself and your mother.

And then one day it hits you that you aren't as happy or as in control of your life as you expected or wanted. Usually, a crisis or an

emotionally-charged event sets off this temporary anguish and awareness. Perhaps you just broke up with another wrong-for-you boyfriend
or you are the last of the single women among your friends. Or perhaps
your marriage or relationship with your existing partner isn't going
very well. Another holiday with your mother aggravates you. Whatever
the reason, you come away with a very bad case of the blues.

Even worse, you sense that your mother is angry with you. You
detect a resentful tone in your mother's voice or in the look in your
mother's eye. She now makes snide comments or she snorts when you
talk about getting a promotion or meeting famous people. She hounds
you for details about the rich and famous, but she still ends up making
negative comments about them. Learn more about yourself and your
mother in this next exercise.

I Sense My Mother's Resentment— or at Least Her Confusion about Me

Complete this sentence:
I think my mom has difficulties dealing with who I am, because
lately or in the past she's said or done things such as:

If your mother's conflicting messages of being happy and unhappy
for you confuse you, then you are probably grappling with what mental
health professionals call the double bind message. Families often send
contradictory messages to their children. Women in my study often
experienced the conflicting messages of "You can be anything you want"
but "Don't be better than we are and then make us feel that you left us
in the dust."

If the daughter is psychologically astute, she knows her mother
is broadcasting a message about her own feelings of loss. Collectively,
these messages go like this: "Who do you think you are—have you forgotten where you came from? Don't you respect me and what I did for
you? What—are you too good to live in this neighborhood anymore?"

You feel a strange brew of pity and guilt for leaving your mother.
You probably hoped that your accomplishments would make your
mother proud. You assumed that your successes would insulate you
from living your mother's hard-knocks lifestyle. But perhaps your

mother experiences your achievements as a rejection and judgment of her life choices and plight.

YOU BEGIN TO SEE HOW YOUR PITY AND GUILT FORM A THIN COVER FOR YOUR SUBMERGED LOYALTY AND IDENTIFICATION WITH YOUR MOTHER.

Your mother's critical tone and words are contagious. Your life seems to be in a rut and it hits you: Your life might vary in detail from your mother's, but you are left feeling a similar pain of loneliness and disillusionment. You might be successful at work, but success in love has eluded you. You are shocked to find yourself choosing inappropriate partners who hurt you in ways similar to your mother's relationships.

"How did this happen to me?" you wonder. Your mix of empathy and respect for your mother facilitates this identity. As Nancy, one of my clients, said, "It's like there was this demon of doom and failure all along in me that I didn't know about."

Unknowingly, you have joined the "Unlucky in Love Mother-Daughter Club." Surpassing your mother and succeeding where she did not can create surpasser's guilt.

Even if you do triumph in love and work, it can occur to you that you might as well have just slapped your mother in her face, *because she could easily construe your lifestyle as a rejection of her.* Suddenly, you risk forsaking your membership in the mother-daughter society—and it doesn't feel all that good. You feel more than guilty—you feel surprisingly scared. What if you lose your mother's emotional support forever?

In one of my focus groups, Katherine expressed the power of this guilt. Katherine said she felt "swallowed up" by her mother's veiled messages to remain at home—or at least live a different kind of life. "I felt that I was shrinking or even disappearing," she said. "It seemed I was willing to give up my whole lifestyle to keep my mother's care and support." Tease out your own guilty tether to your mother in this exercise.

You—without your Mother

Imagine that your life and love choices make your mother turn her back on you. She won't talk to you or return your phone calls or e-mails. She doesn't want to know about your accomplishments at work or about the good things in your love life.

For example, she won't be there when you get married or have a child. On Mother's Day, you have no one. At the holidays, even your celebrations with loved ones feel bittersweet because she won't be there. If your mother is deceased and didn't approve or understand you, think about her being alive and doing these same dismissive acts. Write down the words or phrases that best describe your feelings.

YOUR FEAR OF ABANDONMENT EMERGES, BUT YOU QUIET IT EITHER BY ADMIRING YOUR MOTHER OR BECOMING LIKE HER.

Why would a grown and successful woman fear losing her mother's love? Knowing and accepting that your mother didn't like or approve of you puts you on the road of life without her—or even alone.

Letting go of *trying to get love* from a parent who has given up on you is one of the most difficult tasks you might have to face. Once you stop *trying*, you have agreed to live without their approval and applause.

Because the fear of total disapproval and abandonment is so high, you risk unknowingly converting your anger into admiration. Admiration allows you and your mother to sustain a relationship. Anger puts you on the path to losing her.

This twist and turn in feelings is not unusual. Martha Saxton, the biographer of Louisa May Alcott, the author of the much-loved novel *Little Women*, discusses at length Louisa's recasting her resentment of her mother into admiration. The Alcott family endured a lifelong struggle with poverty. Mr. Alcott's philosophy did not permit working for a living. Louisa witnessed her mother's struggles to rein in her own desires, needs, unhappiness and, most importantly, her anger at her wayward, dreaming husband.

To gain the approval of both her parents, Louisa, too, had to temper her aspirations, personality and observations of a family that lived off the generosity of others. Louisa saw her mother's exhaustion as noble. She even accepted the family's belief that the role of girls and women was to obey, bury—and atone—for their lapses into ambition and individuality.

The ruse worked for a while, but Louisa's anger at not being allowed to be the strong, independent, devil-may-care woman of her character

Jo in *Little Women* drained her emotionally. She would forever try to turn her anger at her mother into a sense of duty and admiration.[1]

If you are smart, you will build love from within. You will not need to seek as much affirmation from others—especially your mother and men. You will always feel the anguish of the loss or reduction in your mother's love for you, but you will manage it. When you are with her at holidays, for example, it might be more painful, but you can calm yourself and not feel as sorry for her or as guilty or frightened of the loss.

If you can't deal with this fundamental fear of abandonment, then you leave yourself vulnerable to becoming too much like her. A strange thing happens: unconsciously you find a way to keep your mother. A daughter's poor choice of mate may be her deeply-rooted way of saying: "Don't abandon me, because I didn't really abandon you. Because I am like you in some way, I still keep a part of you in me."

This phenomenon of partially keeping a parent's love by *becoming* somehow like them is very evident when a parent dies. One way of keeping that parent alive is to become like them in some way. This barely experienced identification is almost hard-wired into our biology.

Few people are aware of this process. But perhaps you've met someone who lost a parent, and then morphed into becoming more like the deceased parent. This incorporation is the human mind's way of keeping that person alive—and thus reducing the sense of abandonment. Think about how even the smallest memento—a ring or set of dishes—from the departed makes you feel closer.

An unwanted identity—no matter how small—does not have to *ruin* your life and happiness. It's hard, after all, to leave home completely, and becoming even a little like your mother can actually be a good way of keeping her close. This new form of closeness weakens the combined power of your pity, empathy, guilt and fear of abandonment.

This potent power of keeping your mother close—without having to appease those feelings by *over*-identifying with her—is to *select* the positive aspects about her that you want to incorporate in you. Despite your childhood experience in your family, it is unlikely that there was nothing positive to get from your mother. Don't throw the baby out with the bath water by trying so hard to be nothing like your mother that you risk tossing out good traits. Do this next exercise to find good ways to stay connected to your mother without impairing your life.

Good Things to Keep about My Mother

What do I like about my mother? Here is a list of those qualities or skills.

What can I do to keep my mother "alive" in myself?

I will write a note to my mother to thank her for giving me these good things, such as (make a list). I might revise the note and mail it to her. After she's had time to read it, I might arrange to see her or talk to her about my gratitude.

Finding ways for *you* to be the main source of approval and to keep good aspects of your mother in you also reduces your chances of getting stuck for too long in a punishment-reward cycle. Overeaters get trapped in this cycle frequently. They eat when they are stressed. The comfort food makes them feel better for a while, but then they start eating more. The carbohydrates make the eaters crave even more carbohydrates. Sugar highs and lows require more highs.

Soon the shame of overeating prompts them to eat *more* to punish themselves for being so bad. "I was on a roll—literally. I felt like I couldn't stop," one woman said. Overeaters also eat when they want to celebrate something. But now, if there are conflicting feelings about mothers and successes, they might get caught in that same punishment and reward cycle by not only eating more but also—as incredible as it sounds—finding a way to remain loyal to their mother by reproducing relationship unhappiness.

Don't give up. The *best* way to honor your mother is to succeed in love, life and work.

Tips for Not Reproducing your Mother's Unhealthy Choices

Acknowledge that you are afraid of being alone and abandoned. These are normal feelings. Become mindful of how these feelings can lead you to make unwise love choices or relive your mother's unhappy life.

Expect to feel guilty about surpassing your mother and family. These feelings are smokescreens to keep you in line with the family's style.

Keep your loyalty to your mother alive in yourself by incorporating positive things about her. Cherry-pick her good qualities and behaviors, and do not toss out the baby with the bath water. Refine these good things and make them your own. You have far more choices between the extremes of being just like them or not being anything like them.

Don't get into a punishment and reward cycle. Give yourself permission to be yourself. Build internal controls to help you tolerate any potential losses of your mother's approval. Say no to unhealthy behaviors such as overeating.

Thank your mother for what she's done well or taught you. Tell her that you are not rejecting her, but, instead, you are becoming what she probably really wants—for her daughter to become a productive, independent and happy person. Tell her she has reasons to feel proud!

Part III

Getting Mindful about Dating, Mating and Loving

Chapter 7

Myths, Facts, Cultural Messages and Affairs

Too many women are upset with the discouraging statistics about their poor odds of finding a good match. Demographics show that women outnumber men, women with post-college degrees get divorced more frequently and older women have trouble finding a mate. But statistics are only as valid and trustworthy as the methodology and interpretation. Even if certain pessimistic facts about marriage, divorce or cohabitation are true, that doesn't mean that they apply to you—or that you have to give up on love. Many women in my study said they couldn't "turn down the background noise" about what to do about love and sex.

But demographics are not the only challenge. Holding onto myths and certain cultural messages can also impede your romantic life. Lectures, articles, books and entire college courses deliberate the intertwined issues of women, work, love, society and happiness. "More noise," the women said.

This chapter targets my findings and your questions and fears about this tangled knot of statistics, social expectations, sex and relationships. Later we'll discuss in more detail the impact of cultural pressures about work on women.

IS THERE A "MR. RIGHT?"

This question plagued almost all the women in my study. The chorus of voices tells you "don't compromise, don't settle. Wait for *him*." The voices come from characters in romantic comedies where women sit around tables in restaurants to talk about their latest dates and their pessimism about finding love—until thwack!—it hits them that their guys who are just friends are the ones who should be boyfriends.

The voices come from romance novels where the heroine, after fending off a charismatic man who seems wrong—but to whom she is nonetheless attracted—either realizes he really is the right man or succumbs to some of his advances and *then* realizes he is the right man. Mixed messages from articles in women's magazines teach to either hold out for *him* or not to.

To make things worse, many of my participants said that when they brought men home to meet their parents, the women waited for a stamp of approval from the family. They wanted confirmation that these men were good matches. In the workshops many said that their family sighed in relief and said things such as "this is it" or "finally" when they brought men home for inspection. "It didn't help," one woman said, "when my own mother said, 'He's *the one*.' Still, I wondered. But I was so thrilled that I overlooked some important things."

How much do all these noisy voices get to you? Answer these questions. I want you to tease out some of the ideas floating in your head and heart. Circle or underline the choice that best describes you.

Awareness of Believing in *Mr. Right*

1. I really do think there is a *Mr. Right* for me.

   Yes   Probably   Sometimes   Probably Not   No

2. I'm holding out for a man who matches all the things I listed on dating sites.

   Yes   Probably   Sometimes   Probably Not   No

3. I am willing to compromise in my choice of mate.

   Yes   Probably   Sometimes   Probably Not   No

4. I'm looking for that feeling of having found a soulmate.

   Yes   Probably   Sometimes   Probably Not   No

5. I'm unhappy with my current partner because he just
    doesn't give me that special feeling.

    Yes   Probably   Sometimes   Probably Not   No

6. I know right away—often in seconds—whether a man is
    right for me.

    Yes   Probably   Sometimes   Probably Not   No

7. I am very discouraged about finding love because there just
    don't seem to be any good men.

    Yes   Probably   Sometimes   Probably Not   No

Look at your answer to number three. Did you indicate "Yes"? That
question is most likely a key indicator of your wisdom, maturity and
flexibility in choosing and loving a man who is good for you.

Earlier, I talked about the differences between settling and compromising. Settling requires you to sacrifice your values, your identity
and your unique needs. Compromising means that you don't get everything you want in a man, but you do get most of the things that are
crucial to you.

If your answers to the other questions placed you close to "Yes,"
then you might be setting yourself up for being alone. I say *might*
because interpretations about what constitutes *Mr. Right* vary from person to person. I'm trying to give you a general sense of what you might
be over-using from the cultural messages about finding *the one* or your
soulmate.

ISN'T IT TRUE THAT WOMEN DON'T REALLY NEED MEN? AND THAT'S A GOOD THING SINCE THERE AREN'T ANY GOOD MEN ANYWAY, RIGHT?

Internalizing the cultural message that you don't really need a man or
believing that all the good ones are taken is a powerful way to justify
your lifestyle choice of being single or plodding along in an existing relationship because, well, it's just too complicated to break up. Besides,
you tell yourself, "There's nothing out there anyway." Nothing ventured
in love, no hurt. Women who came of age in the sixties and seventies

might recall a famous poster that said that a woman without a man is like a fish without a bicycle. Look at the next cartoon. Do you see yourself taking Cookie's attitude?

COOKIE HIDES OUT AT WORK

Cookie thinks she's done with men. She hasn't had any luck and she's tired of getting hurt or being disappointed. Thank goodness her back-up plan is to work longer and harder. She didn't hesitate at all to say no to her friends' plea to join them at one of their favorite restaurants. Look at Cookie's "out" box. She's done an excellent job of feeling satisfied with her work effort. So, who needs a man when work fills your time, takes up your energy and makes you feel important and competent?

Yes, work is important. It's true that there are certain things that you should not sacrifice for any man. You should never sacrifice your self-respect, safety or core values, for instance. But too many studies show that social connectedness, love and a mutually-satisfying marriage are good for your health and sense of well-being. Can you still thrive without a partner? Of course you can! But healthy love strengthens your weaknesses, reduces your isolation, improves your health and expands who you are in ways that you'd never expect. Checklists for perfection will rob you of these benefits.

DOESN'T LOVE USUALLY HAPPEN WHEN YOU AREN'T LOOKING?

This belief seems to link you to a benevolent universe that looks out for you. That's a comforting thought. Maybe there is truth in it, but putting your prospective relationships on hold in the hope that the universe or some other force recognizes you doesn't make good sense. You could be waiting for a long time. And you may not recognize the moment when it does happen.

Believing in this saying prevents you from getting out there, meeting men, getting to know about them—and learning from getting hurt. The single women in my workshops didn't like seeing how these myths were self-protective. The women with partners discovered that they used these ideas to pull back from their men and not examine their own behavior in the relationship.

There is just no way to make sound choices or sustain an existing relationship without risking facing yourself or getting hurt or disappointed at times. Don't fall back on handy self-deceptions to support your fears of making mistakes and getting close.

Don't fall for:

If it's meant to be, it will just happen.

CAN'T AFFAIRS HELP RELATIONSHIPS AND MARRIAGES?

You can learn about yourself and your relationship by having an affair. But you are truly playing with fire. When the affair is discovered, just a third of marriages remain together and become stronger.

Affairs are a form of trauma. If your partner cheats, it turns your trust in him, your happiness and your faith in yourself to dust. If you have an affair, it can be a runaway train that temporarily carries your unhappiness on a detour track that is a bittersweet distraction. Your discontent with your existing partner is oddly tolerable. That train speeds you into an imagined future with your new love. It also erodes your respect and values of how to treat another person. You can lose a part of your decency. Rationalizing that your unhappiness made you do it and that lots of people cheat is just that—a convenient rationalization.

Some affairs do lead to love and marriage with a new person. Yet, many of the women in my study who were with a new partner often worried that the affair would become a tool once again to manage unhappiness. Remember this warning:

> ## The Hidden Ease of Having Affairs
>
> Once that trust barrier is crossed, violating it again by having an affair might be easier.

WHAT IS SO BAD ABOUT HAVING CASUAL SEX AND BELIEVING IN "IF YOU FEEL IT, DO IT"?

The pill and other modern, reliable forms of birth control have allowed women to separate sex from love, reproduction and marriage. However, in some cases the pill has also allowed women to sever their heads and hearts from their bodies and emotional management.

The message of "if you feel it, do it" actually strips you of your power to take charge of your feelings, beliefs and actions. We human beings have the benefit of a head-heart dialogue. We don't always do what we feel. Our thoughts allow us to weigh and rein in unwise actions. But if you fall for the belief that you *are* your feelings, then you risk losing your ability to self-monitor and develop *more* choice about what you want to do—or not do.

DO I ALWAYS HAVE TO CONNECT SEX WITH LOVE OR MARRIAGE?

Your personal values will determine whether sex is only permissible within marriage. But if you believe that lovemaking can occur before marriage, then you have lots of decisions to make. Casual sex permits the downgrading of the special bond from lovemaking to just having sex. Many of the women in my study looked back on their sexual experiences and didn't like that they bought into the belief that sex is no big deal.

Societal views of women and sex, despite the sexual revolution for women, still value—if not virginity—then sexual experience that is low in number of partners and high in personal meaning. Brief stints of sexual wildness and experimentation are deemed acceptable—as long as the woman comes around to valuing the integration of sex with mutual, mature love and intimacy.

Impulsive sex or sex too early in a relationship has become an acceptable craving—not worth much more anguish than the emotional beating up you do when you eat a pint of ice cream or a box of donuts in one sitting.

Your mind can exonerate you from just about anything you do sexually. Women and girls' current and centuries-old fascination with vampires is one potent example of the longing to be seduced by a sexual force more powerful than reason. Dracula, it seems, has become the perfect lover—the mysterious, commanding, buff and unattainable being who can make you lose yourself—which is emotional code for letting yourself off the hook for taking any responsibility for your actions.

But women today don't need a vampire to give them permission to experiment sexually or to be wild and drop their sexual guard. Women of the twenty-first century feel they have plenty of that any time they wish—and without the need to make any excuses.

Instead, Dracula's power lies in offering women the chance to drop their sexual guard with men of authority, status, wealth and sexual prowess while retaining the emotional guard of their hearts. Sex, yes; closeness and true intimacy, no.

Stephenie Meyer, the author of the *Twilight* series, addressed this problem by having the heroine, teenage Bella Swan, build emotional intimacy first with Edward, a vampire, marrying him and then having sex. Bella had to examine her strong feelings for her other potential love interest, a werewolf named Jacob, to determine whether he was a good love match. Depending on your values, you can adjust Meyer's model of at least putting love, closeness and self-reckoning before sex, and use it as a guide.

Unfortunately, as the social rules about sex fade away, one rule you must cling to is to have safe sex. So, if you are hungry for it and there is an appealing man, why not? Ask yourself just how appealing is it the next morning—or even the next hour—to know that your freedom to have sex with whomever you please has left you feeling a little empty?

Almost all the women in my study said that, looking back at their sexual activities, they "could have done without most of them." No matter how much they convinced themselves that the fling was a fun departure from themselves and their boring or restricted life, many of the women also said that they still longed for a phone call from the man.

There may be social acceptance to say yes, but there doesn't seem to be as much social acceptance to say no—except, of course, to rape and abuse. Society's current message to take charge of your health and body seems to have missed the part about your mental health and emotional maturity. Ask yourself: What is the downside of linking sex with mutual, mature love?

ISN'T MARRIAGE JUST A PIECE OF PAPER?

For the moment let's say this statement is correct. Now, let's test it. If marriage is a socially meaningless piece of paper, then why not get married—since it doesn't matter one way or the other? When I asked this question of women in my study, they became silent.

The emotional dissimilitude between living together and being married may as well be the distance of a light year. Even if you pool your money, share your purchases and raise your children together, living together does not raise the *emotional* investment to the highest level. Love and marriage are *too* important—and therefore scarier. Not having a marriage license gives you an escape hatch and *false* protection against making a mistake.

Why Love Can Hurt

As the importance of the relationship increases, so do your automatic defenses against getting hurt or abandoned. And that's why love hurts so much when it goes wrong. But it's worth it.

WHY SHOULDN'T I BELIEVE THE STATISTICS ABOUT WOMEN, MARRIAGE AND DIVORCE?

If you want to duck and cover from the hard work of self-reckoning and managing emotional hurt and disappointment, then rely on the negativity of statistics about women and love. Here are top stats that both single and coupled women in the study used to explain their pessimism. Circle or underline the ones that have tied up your heart. Add your own.

STATISTICS THAT YOU USE TO CONFUSE AND CLOSE YOUR HEART TO LOVE

Women outnumber men. Yes, that's true, because you need more women to perpetuate the species than men.

More men have affairs than women. True again. Large surveys such as Director Tom W. Smith of the General Society Social Survey's "American Sexual Behavior" revealed that 28 percent of men report having affairs and 18 percent of women report having affairs. Other surveys showed similar numbers.[1]

So, not everyone cheats. Also, there is no clear agreement on what constitutes infidelity. Is it kissing? Having sex? Falling in love? Spending lots of time together?

Women with post-graduate degrees in areas such as law or medicine have higher divorce rates. Yes, but the rise is only slightly higher than the national average, which now is below 50 percent.[2] Possibly the increase reflects the women's economic independence. This study is based on the 2006 findings of Washington and Lee University law professor Robin Fretwell Wilson's study of 100,000 women.[3]

White women with college degrees are also less likely to marry compared to less educated women. In 2010 economist Betsey Stevenson and graduate student Adam Isen of the Wharton School of the University of Pennsylvania presented this finding to the Council on Contemporary Families in a paper, "Who is Getting Married?"

However, when these women do get married, they are less likely to get divorced. And black women with either some college or college degrees are more likely to marry than less educated black women.[4]

The marriage rate is down, especially in younger adults. The 2011 Pew Research Center found that only slightly more than half the United States population is married. Yes—but that's still a lot of married people. And younger adults are delaying marriage, in part, to complete advanced training and education.[5]

Divorce rates rise in marriages when couples are in their early to late forties. The 2010 U.S. Census did find, however, that the percentage of women married or divorced remained steady until the women were age sixty, when death of the husband is more likely to occur.[6]

Only thirty of 1,000 women between the ages forty-five to sixty remarry in a given year.[7] Yes, but that's still in a one-year span. And who says you can't be one of the thirty? This kind of statement is similar to those that say that every three seconds someone in the world is performing a specific action.

Of couples who divorced, 20 percent cohabitated. The 2011 Pew Research Center found that the rate of people thirty to forty-four years old who cohabited before marriage and then divorced has increased dramatically since 1960. But does the divorce rate mean you shouldn't live with someone? Not necessarily. Only 12 percent of couples who moved in together *after* they became engaged got divorced.[8]

This information can be very confusing. Statistics are only as good as the methodology and the analyses. As Mark Twain said, "There are lies, damned lies and statistics." Statistics consist of data about populations, not necessarily about the fate of one person: you!

When Dr. Stephen Jay Gould, the well-respected scientist and author of noted books such as *The Flamingo's Smile*, learned that he had the asbestos-caused lung disease mesothelioma, he looked at the life expectancy percentages for people with the disease. They weren't good. But the odds of living for many years and not dying within a few years of diagnosis were not zero either. He decided to take the attitude that he belonged in the group that lived the longest. And he did.

If you want to convince yourself that you are a victim of social trends, then you will see your chances at love as a glass that is half full. The lesson to take away is that you—your attitude and behavior—can trump the negativity of statistics about love and marriage.

HOW CAN I GET MORE FLEXIBLE AND SMART IN CHOOSING AND LOVING A GOOD MAN?

GIVE UP YOUR SCRIPTS, FANTASIES AND SOULMATE SEARCHES.

Open your mind. Don't fool yourself by trying to fill your checklist. Knowing your values and needs in a relationship is part of the foundation of making wise choices. But looking for these things is not the same as having an impossible-to-fill checklist.

That kind of checklist is like going to the grocery store and not coming home unless you find the most perfect apple, pear, grapes, melon, potato, zucchini, steak, fish and pie in the whole store. You will be there for hours holding up each pear, weighing it in your hands for heft and ripeness. You will have to examine all the fat veins in the steak or smell each piece of fish in the showcase. You're never going to come home—and you're never going to find a man—or even discover that the man with you is a right-enough match. Keep this thought in mind:

Looking for *Mr. Right*

Give up the notion of *Mr. Right*. But there sure are lots of *Mr. Right-Enoughs*.

Margaret's story is a great lesson in choosing *Mr. Right-Enough*. She and her three sorority sisters from college rented a huge, four-bedroom house in a major city. They went to graduate school and training programs during the week. On Friday and Saturday nights they looked for men at bars, parties and local events.

They all got good jobs after graduation, but five years later only Margaret was married. At first, none of her friends liked George. They thought he was a little flabby and they didn't like his thinning hair. He tended to be quiet. But Margaret and he shared an interest in art, and on weekends they would take walking tours of architecture in their town. He worked as an industrial designer and Margaret was a book illustrator. They had met in a bookstore.

She liked his analytical nature and he liked her gentleness. She learned to be more objective, and he learned to see things in shades of gray. They both had families that were neglectful. As children, each escaped the sadness by reading. She wasn't looking for perfect. They were very happy together and after two and a half years of dating, they married. Margaret's girlfriends found fault with all of George's friends at the wedding.

Margaret's sorority sisters are still not in permanent relationships. Their checklists were so specific that no man could ever qualify—which was the whole point of having such an exacting list. They were afraid to risk love. You don't have to be like them.

No man is perfect and there are lots of men out there who would make good matches for you. It doesn't make sense to think that in the millions of men in the world there is just *one* man whom you haven't had enough luck to find.

Unfortunately, the stories of princesses who hold out for that one Prince Charming are still part of the romantic fantasies of today's women. In my workshops, when women had to list their ideal scenarios for finding love, they often resembled contemporary versions of *Cinderella* or *Sleeping Beauty* where the perfect man was the one person who recognized the woman's true worth. These men were rich, handsome, famous and able to read their minds and hearts. They surprised their women with expensive gifts and grand estates far, far away from it all.

These women so disbelieved in their potential to love and be loved that they protected themselves from hurt by constructing an impossible profile of that one man. Just in case reasonable enough men came along, they also added a checklist of goodies such as certain looks or income levels that they had to have so that no man could qualify.

For example, Bonnie believed her salary and position as Marketing Director of a national wine distributing company entitled her to have an extensive checklist. In addition to fame, fortune and status, she added that *Mr. Right* had to be knowledgeable about the contemporary art scene, love wine and have blue eyes and straight blond hair just like hers.

Bonnie found a man who fit the description to a T, but eventually she learned that Prince Charming's looks and financial assets did not make her feel loved. Her prince turned into an ogre. After four years with him, Bonnie accidentally discovered that he had a wife and family in another town. She broke up with him and didn't date for a long time.

Then one evening at a charity wine-tasting event, she saw a man with dark, curly hair offer an elderly woman a napkin from the buffet. The act was a small gesture. Bonnie watched him for a while and the man noticed her looking at him. When he came over to her, Bonnie was too embarrassed to turn down his request for a date.

This new man, Donald, didn't have a grand estate, but he did have a solid career and a caring personality. She taught him about art and wine and he taught her about travel and economics. They shared a common bond of being on their own since childhood and relying on themselves. Bonnie said that Donald's act of kindness spoke volumes about his character. And they lived happily ever after!

There are lots of everyday princes out there and if you want to find one, search for the many variations on the right-enough man.

THINK OF DATING AND LOVING AS AN ADVENTUROUS VACATION THAT LASTS A LIFETIME— WITH PITS, POTHOLES AND ROADBLOCKS—BUT STILL IS SOMETHING FOR WHICH YOU'D LIKE TO SIGN UP!

Vacations get spoiled unless the traveler accepts that there will be times when she will be hungry, tired, cranky, dirty, lost or disappointed by food or accommodations. One wonders why anyone would leave home. But women seek out new sights and locales all the time.

Getting to know men is another way to seek out the world of love and knowledge about self and others. It can actually be enjoyable—as long as you acknowledge that the journey of choosing wisely involves detours, wrong turns, anxiety, disappointment in the current trip and inaccurate assessments of what you need or want.

The point is to go! Yet, too many women protect themselves from emotional hurt and disillusionment by getting lazy and falling for beliefs about finding love. One of the main things I've learned from my study is that women today are very lonely. They find the task of meeting men so overwhelming that they quit their efforts too soon. But quitting is another form of lying to yourself to protect from getting hurt and feeling the pain of your loneliness.

You have to treat your search for *Mr. Right-Enough* as another job. Attend events that interest you, ask others to fix you up, use dating companies and just get going. Unfortunately, other than dating sites and companies, there are few ways to meet lots of single people at once. Throughout the eighteenth and nineteenth century in England, for example, there were huge social balls where young girls "came out in society" to announce their eligibility. Twentieth-century America had debutante balls to serve the same purpose.

The world still uses variations of this social tradition, but I don't recommend that you rely on them. You have to hunt for smaller social offerings such as business network meetings, church events, matchmaking services, charity activities, political gatherings and your community's free weekend events.

HERE'S A NEW MYTH YOU CAN BELIEVE: "YOU HAVE TO KISS A LOT OF FROGS" UNTIL YOU FIND A GOOD-ENOUGH MATCH.

This truism only works, though, if you increase the number of men you go out of your way to meet or speak to—and if you give up the idea that your frog still has to be as mighty as a prince. Searching forever for that elusive and powerfully perfect man in the forest of life is the equivalent of hunting for a unicorn.

A better strategy is to open your mind and eyes to the fact that the good-enough man comes in many varieties. Think of all the types of good-enough men. In the workshops, the women got very inventive. They vowed to stop being dinosaurs by clinging to an outmoded hunt for the perfect man. This next exercise will expand your list of eligible men and help you become braver in dating and loving men who are different from your usual choices.

No More Dinosaur Ideas Exercise

Think about your past relationships. If you are with a man now and you feel you are falling out of love, think about what might be making you cool your feelings. It is, of course, possible that your man is not good for you. Maybe he is an abuser or a liar. Perhaps he does not respect you. Perhaps you don't share certain values. But if your man is a good man, you might be falling out of love because of your scripts, intolerance for differences or difficulty in being your best self that enables your man to become his best self.

Now think about animals that represent qualities you like in a man. Do you like turtles because they take their time and are not hasty? Do you like foxes because they are cunning? Or do you like elephants because they take care of each other? If you can't think of a favorite, invent an animal.

Here are two examples of how the women in my workshops opened up their minds:

Mary's Story

Mary said that despite her success in academics, growing up and living in the hills of West Virginia made her feel limited. Mary's husband was also an academic from a small town, and she said that their marriage was like "the blind leading the blind." When he died, Mary vowed to choose a smart man. "University life is good for me—it's like a little world. But I think I need a man who can offer a competency that I don't have." Mary knew she had to look outside the academic world. "It scared me a little," she said.

She asked her friends to fix her up. Her only requirement was that the man should have skills in life experiences such as reading people, taking wise risks, traveling and relating. She told them that she was looking for someone who could leap into life and feel at home covering a larger territory. The dolphin came to mind because she said she learned that dolphins were great communicators, intuitive decision-makers, good caregivers and brave hunters.

At first, Mary said she felt awkward dating a variety of men. She was embarrassed to admit it, but she didn't realize that people outside the university could also be knowledgeable about history or the arts. "Guess I was wrong," she said.

She met Ricardo, who owned a home construction company. Ricardo grew up on opera and classical music. Mary said that they shared common interests and family values, and she especially liked that Ricardo's skills in business and finance expanded her world. "I would never have picked him," Mary said. "He was that dolphin I was looking for—smart, good at communicating with me, brave and caring." She learned from his ability to take risks, assess situations and not be afraid to try new things and visit unfamiliar places.

Linda's Story

Linda was a high-powered certified public accountant who lived for her job. She felt "all thumbs" when it came to people. She was abrupt and had no patience for mistakes. All her previous men were either exciting bad boys who brought her out of her shell or clinging men who turned her home into another kind of shell. She said she knew that she needed a more outgoing but also a smart and caring man. Yet, she was scared to venture outside of her usual patterns.

I asked her if she became brave, what kind of animal would offer her a different love pattern. She thought for a while and said she wanted a cross between a dog and a horse. She chose a dog for loyalty and love, combined with the tame but still exciting, smart and loving horse.

As Linda dated, she kept pictures of a dog and a horse in her handbag. "I wanted a kind and loving person who was still his own man," she said. With the help of several girlfriends, she pushed herself to get fixed up and use dating sites. "I really did 'kiss a lot of frogs.'"

It took Linda over two years to meet Marvin. He was older than she by ten years, but Linda said he was "younger in spirit" than she was. He was a retired attorney who loved to travel. Linda avoided traveling for pleasure. "I hated the idea of traveling alone, but I didn't want to go on one of those group tours where you can't get away from people."

Linda took the same attitude toward anything that involved stepping outside her safety zone. Most of her friends were accountants. But Marvin helped her break out of her shell. She tried new foods and even wore different styles of clothes. Marvin respected her competency and liked her reliability. They each borrowed from the other's qualities.

If you were brave, what kind of animal or animal combination would you choose?

Tips for Breaking through Cultural Myths and Messages

Don't look for *Mr. Right* or your soulmate. There is no perfect man, and looking for him is just a way to protect yourself from hurt, self-reckoning and the real responsibilities of love.

Don't let statistics about women, love and marriage turn you into a pessimist. Statistics are about lots of people. Don't see the glass as half full as another way to hide you from your fears of getting close. Educated and older women can find happiness.

Be aware of the cultural messages about women and sex. Don't fall for beliefs that sex is no big deal. Respect the union of your head and heart. Empower yourself by saying no to sex without mutual love.

Be aware of other cultural messages that downplay wanting an intimate partner or marriage. It's normal to want companionship and love. However, there is a world of difference between marriage and living together indefinitely.

Focus more on your needs and values so you can expand your love choices. Love comes in many varieties. Don't limit yourself to scripts. Flexibility allows for growth and inner strength.

Chapter 8

Sex, Chemistry and Intimacy

Let's have that sex talk and expand on the cultural messages that we've discussed. Are there really rules? Many of the women with whom I spoke lamented that there weren't enough clear ones. Even though the twenty-first century women in my workshops enjoyed the freedom of sexual choice, they valued the Victorian view that love, marriage and sex were seen as a package deal and you took time to know a man by including him in activities with friends and family or attending elegant balls. Almost all the women said that they had moved too quickly in relationships.

When I mentioned that British novelist Jane Austen had remarkably astute observations about the problems of sex, love and courtship in the eighteenth century, Gayle raised her arms in the air in exasperation and said, "So what century should we date in?"

My best answer is to date and love in your unique time zone that mixes the values of the eighteenth and the twenty-first centuries with your customized use of them. A great book to read is *The Jane Austen Guide to Happily Ever After* by Elizabeth Kantor. Your goal is to become an expert on sex, love and dating for *you,* so you can break through the personal obstacles in your love ceiling.

This chapter will help you get a better understanding of the main issues and the skills needed to manage them.

WHY IS SEX SO POWERFUL?

Sex is one of our fundamental needs. Reproduction is a biological imperative for survival, along with our other requirements such as our needs to feed ourselves and develop defensive strategies of fight or flight against threats to our existence.

Reproduction includes finding and securing mates. Human beings are among the most sexually active animals. We, along with dolphins and bonobo monkeys, have sex for pleasure. We tend to like sex because the experience of it usually feels very good.

Sex and food can become addictive because they are hard-wired in the brain to be both important and enjoyable—and therefore repeated. Food may keep you alive, but sex seems more powerful. It can be emotionally transformative and make you feel calm, loved, vibrant, valued, healthier, self-accepting and close to another person.

Sex also has a strange way of perpetuating relationships past their expiration date. Having satisfying sex arouses the neurochemicals of endorphins and oxytocin in the brain. Oxytocin has been called the love hormone because it is essential for mother-child bonding. It is also known as the attachment hormone because sex activates it and then can fool you into thinking you are close to that person. Common sense and mindfulness are forgotten and you end up wanting to be with a man you may not really know.

COOKIE GETS CARRIED AWAY

Cookie had never met anyone like Nick before—the kind of successful man she felt she had earned. Nick was a maverick, an independent soul just like she was. She felt different from her mom, who seemed so desperate for love that she settled for anyone.

Nick was so different from her other men, like Tim who was sweet but unreliable. Cookie thought about what life would be like with Nick. Maybe she'd give up being an attorney. She was beginning to get burned out.

Dinner with Nick was amazing. She loved his knowledge of seasonings and sauces. Standing next to him on his balcony that evening was even more amazing. It was like having a private view of the world. Imagine actually owning a view like this.

She usually wasn't one to fall this hard for a guy. But it just felt right. There was no question sex was going to happen. He knew it; she knew it. Why play games?

The next morning gave her the right answer. Cookie felt oddly empty inside. Sure, the sex had been good. Well, not like the attentiveness of Tim. But Tim had become so cloying. She liked Nick's masculine style. At least she thought she did. Nevertheless, something was missing—like knowing where she stood with Nick and wondering if he'd call or even if he had a girlfriend or an ex. Suddenly she realized she didn't know that much about him at all.

Do you see those sailboats which resemble shark fins in the water near Nick's lighthouse? Cookie didn't see this similarity because her brain was already flooded with the neurochemicals of pleasure. It seemed as though her good feelings for Nick were not much more than a love potion of hormones and hope. Like Cookie, at this point, you may be wondering how soon to have sex.

WHY IS IT A GOOD IDEA TO POSTPONE SEX AT THE BEGINNING OF DATING?

Postponing sex in a relationship requires the management of anxious feelings, an awareness of the impact of your childhood and the ability to live with the uncertainty of how the man feels about you. Happy, smart women mastered these tasks and didn't rush sex for the sake of closure. They knew that pushing the relationship would cause more anxiety than taking time to learn about their man and building friendship first.

If you found yourself in bed with a man too soon in the relationship, your situation is similar to some women in my study. Twenty percent said if they really liked the man, they didn't mind having sex on the first date. Almost a third described themselves as women who fell in love quickly and tended to have sex by the third date.

Even if intercourse didn't occur, slightly more than 40 percent of the women said that they acted against their better judgment about issues such as going out with a man in the first place, going back together to one of their homes near the end of the date, getting too high on alcohol or drugs with him or doing more than kissing, such as everything-but-intercourse. The women said they closed their eyes to their problems, took the plunge off the emotional pier and "just wanted to see what would happen." Life is short, they reasoned, so what really could be the harm?

These women played with fire. Going back to a stranger's place is perilous enough. But being even a little high and closing down your self-understanding and your mindfulness are equally dangerous. Tempting fate is never a good plan. Major crimes have occurred when a woman takes just one wrong turn in her behavior and ends up hurt, robbed or dead.

If, as in the cartoon about Cookie, the man seems an amazing catch, then emotional self-control becomes more difficult. You might convince yourself that you are the one who can land this man—and then permit sex to speed the connection. Next let's look at Trina's story, a lesson about lapses in emotional and sexual judgment.

Trina's Story

Trina knew about Dan. She imagined his personal advertisement: Rich bad boy. Killer looks. Single. No baggage. Looking for same minus the income. Must be pliable.

Still, she couldn't resist bidding on him at a charity auction. The moment she won, she started fantasizing about their future together. She could land him. Men liked her exotic beauty and sense of fun, and were always shocked when they found out she was an architect.

On Trina and Dan's first date they flew in his plane to a neighboring state for dinner at a famous restaurant and had sex the first night. Trina said his tenderness made her "feel like a princess."

Trina came from a southwestern town of dust and sun that no one seemed to leave. As a child, she sat in the park and drew pictures in the dirt of her dream houses that were many times the size of her family's cramped quarters. A college scholarship was her way out.

In the beginning, her life with Dan was filled with excitement—weekend trips with the rich and famous and shopping sprees to designer stores, where he'd buy her tight dresses and high-heeled shoes. He liked his women sexy-looking. Trina cut out photographs of them from the society sections of the newspapers.

"The trouble just crept up on me," Trina said. "It was drugs." Marijuana led to prescription pills and the best sex that Trina said she had ever experienced. She felt alive. Her dusty childhood disappeared like tumbleweed.

She was not addicted but she became exhausted from the late hours and drugs. Monday at work turned into a Tuesday morning. She was behind schedule and when Dan complained that she wasn't as available to him as he wanted, she gave in. When her work piled up and the complaints came in, she looked at herself in the mirror and saw a tired face. "What are you doing?" she shouted at her reflection.

Trina learned that the real danger of sex too soon was not just that you risk your physical well-being and safety, but that you also risk losing your self-worth, your inner control of your needs for love and companionship and, most importantly, your strength and skills in soothing yourself from within. "I was really looking for someone else to make me happy," she said. "Falling in love quickly and totally was my legal drug."

The women in one of my workshops were very moved by Trina's story and her ability to pull herself away from Dan. If Trina's situation sounds like something you'd never allow to happen, think again. We all test our limits in different ways. And when you add hope, hormones, fantasies and disappointment in your life, you push your luck in love.

The bigger problem for most of the women in my study was detecting the more subtle—but equally as telling—hints about a man. Amber's story is about how kissing with your mental eyes closed blocks out the less dramatic signs.

Amber's Wake-up Call

Amber couldn't believe David had met someone and gotten engaged and married within six months of their breakup. She and David were both certified financial advisors, and before the breakup she had imagined them as a team on financial television shows and at major conferences. Marrying him would prove to her parents that she was not the ugly duckling nerd of the family. But David chose to marry Suzy the Homemaker, Baby Maker and Bread Baker—everything Amber wasn't and was never going to be.

Later, when a friend fixed her up with Andrew, Amber thought he was the one. He was also a financial analyst who lived in a city that was several hours away by car. They connected online for a month. She couldn't believe how much they had in common. They even had similar childhoods, growing up in rusted-out towns with no opportunities for advancement.

The moment they met, they had sex. "It felt like love," Amber said. He made her feel beautiful for the first time in her life. Amber was built like her large, barrel-chested father, and her mother told her she should be grateful if a man found her attractive.

Every weekend, Amber drove long hours to see him. He couldn't get away, he said, because he had to help his elderly parents on weekends with household chores. His parents had moved to be near him and his two other brothers so they could take care of the parents' health needs.

On the sixth weekend of driving to see him, Amber wondered why his two other brothers couldn't take over some of Andrew's chores once in a while. But she batted away that thought. She didn't want to rock this perfect boat.

Andrew and Amber went to a party and Andrew seemed distracted. When a woman next to her dropped her wine glass, it shattered as it hit the ground and cut Amber's foot. Andrew just stood there and told her that she'd better get to the bathroom right away. It didn't even occur to her that Andrew should have at least grabbed a napkin to stop the bleeding.

That night, after sex, he told her that he was dating other women. She rationalized that they really didn't have an exclusive agreement, but she cried on the long ride back to her place. As she pulled into her driveway, she received a text message from him: "Good times. Breaking up best 4 me. Met someone. Thnx. Talk if u wnt."

Amber almost collapsed. When she told her friends that the friction between her and Andrew was "hard to understand," her friends set her straight. "Not hard at all," they said. "It's easy—he never made an effort. It's over and there is nothing to talk to him about."

Amber realized she had closed her eyes to the warning signals—and to her intense desire for attachment to a man. Later, she learned that the woman who broke the wine glass was Andrew's new girlfriend. Amber had sensed something when they were at the party together, but she had dismissed the feeling.

Most of the women's disappointing love experiences resembled Amber's more subtle but still flashing warning lights. No matter how small the incident or your reaction, make sure you are mindful of your inner voice and feelings.

I asked women in my workshops to make a list of why they continued to date and have sex with a man when they truly sensed it was not in their best interest. Here are their top reasons. Check the reasons that sound like you.

Checklist of My (Wrong) Reasons for Continuing to Date and Have Sex Against My Better Judgment

❑ I was lonely, especially compared to my married friends.

❑ I wanted to make myself feel better by creating a tomorrow with this man.

❑ Having sex again and continuing the relationship made me feel like a good girl and not a one-night stand.

❑ I wanted to please my parents who really liked this man.

❑ My biological clock was ticking.

❑ I wanted to stop being picky.

❑ I wanted to feel chosen and special.

❑ I was taking a holiday from myself.

We all make love mistakes. Instead of going backwards and being harsh on yourself for stumbling, go forward, get brave, look deep within yourself and learn.

IS POSTPONING SEX THE SMARTEST WAY TO PREVENT GETTING HURT?

Remember this cautionary statement:

A Warning about Postponing Sex

You can postpone sex, take your time to know a man and still end up disappointed, disillusioned and harmed emotionally, physically or financially.

When I said these words in my workshops, women responded by saying something like, "thanks a lot." Don't fool yourself into thinking that just because you didn't sleep with him that you have protected yourself from getting hurt or used.

There are never any guarantees that you won't get hurt in love. Some men are just too good at hiding their motives. Think of all the television shows such as *Dateline* or *48 Hours* where the man was an expert dissembler—often for a long time before he launched his plan and uncovered his real nature.

Your remedy is to stay mindful by asking yourself questions about your physical and emotional reactions during and after your times with your man. Practice this exercise.

SUSTAINING MINDFULNESS

Calm down and connect with your reactions. Be present and in the moment so you can become tuned in to yourself. Do deep and slow breathing exercises at home before your time with your man. See what comes to mind and don't judge yourself. You might discover why and how you prevent yourself from awareness. The best way is to do this in a quiet place before and after an experience. Some women were able to do a mini-version of slow breathing while with their men.

Observe sensations that you are feeling in your body.
Notice your heart rate and activity in your stomach or other physical reactions. Learn about your typical warning signs.

Think of words that describe your feelings.

Think of observations about him that you have minimized.
Replay them in your mind.

SHOULDN'T I JUST LISTEN TO MY HEAD AND MY HEART TO DECIDE WHETHER TO HAVE SEX?

You've been taught that if your head and heart say yes, then you are out of love's danger. Is that correct? Once again—yes and no. You can still be surprised by your man.

One of the biggest culprits when you move toward sex too soon is relying on listening to your head and heart when they could be *wrong*. If you remain perpetually mindful, you reduce the chance of making a mistake. Challenge any agreement between your head and heart. Ask yourself the following questions:

The Head and Heart Challenge

Am I emotionally vulnerable right now? Am I going through emotional or financial difficulties? Am I turning a certain age or getting divorced? Are my children leaving home? Does this time of year include an important anniversary such as the death of a loved one?

Am I using love as medicine for loneliness? Is my life all work and no play? Am I waiting for a man to be my *main* source of feeling vital? How can I create a richer life?

Do I tend to rush sex because I feel attracted to the man? Do I have a history of moving too quickly? Do I rely on sex or expedient relationships to soothe me?

Have I really been mindful of my physical and emotional reactions? What have I learned?

HOW DO I FILTER OUT WHAT I THINK I "SHOULD" DO ABOUT SEX?

MINDY'S AUTO-PILOT RESPONSES

There are other sexual traps. Cultural messages and behaviors can also get you in hot emotional water. On Mindy's third date with Jeff, she felt a mix of excitement and dread. Like many women I've worked with, she believed that accepting a third date signaled the man to expect sex that night. After dinner at one of the best places in town, she invited Jeff to her apartment and, not surprisingly, they had sex. It seemed like the most natural thing to do. Besides, *What's the big deal*, she thought. She was a big girl. But the next morning, Mindy regretted her decision. She couldn't wait for Jeff to leave. Let's see what Mindy could have done on her date to feel better about herself.

BECOMING MINDFUL OF "SHOULD" MESSAGES

Don't use the "third date auto-body rule." Don't buy into the belief that accepting a third date equals consent to sex.

Sex is not tribute. You don't owe a man sex for any reason. Don't fall for the belief that you have to finish what you started—even if you weren't sure but you started it anyway. Say no. If you owe anyone, it is yourself and your values and self-respect.

Don't tempt fate. Don't go to his place or yours at the end of a date unless you are absolutely sure you want to engage in sexual activities. I know it's the twenty-first century, but don't set yourself up for the privacy, soft music, bottle of wine and dimly-lit rooms that raise expectations that you don't want.

Get inventive about where to go afterward. If you want to continue the evening, go to a diner.

Don't fool yourself that sex is no big deal. Sex most certainly is a big deal. As we previously discussed, very few women have sex and then wake up the next morning without wondering whether he'll call—or whether it's normal to feel too uncomfortable to call him. If you're wondering, then you're having sex too soon. You should know where the two of you stand with each other first. Sex is not separable from you.

Don't use sex to get a man. It's one of the oldest tricks in the book and, unfortunately, it does work at times. There may be plenty of other women who would gladly sleep with your man right away, but having sex too soon creates potentially serious problems for you such as ending up in a relationship that you don't want.

Remain mindful. Remember that sex is not the only thing that clouds your vision. Stay present in the moment about all of your reactions.

WHAT IS THE DIFFERENCE BETWEEN SEX AND INTIMACY?

Somewhere out there, in western culture at least, is a saying that goes something like this: A man uses sex to feel good and to feel good about himself. A woman relies on sex to feel special about both herself and the relationship.

In the beginning of relationships, sex is the emotional river that takes men to feelings—and to feeling close. It is often difficult for some men to access and express their feelings of closeness. Sexual pleasure can be a gateway experience for them to arouse the brain's attachment neurochemicals.

For many women, however, sex works best emotionally when women can derive personal meaning and value. Despite the cultural range of women's choices from one-night stands to lovemaking, women tend to combine love, sex, meaning and a future with the man.

Men want to fall in love, too, though. They really do. There certainly are differences between the brains of men and women. Men's brains, for instance, are larger. Women's brains have more area and neural connections for relating—probably a survival mechanism to enhance the caretaking of infants and children. There are actually *more* differences in brains between people of the same sex than there are between people of opposite sexes.

Intimacy develops when both partners experience the building blocks of closeness, bonding, affection, safety, warmth, teamwork, empathy, complementary styles, shared values and mutual respect. Marital researcher and author John Gottman, who wrote the bestseller

The Seven Principles for Making Marriage Work, discovered that the shared happiness of long-term marriage rests on the power of loving communication that does not use criticism or tuning out. Instead, you act with respect for each other and yourselves. Sex, along with commitment and companionship, is part of the mortar that holds these blocks together.

Delaying sexual intimacy may be difficult, but you are fooling yourself if you think that it is easier than emotional intimacy. As I said before, sex is no substitute for closeness—even if it feels like it. Sex hurls you too quickly and blindly into the future. Your focus shifts from being mindful to plotting out your life with him. When you plot, you blot out your accurate vision of him and you end up kissing with both eyes closed.

The process of getting to know a man and developing feelings for him over time is not always pleasant or easy because it requires that you allow him to know you. The really hard task and test of intimacy is being known. It means that, eventually, you have to drop your guard and make available the details of your past, your shortcomings, struggles, needs, quirks and fears.

Romantic comedy films mine this dilemma with great invention. Think of the movies that center on lies and misrepresentations such as not letting the other person know that you are a reporter or are really rich. At the heart of this movie genre are incorrect assumptions about a person because they are based on a mistaken identity—a madcap tool that goes back at least as far as Shakespeare. Lovers are unknowingly on the wrong side of politics or parents' wishes or professional agendas. Just think of your favorite romantic comedies and this theme of the lovers not knowing the truth about each other will probably be part of the story.

This plot trick is a shortcut to addressing your fears of being known, found out and then—oh no!—possibly rejected. But if you don't risk being revealed and known, then you can't ultimately find love that you can trust.

WHAT ABOUT CHEMISTRY?

What is instant chemistry? Chemistry is often a mix of hormones, hopes, family history and timing. Look at the next recipe for instant chemistry, but don't use it, because the recipe is unsavory.

How to Make Instant Chemistry

Mix the following ingredients into a big bowl:

- Half cup each of finely ground unhappiness and loneliness; add an extra half cup if you are currently going through hard times for any reason

- Two cups of an unhappy childhood; add an extra half cup if your mother was unhappy

Stir all these ingredients until they are well-mixed and pour the mixture into a pot.

Sprinkle generously with your hand-picked spices of what attracts you to a man.

Stir for a long time over a hot stove.

Add a dollop of both desperation and luck.

Do you really want to rely on this concoction to decide whether to date a man—or have sex with him? Be aware of what life and emotional circumstances you are bringing to the situation. Passion and the neurochemicals of arousal and attachment can land you in a soup that you can't get out of so easily.

Notice that one of the largest ingredients is an unhappy childhood. Like it or not, in various disguised forms, you repeat the patterns and problems of your parents and other main caregivers. It's important to note that it is one of the chief components of instant chemistry. Remember this important concept:

Warning Label for Instant Chemistry

It is just as easy—and comforting—to fall in love with the wrong person as the right one.

Why? We tend to feel emotionally comfortable with people whose personality and problems prompt us, consciously and unconsciously, to act in ways that reproduce how we acted in our family—or how our parents acted toward each other. If your family life was not healthy, then you risk repeating some of these patterns and issues.

Your family's influence over your choice of partner and the relationship structure you create with him are so potent that, despite how much you might think you are over your past, it can influence your feelings today.

Sharpen your awareness of your emotional comfort zone. It could lead you astray. Unfortunately, because the men you choose are most likely not thoroughly horrible people, it is difficult to see how the recipe for instant chemistry can harm you.

It can—otherwise you may not have chosen some of the men who made you unhappy or—even worse—harmed you. Relying on chemistry early in the relationship can limit your number of possible matches. Feeling instant chemistry also stunts your awareness of the quality of your new relationship.

WHAT CAN I DO TO USE CHEMISTRY MORE CAREFULLY?

Good matches come in all kinds of shapes and sizes. Sit down on a bench in a shopping mall one day and observe couples. You will probably think, *What an odd couple some of them make.*

Many of the women who attended my lectures or workshops told stories about how foolish they were to restrict themselves to men who were very handsome. Often, these relationships didn't work out for various reasons and the women said they learned that the men's physical appeal didn't sustain the relationship.

Over time, less physically attractive men became good looking. "My boyfriend has this big nose," Bobbie said in a workshop, "but he's such a good man. Now I see him as sweet and charming with a very endearing face." Yes, sexual attraction is important—but it's usually not a good idea to lead with it. Attractiveness grows with love and time to know a man better.

If you are serious about finding a suitable partner, date lots of *different* men. It's a numbers game where the more men you meet, the more you increase your odds. But dating different men requires you to date against your type. It's not easy to date against type because, at first, it feels so wrong. But if you aim to tolerate the initial discomfort of stepping outside your emotional comfort zone, you might learn about yourself and be surprised by your man and your assessment of him. Besides, your usual type hasn't yielded happiness.

Dating a variety of men also builds in the flexibility necessary for giving men chances. Many of the women in my study berated themselves for passing up men whom they now saw as viable partners. They rejected men immediately and did not give good men a second chance.

We all can mess up at times and not put our best selves forward. In baseball, the batter gets three strikes before he's out. Give most men at least one more swing of the bat. Make a list of things that concern you about him and, as you get to know each other, see if you are right.

IS THERE SUCH A THING AS LOVE AT FIRST SIGHT?

Surprisingly—yes! It's rare but possible. Some couples experience immediate, healthy chemistry and love at first sight because they have an emotional state of preparedness. These couples are adept at reading people: They pick up behavioral cues, know their healthy needs, reduce their defensiveness and manage their emotions and fears.

A few of the women in my study said they knew within twenty minutes that their men were the right ones for them. Their feelings of trust and attraction accelerated their willingness to disclose personal information and painful experiences to establish emotional intimacy. In general, however, instant chemistry and sex on a first date can be cruel seducers. They can lead you to choose the same type of wrong man again and again. Here is a recipe for good love at first sight.

How to Bake a Healthy Cake of Love at First Sight with a Good Chemistry Filling

Mix in a large vat:

- Two cups of healthy family role models or two cups of your ability to forge healthy relationship models that differ from your family
- Two cups of ability to read others and yourself
- Two cups of being able to withstand self-examination

Blend in one cup each of shared values and goals, good timing in both of your lives, flexibility in accepting different kinds of people.

Moisten with half a cup of luck.

Bake in a medium oven until ready.

Sprinkle with love, kindness and maturity.

The advantages of the combination of postponing sex and being mindful are crucial to personal growth. Put a mark next to the suggestions on this next review list that you did *not* do in your past relationships. Refer to this list of reasons to wait for sex when you feel the urge to skip the preliminaries and head for the finish line in the bedroom.

Tips for Sex, Chemistry and Intimacy

Hold back your urge for sex so you can be more mindful about your emotional and physical reactions before you attach too quickly. Although some women do snag a man with sex, it's wiser to know that a man fell in love with *you*. Take your time. Don't allow the sex hormones to cloud your ability to read men accurately. Waiting also helps you focus on the *You Who Is You* in the relationship *before* your brain's attachment hormone of oxytocin ramps up too much.

Delaying sex also gives you time to examine your values. Some women decided to wait for an engagement ring and wedding date or marriage to have sex. This decision rests on your assessment of your beliefs and values. It's a highly personal and important choice, so take your time to know how you think and feel.

Don't confuse sex with intimacy. Intimacy requires risking closeness and becoming known. Sex may seem easier at first, but it will not necessarily lead to a fulfilling relationship. Postpone sex until there is mutual love and respect. Waiting turns you into someone who can choose to take action—instead of only *reacting* to a man.

Don't use sex as medicine for loneliness or anxiety. Turn down the volume on your romantic fantasies of being swept away or given an instant life. Focus on being able to self-soothe without using food, drugs or sex. You become stronger, because you are no longer a slave to your needs or the fundamental fear of abandonment.

Take better charge of your dating choices and environment. Say no to going to his or your place. Get inventive and find other things to do other than visiting romantic restaurants. Don't get trapped into thinking that you owe him sex just because you've been seeing each other for a while.

Doubt any agreement between your head and heart. It's too easy to convince yourself to fall in love or jump into bed with a man you find attractive.

Forget about instant chemistry with *Mr. Right*. It is just as easy to fall in love with the wrong man as it is the right one. Date against your usual type and date lots of different types of men. Lose the extensive "checklist." Replace it with reasonable, realistic, solid values and needs. Give up the idea that there is *the one*.

Chapter 9

Your Body's Messages

In my research and survey, the most common questions I was asked were: "What were your top findings?" and "What do you think women need to learn about love?"

In our journey together through this book, my analysis and recommendations address the importance of mindfulness, emotional bravery, psychological self-examination and best-self behavior—the four pillars that support women's success in love.

One of the main problems I discovered was that women had shut down their mindfulness of the connections between their thoughts, feelings, behavior, physiological reactions and observations of men and themselves in any given situation. They not only failed to sense their emotional and physical reactions, but they didn't *value* the power of this information about the self.

By closing yourself off to *feeling* your body's experiences with men, you weaken your ability to understand this self-knowledge and apply it to your relationships. When you limit your accessibility to the bridge of mindfulness toward your reactions in the moment, you also diminish your capacity for the emotional bravery necessary to face your fears, push through them and master your emotional management of them. It's as though you close your eyes to the connection between yourself and the world.

Knock out these two bridges of mindfulness and bravery and the other two bridges of psychological self-examination and best self crumble. Psychological examination includes respecting—not blaming—the powerful influence of your childhood. Too many women said that "the past was the past." Yet, the present always includes your past—your hurts and triumphs and what you've learned from them. The bridges are connected, so you need all of them to get over the troubled waters of your fears. This chapter will focus on the bridge of mindfulness.

Mindfulness > Emotional Bravery > Psychological Self-Examination > Best Self

---

COOKIE FEELS SOMETHING

Cookie fell for a successful and exciting man who had a touch of danger. Now she has a taste of his cruelty. Notice how her boyfriend not only criticizes her, but he walks away from her, even after she says she doesn't feel well. Cookie hasn't felt well all evening—perhaps even earlier than that. She isn't connecting her stomach upset to the disturbance of being with this man.

WHY IS IT SO IMPORTANT TO BECOME AWARE OF MY BODY'S REACTIONS?

We've previously discussed the peril of allowing yourself to be so swept away by a man of wealth, charm and daring that you accommodate to mistreatment. On the flip side, that intense longing for affection, closeness and warmth from a man can prompt you to minimize his inadequacies, self-centeredness and insensitivity.

Regardless of your relationship pattern you can end up tolerating the intolerable. And then one day, something makes you open your eyes to the emotional crumbs you have accepted. You are shocked and even ashamed of your situation. There were signs all along in both your behavior and your body's responses to being hurt, disappointed, disillusioned or diminished emotionally. Your physiological reactions such as headaches and stomachaches were clues, too, but you didn't detect any of these warning signs.

Keep the sentence in the next box in your mind. It answers the question of why you should become aware of your physiological reactions.

The Importance of Body Awareness

What contributes to your complicity in accepting hurt is how tightly you shut down your mind's eye—your mindfulness—to cues from your body.

WHAT WARNING SIGNS AND SYMPTOMS SHOULD I OBSERVE?

Your body sends lots of signals to you about your feelings. The topic of mind and body connection is complex, so I'm limiting this chapter to a quick way of using the information to boost your awareness and reduce your potential for unhappiness or harm in love. If you'd like to learn more about listening to your body, I strongly recommend Dr. Jon Kabat-Zinn's book, *Full Catastrophe Living*.

Let's start with raising your overall awareness of yourself. The following statements come from my survey and the questions that I asked women in workshops. Underline or circle the word that best describes your level of agreement to the statement. The goal of this exercise is not to get a particular score but rather to kick-start your mindfulness of the connection between your body's reactions, your behavior and situation and your feelings.

Beginnings of Mindfulness

1. I do not have any difficulty controlling my use of alcohol, cigarettes, drugs, shopping, gambling, food or any other addictive behaviors.

    True   Mostly True   Mostly False   False

2. It has been more than two months since I had a good belly laugh.

    True   Mostly True   Mostly False   False

3. Other than work-related things, I haven't found anything that really interests me.

    True   Mostly True   Mostly False   False

4. I have trouble falling asleep at night or staying asleep.

    True   Mostly True   Mostly False   False

5. I often get physical reactions such as headaches, stomachaches, overall body aches, tiredness or agitation when I interact with my partner.

    True   Mostly True   Mostly False   False

6. I often wake up anxious.

    True   Mostly True   Mostly False   False

Let's see what these questions and your answers can teach you about you and your body. Look at numbers four and six. Sleep disturbances seem to be a national—if not international—problem. Somewhere between a quarter and a third of people report having chronic sleep problems.

A third of the women in my study said that they experienced difficulty falling asleep or staying asleep. "I dreaded going to bed," many of the women said, "because it didn't do much good. I couldn't turn my mind off to my problems." They tossed and turned, their hearts raced and they woke up anxious. A 2010 survey in *Self Magazine* revealed that one in three women reported experiencing anxiety.[1]

Sometimes, though, your behavior can mask your anxiety. Reflect on your answer to my first question in the Beginnings of Mindfulness exercise. More than a quarter of the women queried said they either ate too much or too little. Almost 30 percent said they had more than two drinks a day. Addictions of various kinds were among the ways that more than a quarter of the women used to calm or escape their anxiety or unhappiness.

Now look at your answers to numbers two and three. Losing interest in life, limiting it and not expressing joy and laughter could indicate a depressed mood, or at least a bad case of the blues. More than a third of my research participants said that they had not taken up any non-work related interests. What surprised me even more, though, was that more than 20 percent said they hadn't had a good laugh in months. Other signs of depressed mood also include experiencing the non-specific but persistent physical symptoms in statement number five.

The 2010 *Self Magazine* survey found that one in five women reported being depressed and my research found that more than a third of women showed warning signs of depression. The magazine also noted that almost a third of women were unhappy enough to talk to a counselor.

The overall portrait of being a woman today clearly includes elevated levels of anxiety and low mood. Your responsibility to be your best self begins with paying attention to your feelings and behaviors. A diagnosis of depression often rests on whether the following typical symptoms last more than two weeks. Sometimes, as in having suicidal thoughts, it takes just one symptom to sound alarm bells.

Look at this next list of depression symptoms. Seek help if you experience these reactions. You know the expression, "It can't hurt to..."? Well, I say it *can* hurt if you don't err on the side of caution. You deserve to pay attention to yourself. Don't ignore the warning signs. Open your eyes, become mindful about your body, feelings and behavior and don't ignore symptoms out of fear of upsetting your relationship. See a counselor when in doubt.

Depression Checklist

Check the items that apply to you.

❏ Frequent headaches, stomachaches or body aches

❏ Increased tiredness or exhaustion

❏ Energy fluctuations from too little to too much

❏ Eating too much, too little or binge eating

❏ Reduced interest in life, work, relationships, friends, family and both new and old activities

❏ Difficulty concentrating

❏ Persistent problems falling or staying asleep

❏ Increased anxiety, agitation or anger

❏ Sex drive too low or too high

❏ Suicidal thoughts, plans or actual attempts

❏ Decreased self-esteem or feelings of guilt

❏ Increased hopelessness or sadness

HOW ELSE CAN I USE MINDFULNESS TO HELP ME?

The concept of mindfulness often carries specific definitions and steps. It's a good idea to develop a basic understanding of how to enhance this mind-body connection so you can become more adept at understanding and managing your emotional pain and fear.

My next discussion has as its basis the mindfulness practices and explanations of Jon Kabat-Zinn's, which are explored in his book, *Full Catastrophe Living*. Dr. Zinn's ideas have become a landmark in teaching how to use mindfulness and meditation for healing, stress reduction and managing your feelings. You don't have to do every-thing—or even everything exactly as suggested. But it's a good idea to start with a brief orientation to what Dr. Zinn means when he uses the concept of mindfulness.[2]

Mindfulness is a way of activating your ability to become aware of yourself and your surroundings, emotional and physical reactions, and behavior *in the moment*. The knowledge you gain about yourself adds depth, emotional bravery, stress reduction, improved quality of life and personal acceptance as well as growth.

To benefit from this approach you need to get into a mindset of focusing on how your body's functions and reactions *feel* to you. You need to turn off any tendencies to judge these sensations, feelings and your experience of them. There is no right or wrong about the process. It just *is*. You aren't trying to change anything or accomplish anything. Your goal is to pay attention to what's going on in the moment.

You will need patience to maintain this focus on your reactions. Your mind may have a tendency to wander off to subjects like paying the bills or answering e-mail. Let those thoughts drift away and resume your focus. It might feel frightening to concentrate on feeling your sensations, but this reaction is normal. You have within you an innate ability to feel and be aware of your body's functioning.

Dr. Zinn recommends that you become aware of your breathing. He explains in detail how your lungs and diaphragm enable breathing. But for our purposes, you might want to sit or lie down and just breathe slowly and focus on *experiencing the feeling* of the filling and emptying of your lungs and of the air passing through your nose. Breathing is a great way to start your mindfulness skills because, well, you have to breathe! You don't need lessons in how to do it. So why not concentrate on improving your awareness of what you do every day without noticing it. Do this exercise for at least three minutes and then increase the time on each new attempt.[3]

Improving your attention to one bodily function helps you pay attention to others such as your heart rate or fluttering, perspiration, stomach churning, body aches, headaches and other processes. Remember, you are not separate from your body's reactions or your feelings. If you are anxious or frightened, that feeling will find expression in your muscles, tendons or blood flow. You might feel dizzy or nauseous. So why bother doing something that takes time—and might result in not feeling so well? Read the words in this box carefully:

What You Gain from Mindfulness

The benefit of body awareness exercises is a *feeling attune-ment* to the connection between physical and emotional reactions *as* they are happening—including interacting with your partner—so you can learn about yourself and thus manage your stress, fears and knowledge of your life choices, including your interactions with your partner.

After the women in my workshops experienced mindfulness in breathing, they did the next exercise that helps you zero in on the body's fear reactions. You don't have to do the exercise in this exact order, but this approach yielded the most useful information.

This exercise takes time. Don't give up on yourself out of laziness. Laziness is a feeling that masks fear. Don't fall for it. The purpose of this series of tasks is for you to build your own alert system for experiencing fear, anger, frustration and hurt in your relationship. If you don't know what you are feeling, then you can't know what's happening or what to do about it.[4]

The Movies, You and Your Reactions Exercises

1. **Go to a scary or exciting movie that you have not seen yet.**

   A. Go alone or with a friend—but not your partner. As you watch the movie, become aware of *feeling* your body's fear responses such as being startled, jumping in your seat, leaning forward, turning away, putting your head down, closing your eyes, clenching your fists, breathing quickly, holding your breath, heart racing, perspiring, throat closing and any other feelings you have.

   B. When the movie is over, think about what you were *feeling emotionally and physically*. Look at the list above and underline any that apply. An alternative is to bring

a pen and big piece of paper, and write in the dark
a key word or phrase such as "fast heart." After the
movie, read your notes or think about your feelings and
reactions.

C. Now pay attention to the thoughts or memories that
these feelings evoke. There are no right or wrong
answers. You are just trying to access any connections
between feelings, physical reactions and your associated
thoughts and memories. Write down these thoughts
and memories. Read them several times. What are you
learning about yourself, your reactions or your life and
relationships? Can you connect these observations with
feelings you've had with your partner?

2. **Go to a romantic comedy or tear-jerker that you have
not seen.**

A. Go alone or with a friend—but not your partner. As
you watch the movie, become aware of *feeling* your
body's responses such as headache, tight jaw, trouble
swallowing, eyes filling with tears, crying, feeling
sadness or loneliness, lowering your head, heaviness
in your chest, rapid heart rate, fast or slow breathing,
stomach churning, nausea, dizziness, fidgeting hands
and legs and any other body feelings you have.

B. When the movie is over, think about what you were
feeling emotionally and physically. Look at this list and
underline any that apply. An alternative is to bring a pen
and big piece of paper and write in the dark a key word
or phrase such as "sadness." After the movie, read your
notes or think about your feelings and reactions.

C. Now pay attention to the thoughts and memories
that these feelings evoke. There are no right or wrong
answers. You are just trying to access any connections
between feelings, physical reactions and your associated
thoughts and memories. Write down these thoughts
and memories. Read them several times. What are you
learning about yourself, your reactions or your life and

relationships? Can you connect these observations with feelings you've had with your partner?

3. **Watch one of your favorite romantic comedies or tear-jerkers.**

   A. This time it's better that you watch it alone. As you watch the movie, become aware of *feeling* your body's responses such as headache, tight jaw, trouble swallowing, eyes filling with tears, crying, lowering your head, heaviness in your chest, rapid heart rate, fast or slow breathing, stomach churning, nausea, dizziness, fidgeting hands and legs and any other body feelings you have.

   B. When the movie is over, think about what you were *feeling emotionally and physically*. Look at the list above and underline any that apply. An alternative is to bring a pen and big piece of paper and write in the dark a key word or phrase such as "loneliness." After the movie, read your notes or think about your reactions.

   C. Now pay attention to the thoughts and memories that these feelings evoke. There are no right or wrong answers. You are just trying to access any connections between feelings, physical reactions and your associated thoughts and memories. Write down these thoughts and memories. Read them several times. What are you learning about yourself, your reactions or your life and relationships? Can you connect these observations with feelings you've had with your partner?

4. **Watch a romantic comedy or tear-jerker—new or previously seen—but now watch it with your partner.**

   A. As you and your partner watch the movie, become aware of *feeling* your body's fear responses such as headache, tight jaw, trouble swallowing, eyes filling with tears, crying, lowering your head, heaviness in your chest, rapid heart rate, fast or slow breathing, stomach churning, nausea, dizziness, fidgeting hands and legs and any other body feelings you have.

B.   When the movie is over, think about what you were *feeling emotionally and physically*. Look at the list above and underline any that apply. An alternative is to bring a pen and big piece of paper and write in the dark a key word or phrase such as "loneliness." After the movie, read your notes and think about your reactions.

C.   Now pay attention to the thoughts these feelings evoke. There are no right or wrong answers. You are just trying to access any connections between feelings, physical reactions and your associated thoughts and memories. Write down these thoughts and memories. Read them several times. What are you learning about yourself, your reactions or your life and relationships? Can you connect these observations with feelings you've had with your partner?

5.   **Finally, review what you've learned from all these steps. Become mindful of these same or similar emotional and physical reactions when you are with your partner.**

KAYLA'S MINDFULNESS

When Kayla did this exercise, she became increasingly aware of the connection between her racing heart, fear, heaviness in her chest and her anger at her boyfriend whenever he criticized or demanded unrealistic things of her. "He was always finding fault with my work schedule, criticizing me for not sitting with him longer, not making fancy enough meals. He knows that tax season is my worst time, but I just jumped and did what he wanted whenever he spoke up. I was terrified of losing him."

Instead of breaking up, Kayla practiced best-self approaches and sat down and explained her work situation and her shared frustration about not being together more. She and her boyfriend came up with a plan that after tax season, they would always go away for a brief, romantic vacation.

Marla's Story

When Marla watched a romantic movie with her husband, she said "all my awareness just tumbled onto me. It made me think of opening a stuffed closet and having all my things hit me on the head." She said her awareness of her dips in mood, her exhaustion and feelings of heaviness in her chest felt like her entire life with her husband. In the past she had excused his shoving and yelling and pushing because, in her words, "he never really harmed" her. Now she realized that she indeed allowed him to harm her self-esteem. The romantic movie scenes brought into focus that her husband had rarely gone out of his way to be kind or caring. Her reactions to the scary movie made her more aware of experiencing danger.

She and her husband went to counseling, but her husband bolted. His anger increased to the point that he hit her and she divorced him.

All the women in the workshops used some version of this long exercise. Treat yourself well and put yourself on a mindfulness path so you can become your best and bravest self. When you can *feel and link* your emotional and physical reactions to fears and relationship unhappiness, you increase your self-awareness and your power to be good to yourself.

Tips for Building Mindfulness

Value the power of mindfulness. Mindfulness of your feelings—emotional and physical—is one of the best ways to gain control of your life, stress, fears and maladaptive coping mechanisms.

Step back and observe your life right now. Are you limiting your activities? Do you have any aches and pains in your body? How are you managing your drinking, spending, eating, sleeping? When was the last time you laughed?

Learn about serious symptoms of depression. Value yourself so you can take your symptoms seriously. Don't brush them under the rug out of fear of rocking the relationship boat. You are worth caring about.

Practice mindfulness. Sustain mindfulness by *feeling* your body's reactions. Use the breathing exercise as a refresher course.

Connect your reactions emotionally and physically to your relationships. Learn from this awareness. Aim to put your best self forward and work with your partner as a team to address the problem. Seek counseling before ending a relationship too soon.

Part IV

Taking Charge of Work's Power over Your Love Life

Chapter 10

Cultural Messages about Women and Work

Many women have listened to cultural messages about achievement and independence. Work and career success has become the entrance ticket to securing these goals. Like men, many women see their jobs as their identities rather than work they *do*.

Women earn more college, masters and doctoral degrees than men. According to the 2010 Census, 36 percent of women between the ages of twenty-five and thirty, or almost thirty million, have college degrees or higher.[1] Among physicians, 34 percent are women.[2]

Women's presence in middle management and law are rising, too. There are 338,000 female attorneys and over 31 percent of them are partners. By 2007, almost eight million women owned businesses. By 2009, 59 percent of women or seventy-two million were in the workforce.[3]

However, there is a downside to this success. According to the recent findings of the 2010 Census Bureau's American Community Survey, women's higher educational levels are linked to increased divorce rates. Women who work full time are 46 percent more likely to get divorced. These high numbers of professional women seem to suggest that because women can take care of themselves economically, they are freer to end unhappy relationships and find new intimate partners.[4]

The Bureau explains that since emotional fulfillment rather than economic stability drives women to marry, when women become dissatisfied, divorce becomes a manageable option. This unhappiness has dropped the birth rate by 6 percent among women age twenty to thirty-four due to factors such as use of birth control, the rising economic uncertainty among both men and women about starting a family, women's increased economic ability to end marriages and cohabitation.[5]

The Center for Work-Life Policy's 2011 report found that 43 percent of Generation X women between the ages of thirty-three and forty-six do not have children. They hold more jobs and college and graduate school degrees than men—but they also work longer hours and carry high debt.[6]

The women in the study were often surprised at this mix of the bad news about love with the good news about education and economic independence. They scrambled to find solutions to burnout, debt, love satisfaction and work-life balance. Just what is going on? Women may have pushed through some pieces of that glass ceiling at work, but they aren't anywhere near the love ceiling.

There's nothing wrong with wanting a career and working hard. And there's nothing wrong either with getting married, having a family and putting your career on hold for a while. And there's nothing wrong with working in a field that doesn't use your degree. And, of course, there's nothing wrong with raising a family and taking an online course, or volunteering or accepting a less demanding and less lucrative position in your area of expertise until your children are older. And there's nothing wrong with...My point is: You have more options about how to craft a fulfilling, successful life than you think.

Yes, there are *always* limitations in life. Sometimes, you can redress your previous decisions with a do-over. You might get divorced, have children later in life or go back to school. Other times, you have to tweak your plans and goals. You may not have all the control and options that you'd like, but you probably still have some choices.

My parents were upset that I didn't get accepted by any college to which I applied. They couldn't understand it. I got very good grades in high school and graduated at the top of my class. But I had two strikes against me: low standardized test scores and a high school which did not have a competitive national ranking.

I decided that I would just go to whatever other college accepted me, focus on my studies and transfer in my sophomore year to one of the colleges of my choice. I was sure I could accomplish this goal. The only person I told of my thoughts was Daisy, the woman who worked for my family. She knew nothing about college. She had to drop out of school after the eighth grade. But she was wise enough to say to me, "Oh, you are a smart girl. There are lots of ways to get to where you want to go." And she was right. My plan worked.

Luckily, today, women in developed countries have lots of choices about how they want to forge their lives. Yet, the women in my study experienced the downside of all these options. First, they had to soul-search to find out who they were, what they were good at and what inspired them. Then, they had to decide how to enact their decisions. Which path was right? Work first? Join the armed forces? Go to school or get trained first? Have children? Get married? Do it all at once?

The result of all these pathway choices is that the women often experienced what is sometimes described as the tyranny of freedom. What made the experience even worse was managing the cultural messages about what they should and should not do.

When I asked women to write down their main concerns and problems in their lives, their topics always included doubts about whether they were doing enough. They crowded their life's agenda with a list of things that they believed they *should* do. The women wondered if it was okay not to work, not to have children, not to have another child, not to accept a high-powered job. Some women said they felt "embarrassed" that they were "just" stay-at-home mothers. Others over-defended why they didn't have children.

Many of the women I surveyed were surprised to discover how deeply they had incorporated so many cultural values about women. Their reactions went something like this: "I just thought I was living my life the best I could and still failing at being in charge of it. I didn't think in terms of a rule book for women. And if I did, I don't think I realized how these messages compete or contradict each other—like 'be yourself but you should do it this way.' And I certainly didn't realize how much I allow them to contribute to my confusion and unhappiness." Look at the next cartoon to see how Cookie handles these messages.

COOKIE BURNS OUT WITHOUT KNOWING IT

Does this cartoon look familiar? Like Cookie, do you thrive on seeing your "out box" full? And by your "out box," I also mean that feeling of finishing other tasks such as picking up the kids at school, attending a recital, finally doing the laundry, picking up dinner, going grocery shopping, changing the oil in your car, rescheduling doctors' appointments, changing meeting times, kissing your partner, putting the kids to bed, getting a sitter, going on a date, seeing friends, taking care of mom, job hunting, finding a new bedspread you like and so on.

Life for today's educated, trained and working women is not easy. You've become a juggler whose skills at multitasking are often barely enough to keep everything in the air. Your body and brain become accustomed to intensity—for a while, at least. However, increased levels of the stress hormone cortisol eventually get to you and you feel burned out. You find yourself doubting your choices, lifestyle, pace and responsibility. This situation leaves you vulnerable to blaming yourself or feeling flawed for not getting an A+ for both effort and results.

Even though you go back and forth between feeling exhausted and exhilarated, you push yourself to get everything done. But how important is it that you do *all* these things and *do all of them over-the-top well at the same time*?

It's time to free yourself from all these messages and rules and learn how to take your life back, modify it or create a new one. In this chapter I'll discuss the women's top struggles and solutions.

WHY CAN'T I HAVE IT ALL?

A movie and a television advertisement use the title and catchphrase "I Don't Know How She Does It." This is meant to be a compliment for such an amazing woman who does it all and has it all. The word "all" implies happiness and stellar success in *every* area of the woman's life—work, appearance, income, education, high-powered job, adorable and brilliant children, gorgeous home—or homes—and an accomplished, wealthy husband who is either handsome or coolly quirky-looking. That's a lot to expect of you.

Why can't you have it all? Some women do, but setting "all" as your goal is most likely going to leave you with depression and anxiety that can actually ruin your health and happiness. Anne-Marie Slaughter, a highly respected foreign policy expert, addresses this issue and more in her brave July/August 2012 *Atlantic* article, "Why Women Still Can't Have It All." She discovered, as did I and the women in my study, that one way to have it all is to make flexible and realistic adjustments to that expectation.[7] Here is a great recipe:

Healthy Recipe for "Having It All"

Prep: Before you start cooking, get into the mindset that it is *your* life that you are preparing—not someone else's recipe for happiness and success. Now you're ready to assemble the following ingredients:

1. **Add a lifelong supply of thinking in terms of gray.**
   Stop thinking in terms of black and white or either/or. For example, you don't necessarily have to choose between having a child *or* a career.

2. **Mix in an equal part of seeing many roads to your goals.** Get flexible. You don't have to go to an Ivy League school, for example, to get a degree. You don't have to swim in a big pond to be successful and to feel gratified.

3. **Mix in another equal part of viewing life as filled with many chances and opportunities.** Don't get trapped into thinking that *every* opportunity is "the chance of a lifetime." True, there certainly could be a one-time chance

at something, but if you are flexible, you might be able to create another opportunity that is also good enough.

4. **Fold in the view that life and priorities come in stages.** You don't have to do everything *at once.* Priorities shift over time in life, so you will probably need to defer some goals. For example, teenagers usually need more supervision and more parental presence in the home than ten-year-olds. If you wanted to return to school, full-time work or a more demanding job, you might need to postpone that decision until your teens are in college, the armed forces or training programs. If you have ailing parents or an ill child, you would then also have to shift your timeline for doing things.

5. **Decorate with slices and pieces of your goals and plans.** You could also work on dual goals simultaneously if you did them in pieces. For instance, instead of enrolling full-time, take a single course. Or, if you cannot work full time, volunteer or work part time.

6. **Sprinkle with patience and dollops of flexibility.** Get into a mindset of looking at the long haul. Realize that goals and dreams can change. As you mature and have more experiences, becoming a "department head of something very important" might not be so appealing.

Now answer these questions:

Creating My Version of "All"

1. *What are my long-term goals, plans or dreams at this time?* You might want to think about schooling, jobs, careers and family.

2. *What are the competing priorities or obstacles?* Think about your time, timing and energy, and what is most important now.

3. *What are the other variations and timetables for achieving these goals?* Think about what's in your life for now and for later. When would it be a good time to begin working on some of your goals?

WHY DO I FEEL I HAVE FAILED?

For many women, a pervasive sense of failure dwells deep inside them. It makes them assume that the failure comes primarily from *within*. Don't lose sight of who should evaluate you—you or them? Whose values will you use? Who knows about you, your struggles or your childhood limitations? Don't compare yourself to others. Life has a random unfairness. Some people get more opportunities and good luck than others. Keep the thought below in mind.

Keeping Your Eyes on You

Talent is given mostly at birth. Yes, you can develop skills, for example, but if you aren't good at reading, it's possible but unlikely that you're going to gravitate toward majoring in English. But it is the character that *you* make of yourself that is truly admirable.

Always bear in mind what you've overcome and your intellectual and physical limitations. Set reasonable and flexible goals rather than aiming for status or pleasing someone such as your parents. The film version of British writer D.H. Lawrence's novella, *The Virgin and the Gypsy*, takes place in the beginning of the twentieth century when women are experiencing more social freedoms. The family lives in a small town in England, and everyone knows everyone else's business. It has a wonderful scene where the parents' wayward daughter is getting fitted for a dress to the local gala.

This daughter—the "virgin" of the title and a rebel at heart—refuses to wear one of the dresses with a buttoned-up neck and a hem to the floor to the affair. Her dress is bright red, with a plunging neckline and a short skirt with fringe that sways with every move. When her parents fret over her dress, she turns to them and says something like, "One day I'll still be alive, and you'll all be dead," implying that she doesn't want to find herself living for the approval of people who are no longer here. Do some serious soul-searching. Answer the next questions:

My Questions

Why do I want my goals?

Whom am I pleasing—other than me?

What fears do I have that will get in the way of my accomplishing my goals and self-definition?

The ability to withstand an honest and deep self-evaluation is one of your most important tasks. It's not easy and it's often emotionally painful. If you don't do it, then you risk short-changing yourself or running yourself ragged for reasons that you don't have to make yours.

Hattie's Story

One of the women in my group sessions, Hattie, came from a family of well-known actors. She was also in the entertainment business, but she had not achieved the level of fame of the rest of her family. Hattie set her sights on getting either a Tony or an Academy Award. Anything less felt like a failure. "I just couldn't get a break," Hattie said. "I began drinking more, and having sex with just about any man in power in Hollywood or New York. One night I drove my car drunk. I almost hit a man and his daughter who were in a crosswalk. Wow—that was some wake-up call!"

Hattie struggled to quit drinking. She went to a detox program where they forced her to face her demons. "It wasn't easy," she said. Hattie worked hard, she was motivated to take charge of her life and she reached those demons. "I saw how I measured myself by my parents' standards. They grew up with parents who had memories of the Great Depression. It was drilled into their heads to strive, strive, strive, money, money, money. I discovered I didn't really have that gene."

Hattie learned that she wanted to teach drama to children and to be part of a theater company outside of New York. "I wanted more freedom, more ability to give back locally," she said. She found a job that fulfilled *her* dream. "I couldn't have gotten there if I hadn't taken a real look at myself."

In one of my favorite poems, "Desert Spaces" by Robert Frost, he speaks of "Snow falling and night falling fast, oh, fast / In a field I looked into going past." He says, "They cannot scare me with their empty spaces."[8] Think of nightfall as the reminder of time and the ending of one day of your years. The white fields of snow are both your past and your future blank slate with still enough room. Step into your own dark spaces of your past, your fears and doubts. Become emotionally brave.

WHY DON'T MY FEMALE FRIENDS HELP ME?

It was very upsetting for many of the women in my study to discover that a sisterhood of women does not necessarily always exist. Many of the comments from them sounded like this: "I guess I was naïve to assume that women would cheer my accomplishments. Some did, but a lot came off really competitive and insecure. It made me feel so lonely."

One topic in my focus groups often was how rare it was to find women who were open and honest about their unhappiness and struggles and who offered real help and empathy. It's not easy to find good friends. Women in corporate or academic positions especially voiced their disappointment that competitiveness had outstripped friendship. One woman, a professor and author, said: "I'd get a phone call from a distant colleague or a woman I just met at a meeting, and I'd get excited. Oh boy, I thought—maybe a new friend. Most often all they really wanted to know was who was my agent and would I read their manuscript? After a while, I began my sentences by saying that I no longer had time to review their work. It made me feel ugly inside and sad."

There were women who had formed long-lasting friendships and support groups that applauded the achievements of others. Here is what they did to increase the chances of making solid friends and getting good advice.

BUILD A WORLD OF SUPPORT AND CHEER

Take time to choose friends wisely. Go slowly. Don't rush
the friendship. Keep in your mind: What do I like about this
person? What do I think she wants from me? Are we a good
match? Look for signs of jealousy. Gloria, one woman with
whom I spoke, said that while having lunch with a new friend,
Brie, a man came up to Gloria and introduced himself. He
recognized Gloria from an article about her in the college
newspaper. He was a professor in another department at the
university where Gloria also taught. "He seemed very nice and
he was single," Gloria said.

Gloria and the man exchanged e-mail addresses and phone
numbers, and they agreed to have lunch sometime next week.
As soon as he left, Brie said to Gloria: "Gosh, Gloria, you don't
even look good today and this guy comes up to you."

At first, Gloria dismissed it as a small reaction out of
jealousy. Gloria knew that Brie was not happy with her life.
But Gloria kept the incident in mind and she watched to see
if there were other signs of Brie not cheering for her. "There
were a few more similar incidents where Brie chastised me
for dating a lot, and so I just stopped seeing her," Gloria said.
Make sure your friends are part of your cheering squad and
realize that those that are not, are not really friends.

Create a different kind of cheerleader. Seek mentors. You
could meet with retirees in your field to learn from their
experiences. Find a virtual mentor by reading biographies and
autobiographies of women you respect. Pay special attention
to how they overcame their obstacles and grew or changed
their goals over time. Get audacious and contact women you
respect but don't know. The Internet is a great way to find out
where they work or whether you can connect with them on
Facebook and other social media and professional sites.

WHY DON'T I VALUE MY NON-WORK ACCOMPLISHMENTS SUCH AS FAMILY OR MY CHARITY WORK?

If you feel that your skills as a good parent and partner and that your contributions of time, money and ideas to charities don't count for much, then you may believe that the only women who do count are the ones who have it all, especially when "all" means high-paying, high-profile, high-status jobs, similarly prestigious husbands and perfect kids who get accepted at the best prep schools and Ivy League colleges and make a huge impact on the world. Anything short of that, you think, doesn't count.

Don't lose sight that two of the most important and difficult jobs are raising children well and helping others. Modern culture can be a toxic brew that only values, admires and respects women whose accomplishments merit being on the cover of a national magazine, the subject of a television show or the winner of any one of an endless number of entertainment awards. The value of the individual in this scenario seems to dictate that you must "be *somebody*." But it is up to you to define for yourself who that *somebody* is. There are millions of *somebodies* all over the world about whom you rarely hear. You don't have to be the next crusader, leader or innovator in order *to matter*. The famous pop artist Andy Warhol captured this imperative to cast a huge shadow with his statement that many people will get their "fifteen minutes of fame."

Don't settle for fifteen minutes. Instead, create a lifetime of doing things that use your abilities and interests, that are central to who you are and what you value and help others. Some women believe that mothers who give up careers—especially to care for their children—who work part time or who do not have big jobs are not living up to their potential. Well, that could be a good assessment if women had evolved into creatures who didn't need to sleep, and who had two brains, an extra set of arms and who could be in multiple places at once.

The real "all" is the freedom to choose and revise your goals, values and self-definition of personal meaning—not to become a slave to ideology. Find your own internal compass and follow it. It is *your* head—not someone else's—that hits the pillow at night.

Tips on Cultural Messages about Women and Work

Don't get trapped in a "have it all" mindset. Few people truly have it all. Instead, focus on the needs and hopes and dreams in *your* life.

Get flexible. You can likely fulfill many of your wishes if you take a longer view of your life. Regard your life as a series of stages, each with different priorities.

Toss out the notion that you have failed. Make sure to measure your achievements with yourself in mind. Learn from others rather than comparing yourself to others. Respect what you've overcome.

Do the tough work of psychological self-examination. Learn about your limitations and why you have them. Discover which ones you can realistically change. Fight through your fears.

Develop female mentors. Get brave and contact women who inspire you. Or, read their biographies and autobiographies to learn from them. Find out about local organizations that can help you meet and learn from other women.

Chapter 11

Office Romances

In past years, one of the most common and successful settings for meeting an eligible man and making a smart love match was deemed to be at your place of worship. When this was the site of a meeting, there was an increased likelihood that you shared similar values. Your families might know each other or he and you could have attended religious classes together.

Religious institutions still provide a great way to meet men but today, another setting offers love opportunities—your job location. Since many people spend more time at work than they do at home, it's no wonder that workplaces have also become environments for dating and mating.

It makes sense on the surface. You and your prospective partner share common interests and talents. Relying solely on the fact that you are in the same or related fields is usually not sufficient, however, for making a good love choice. It's too easy to get caught up in the fantasy of the two of you becoming the next dynamic duo that is going to save the world.

The information in this chapter can help you temper your romantic feelings for co-workers and examine other factors in your life that might make you vulnerable to having affairs or intimate relationships with colleagues or bosses. Let's see how Cookie handles the issue of falling for a colleague.

COOKIE GETS (TOO) EXCITED ABOUT A WORK COLLEAGUE

He called! He called *her*! Out of all the single attorneys at work, Ron called her first. Cookie doesn't know it, but her excitement about the phone call from the new lawyer should have signaled the warning bell for love danger.

She had ended an unhappy relationship with her boyfriend Tim because he was a sweet, money-borrowing lost person with unfocused, half-baked career ideas. To make matters worse, her disappointment in Tim made her swear off men. Her mother's anxiety about Cookie not being married complicates Cookie's retreat from the dating life. Food becomes her companion—until Ron, the new man at work, calls her.

Cookie is not aware that she is too excited. She's too busy feeling ecstatic about not being alone, not eating up a storm of junk food and not disappointing her mother. No wonder Ron's call seems like a life raft.

It certainly *is* exciting when someone you like takes a romantic interest in you. But become mindful of the degree of your excitement. The greater the intensity, the greater the chance that you are adding too much emotional baggage to your enthusiasm.

Intimate relationships with co-workers come in many varieties. You might have an affair with a married man from work, or you might start a romantic relationship with your boss, a top executive or a colleague. Some office romances—including affairs—do succeed. However, be careful. Your married lover might be at a vulnerable spot in his life—or he might be misrepresenting his marriage.

More than just your emotions could suffer. If your employer bans intimate relationships with co-workers, you could be dismissed. Know your company's rules. Don't let the thrill of forbidden love propel you into dangerous territory.

For now, let's pretend that your job permits romance with a colleague. Here is advice about the key questions and issues about love at work.

WHO IS LIKELY TO HAVE A MISGUIDED INTIMATE RELATIONSHIP AT THE OFFICE?

Just about anyone could potentially be emotionally vulnerable to an office romance or affair at work. There is no "type" of person who has an affair, for example. We'd all like to think that we can avoid behaviors that we later regret, but even very good people can make wrong choices. Sara's story is an example of how life always includes the unpredictable.

Sara's Story

When Sara moved to a small town to accept a management position at a national company, she was nervous in a good way. "I had to get out of the big city," she said. "One night when I was walking to the subway after working late, I was mugged and beaten up really badly. I was in the hospital for over a week. My friends and colleagues visited me, but I still felt very alone."

For months afterward, Sara had nightmares. She never stayed late at her job any longer, and even though she took work home with her, she couldn't concentrate. Her performance was suffering. She contacted a headhunter, and swore them to secrecy about her reason for applying for a management position in a smaller and safer town. "An opportunity fell out of the sky— and in a warm place," Sara said, "so when they offered me the position, I grabbed it."

The town was charming, but the new job was, well, just okay. Her days were long and her fear of going out alone at night prevented her from attending events. Making friends with her female colleagues was more difficult than she had anticipated. A few women were in upper management, and most of them rushed home to husbands and families. The female administrative assistants didn't seem interested in or comfortable about socializing with her.

Sara was always one to be friendly with a wide range of people, but she also knew that it took time to make good friends. So, on weekends, Sara rented movies to watch and caught up on sleep.

She wasn't necessarily happy, but she did feel less anxious. Little did she know how much she underestimated her fear and loneliness. Then along came Alec. He was a division manager and he was very impressed with Sara's competencies. Like a shark, he sensed her vulnerability from miles away.

Alec was going through a divorce. Everyone in the office knew about it. His wife and his attorney often called him at work. Colleagues and co-workers felt sorry for him. His wife seemed impossible. Few knew that Alec was the one delaying the divorce, because he didn't want to pay dearly for alimony and child support. It was less expensive to pay the legal bills. He even negotiated a barter system with the attorney. In exchange for his drastically reducing his fees, Alec gave his lawyer access to his plane and golf course membership.

Sara was a great diversion for Alec. He introduced her to the local heads of charities and made sure they included her in event planning. After hours, Alec and Sara had sex in his office and he always made sure to accompany her home when it was dark outside. She felt safe at last.

Then the world crashed in around her. At a charity event that she co-chaired, Sara was in the ladies room in the only stall available—the handicap facility that was tucked around the corner. She didn't mean to eavesdrop, but there was no way to avoid hearing the conversation of two women. "Someone should tell Sara," one of the women said. "What is she—woman number four Alec is using?" The other woman said, "He's never leaving his wife. Her family is old money in this town. He's got too much at stake—especially since he's considering a run for office next term." The other woman agreed. "You better believe his wife's father will reel Alec back in—and keep him there."

What a fool I've been, Sara thought.

In time, the news broke about Alec and his wife's prominent family. Alec moved back into the house with his wife, and he promised Sara that he would get divorced one day. Sara was devastated. It took her almost a year before she began dating again.

The biggest mistake Sara made was not being mindful of her emotional fragility. Her lack of awareness of her desperation and anxiety blinded her to Alec's situation. "He never seemed to make progress in his divorce," Sara said. "He cancelled every meeting with his wife's attorney. That alone should have been my tip-off, but it wasn't. I don't think anything at that point in my life would have opened my eyes."

WHY WOULD A PERSON FALL IN LOVE AT WORK?

Like Sara and Cookie, you might be in the midst of a crisis or in emotional turmoil. Regardless of the situation, you are susceptible. Your usual radar for danger is not working, your defenses against hurt are down and your need for safety and warmth are up.

In workshops and talks, I asked women whose intimate work relationships ended badly to examine this painful experience. They needed to recognize their unique signs of being in a weakened position so they wouldn't have another unwise work affair or a hasty love. Do the next exercise to learn about your warning signs.

Draw You—Before and After the Affair

Draw a picture about how you feel about this relationship now or before. You don't have to be an artist. You can draw a stick figure with a Valentine heart. You could just draw your face, or you could draw images. It doesn't matter what comes to mind. Whatever you draw, think about these things:

- What expression is on your face?
- If your beating heart could talk, what would it be saying?
- What is your brain doing? Is it sleeping? Is it sending out warning signs? How big is your brain at this point?
- What are your other body parts doing? Is your stomach churning? Are your muscles shaking? Are you perspiring?
- Are you in la-la land now? What does it look or feel like?
- Are you filled with regret or confusion?

To get you started, I've given you a few shapes and ideas to start your thought process:

Happy then sad

Glad it's over

A walking
broken heart

Worried that you
could be making
a big mistake

Butterflies in your
stomach

Realizing how
unwise you were

Feel as though
you discovered
an unknown
part of you

The love feels
too confusing

You're too excited
to think

Angry that you
were so vulnerable

Caught up in
the fantasy

Seeing the light

What are you learning about your reactions and the importance you put on this work relationship?

Here are three examples from women with whom I conferred:

Hayley's Story

Hayley drew a stick figure with a heart whose outline consisted of disconnected dashes. She said her heart was working, but it had tiny openings that let in people that her heart would normally prevent from getting through. Her heart was saying, "accept anything that feels good for a while."

Then she drew a stick figure of herself flying over the rainbow. She said, "I was just so excited that Bob and I 'discovered' each other at work that I felt like I was flying high up into the clouds. I had never noticed him before. But he saw me crying in the hallway, and he was such an angel. I was going through a horrid divorce, and he seemed to understand."

Six months later, after Hayley's divorce was finalized, she also discovered that Bob wasn't a good choice. "There was nothing really wrong with him. He was a nice guy and all, but he had no ambition. Our break-up was horrid. Now we just avoid each other at work. It's terrible. He had a good shoulder to cry on and that was really all."

Abigail's Story

Abigail drew a huge heart with wiggly lines around it to show how loudly it was beating. She didn't draw anything else. She said, "I didn't even know I had other body parts. I was just so happy that Eric wanted me."

Abigail was the in-house counsel for a large firm. She was almost forty, never married and kept to herself. She loved her job, and they loved her. She had lots of friends—mostly women who were married or divorced with children. Even though Abigail was outgoing, stayed in shape and looked young, she seldom dated. Her checklist was too exacting. Her perfect man was someone who made a lot more money than she did, had never been married, had no children, loved cooking as much as she did and came from a family whose religion and social status matched hers.

Then Abigail learned she had lupus. At first, she was stoic, but over time, her panic and depression grew. Her friends were great in the beginning but, after the diagnosis, their time together diminished. Outwardly, she seemed fine. Friends were impressed with her coping abilities.

Secretly, Abigail was still very depressed. She could keep it together at work, but at home she felt "dulled and dead." Life was just going to be placing one foot in front of the other. Then Eric was transferred to her company. He was the new assistant marketing director, fifty and divorced, but the marriage had ended on good terms, so Abigail waived that requirement. Eric also had a school-age daughter, but Abigail waived that requirement, too, because his daughter lived in another city and he only saw her on holidays. Finally, she waived the stipulation that the man of her dreams had to come from the same religious and economic background. The only thing she didn't waive was that he had to love cooking.

It was almost a match made in heaven, she thought. Eric asked her out to a new restaurant in town, and they talked about food all night. Within ten days, they had sex. They spent the weekends cooking and making love. During her third week seeing Eric, she told him about the lupus. "He understood me," Abigail said. "He said his mother had arthritis and he knew what illness was like."

After the sex cooled, Abigail realized that their relationship had soured. Eric became bossy and reacted with aggravation to the side effects of her illness. She forgot to ask smart questions such as: Why don't you see your daughter more frequently? Why don't you ever visit your ailing mother? Why are you so insensitive to my illness? And why were you let go from your previous job?

Abigail's questions were good, but they came long after she put her heart out there without being mindful. She eventually saw that Eric was a self-absorbed, selfish person who really didn't like relating to people. He loved showing off his cooking skills and knowledge of food. No one was allowed to know more about food than he. And no one had better make any demands on him.

"He thought that my illness would turn me into a woman who was so grateful to be loved that I wouldn't ask anything of him," Abigail said. The break-up was calm and cold. Abigail didn't date anymore.

Helena's Story

Helena was a force to be reckoned with. She was a beautiful woman with a top-notch education, a spirited personality and talent in the advertising industry. She also had lots of ambition. She vowed to break out of the work groups as soon as possible to head up her own team. Her affair with Randolph, her company's married vice president, started at the company picnic. "We were great at softball," she said.

After contemplating what her relationship picture should be, Helena drew fireworks and her head with the following words swirling around her: "Get ahead. Get out there. Don't slow down. Get ahead. Get out there. Don't slow down." Next to her drawing, she added a light bulb. "Looking back on my disaster," Helena said, "I had all my insides on go. I don't even think I cared about anything else. Even when I think of Randolph, I still don't use his name. He was just a vice president who liked me and who saw my talents."

It wasn't always like that for Helena. She said she felt well-matched with Randolph. They loved sparring intellectually, and he liked that she was aware of financial aspects such as cost-cutting and productivity. The driving force of their relationship, Helena said, was that he saw her as an exciting break from a bored and boring wife and she saw him as a man who recognized and applauded her ability to succeed. "My family would have been happier if I never went to college and instead became an old-fashioned housewife in a small town," she said.

Helena was sure Randolph was going to leave his wife after Christmas. But he stayed with her through President's Day. He stayed for his daughter's soccer championship, he stayed for his son's completion of his first year of college and he stayed for his mother-in-law's birthday. "I didn't want to believe that he was never going to leave her," Helena said, "but when he took his wife on a world cruise and didn't even e-mail me once, I knew it was over."

Helena got her job promotion, yet she said she felt she achieved it not by her merits but by the diversion she offered Randolph. She stayed with the company, but she and her vice president avoided each other as much as possible.

The next list shows the top reasons that women in my study fell blindly in love at work. Add your own.

TOP LIFE SITUATIONS THAT TEMPORARILY DERAILED YOU INTO MISGUIDED LOVE WITH A COLLEAGUE

- Illness of yourself or a loved one
- A loved one died
- Unhappiness with your existing partner
- Loneliness
- Getting older
- You experienced a trauma
- You are the only single or never-married sibling or cousin
- Unhappy with your life in general
- You live for work and have little life outside of work
- Your financial situation has changed for the worse
- You got overlooked at work and feel underappreciated

IF I AM NOT IN A CRISIS OR NOT EMOTIONALLY VULNERABLE, HOW ELSE DO I END UP FALLING INTO MISGUIDED LOVE WITH A COLLEAGUE OR BOSS?

Here's a list of the most common mistakes of mixing work and love:

You fall for the myth that shared work interests will provide the emotional glue for bonding. It's easy to be lured into assuming that men who belong to the "club of people from your profession and interests" are guaranteed to be right for you.

Yes, it is important to find mutual pleasure in shared interests, but those interests don't necessarily have to include being in the same profession. It can seem that speaking the same career language diminishes your need to explain your stress, joys, struggles, accomplishments and crazy work schedule. For example, same-career couples often have long and intense hours. Many medical students often marry each other. As Margery said, "My husband and I are both surgeons. We accept each other's being on call or dashing out for emergencies."

Alyssa and Alan worked for a commercial real estate development company that specialized in hospitals and nursing homes. Alan was the chief project manager, and Alyssa worked in purchasing. Their hours were not only long but also unpredictable. "There was always a new problem because local and state laws about safety changed," Alyssa said. She assumed Alan would understand that she had to stay up late into the night and work weekends to change orders.

Alan's work habits and pace differed from hers and they fought over their use of time. Even though they worked in the same profession, they failed to become a loving team. Alan wanted Alyssa to quit her job so they could start a family. Alyssa, however, wasn't ready to have children.

Other than shared expertise or interests, make sure you have other things in common, such as values, life goals and communication skills. Here are some questions to consider.

Sustaining Mindfulness:
Smart Relationship Questions to Ask Yourself

- What else do we share?
- Are we respectful and kind to each other?
- Can we postpone our needs and issues for a while, if necessary?
- Do we get along?
- Are we good problem-solvers?
- Do we make each other feel safe and warm in the specific ways that we need?

When you collaborate on an important work project, you believe you've fallen in love with a colleague whom you've previously overlooked. The intensity and urgency of the task promotes a sense of closeness that may not have as much depth as you think it does. You stay long hours at work, brainstorm, get giddy from your ideas and feel safe coming up with wrongheaded solutions.

You gobble down pizza like a hungry ten-year-old, and you relax your outer demeanor. You feel comfortable being yourself with this colleague in a way you've never allowed before. Like survivors of disasters, you feel suddenly closer to someone who is in the same crisis mode. You can't imagine anyone else understanding the gravity of your situation and you become intensity junkies together.

Shared perilous events such as surviving an attack create a special fellowship. Some combat veterans only speak about the details of their war experiences with other veterans. Similarly, working on what feels like a do-or-die professional project arouses the same fight-or-flight survival responses in the brain. Your stress hormone levels increase and you and your teammates become a band of colleagues forced to succeed—or else. The television series *Mad Men* depicts this sense of brotherhood and sisterhood in a 1960s ad agency, where winning or losing a contract could determine the fate of the company.

Anna's Story

It doesn't seem a big leap from workmate to intimate mate. But that leap is often bigger than you think. For example, Anna deliberately chose Darryl as her work partner as part of a larger work team at a suicide prevention and treatment center for teens. The agency had received a prestigious grant to develop a program at the regional hospital. They were both nurses and Anna chose Darryl as her co-worker because she wasn't attracted to him. "He was kind of sloppy and too flabby for my interests," Anna said. "He was a safe— but very competent—choice. It would be a work partnership with no chance for romance, I thought. Ha."

One night, three weeks into the project, Anna and Darryl grabbed a sandwich at a local deli, and they began telling each other about their background and unhappiness. Anna said, "We discussed our mutual lack of a love life." Anna's usual guard was down, because Darryl seemed innocuous to her. She felt comfortable with him. After hours, she let her hair get disheveled, and she didn't care if her makeup was flaking a little. Anna loved eating in her usual way of picking at her food with her fingers—her last boyfriend criticized her lack of polish.

Anna and Darryl knew the enormity of the contract they had just won. Their little town was going to be the test case for new treatment protocols. "We were excited about it together and I was calm for a change. He brought out coping skills in me that I didn't have on my own."

Later, though, after Anna and Darryl became intimate, she realized that she had confused work expertise and comfort with relationship viability. Anna discovered a secret side to Darryl. He had wanted to be a doctor, but when he couldn't get into medical school, he became a nurse. His father and grandfather were both physicians and Darryl felt like a failure.

Anna, too, was the disappointment of her family. She was the only daughter of five who did not have a graduate degree or a husband. "I thought our family backgrounds would make us closer," Anna said.

She also discovered another secret about Darryl. When he wasn't at work, he liked to search for pornography on the Internet. He also belonged to several dating sites that specialized in men finding foreign women who wanted to marry Americans. He liked being the boss, and he longed for a submissive woman who would idolize him. At the end of the work project, Anna and Darryl broke up.

You think you know a man because you spend so much time at work together. Work allows you to see a man in action. You respect his competency, and his savvy spurs you to assume that he is equally as able in his private life. At work parties, you see that he often takes the lead. The other men like him, too.

Yet, not every man integrates his work personality with his private personality. Sometimes these areas don't overlap, because the men have compartmentalized them. Gangster movies have shown us how easy it is to have one set of values for family and another set for gangland work. Consequently, you can be fooled into thinking you "know" someone because you work with them.

Vivian's Story

Vivian's love relationship with Christopher began when she saw him in action in the courtroom. Vivian was head of all the paralegals at a prestigious law firm. Recently divorced, she was proud of her ability to take care of herself financially. She had always liked Christopher. He was the company's star and he had only lost one case.

When the firm took on an important criminal defense case, Christopher relied on Vivian's skills. They kept long hours, and one night, after Christopher told her about breaking up with his fiancée, Vivian and Christopher kissed.

For over a year, they kept their relationship a secret, but Vivian knew that it would never last. Christopher was more like a demanding baby than a commanding man. He whined and complained when the smallest thing at home was wrong. From the far end of his house, he'd call out to Vivian to clean up his desk, to run out to get his favorite ice cream or buy a birthday card for his mother. "He went nuts when I bought sheets with too low of a thread count. But when I didn't buy the brand of turkey cutlets that was on sale, he'd accuse me of wasting his money. Nothing he did made sense. He was like a spoiled brat who loved lording over things in a very tiny kingdom," Vivian said. Nevertheless she just couldn't break up with him until the case was over because they had to work so closely together.

You've used affairs before to contain your unhappiness. Perhaps you saw your parents have affairs. Even though their behavior frightened, confused and angered you, this family behavior became part of your submerged and barely known emotional tool box of coping mechanisms. Despite the emotional turmoil of an affair, you feel you can handle it. The situation feels familiar, and there's an odd comfort in dealing with pain that you know.

Tara's Story

Tara and Paul were both unhappy with their spouses. "We'd share war stories after work," Tara said. And then, one late afternoon in spring, they took the long way through the park, and Paul reached for her hand. "It seemed so natural," Tara said. "It was dusk. Families were out with their kids, and teenagers and couples were sitting on the grass. It looked so green and soft, and we almost sat down at the same moment. That's when it all started."

Tara had had an affair with a married man before. Her father's affairs almost broke up her parents' marriage, but Tara's mother always took him back. For a while, they seemed happier than ever. "I never really knew what was wrong, but it seemed like affairs were just part of marriage," Tara said. Her affair with Paul lasted a few months. It ended when Paul wanted her to divorce her husband. "It was too scary for me to take things that far," Tara said.

AREN'T THERE EVER ANY SUCCESSFUL WORK AND LOVE RELATIONSHIPS?

Of course there are! Some of them start out as affairs and some start out with work colleagues who discover they are a good match. Here is a guide for love with a colleague. This is a *guide*—not a guaranteed recipe for success. You can still make mistakes.

INCREASING YOUR SUCCESS WHEN MIXING WORK AND LOVE

Learn as much as you can about him outside of work. What do you know about him? Is he in recovery from an addiction? Is he married or recently divorced? Usually, the office gossip mill knows all kinds of details. Listen to what they say. Develop casual ways of asking questions about him. For example, when Gillian wanted to learn more about Oscar, she said to one of the office staff that he looked very tired lately. Gillian learned that it was the one-year anniversary of the death of Oscar's wife. He had a six-year-old daughter and everyone said he was a great father.

Check your current life situation. Are you in crisis mode? See the *Top Life Situations that Temporarily Derailed You into Misguided Love with a Colleague* list earlier in this chapter. Are you going through rough times such as a divorce or your last child leaving home? Become mindful of your feelings.

Put the brakes on. Go slowly. Don't tumble into love and a relationship. Hang out together with others after work. Meet more often for coffee or lunch. Talk about work. Over time, you will learn about his values and situation as you ease slightly away from talking only about work. If you trust your judgment, think of him as though he were your best girlfriend to whom you can tell all and with whom you can be yourself. He will usually drop his guard, too.

Keep in mind your first impressions of him. Do they still hold? In what ways have they changed? Is there a big gap between his work and private selves? Why?

Think about how others at work regard him. What do your colleagues say about him? How accurate are their assessments?

Discuss coupling and uncoupling. If dating seems a wise decision, make sure you discuss the consequences of becoming a couple. Do you have an exit strategy if your relationship doesn't work out? Do you have a clear way of handling your situation with your colleagues?

When Diana and Lance realized they loved each other, they talked at length about how to tell the staff and how to handle a break-up. Lance said he would put in for a transfer to one of the bank's branch offices if it didn't work out. At a staff meeting, they told everyone that they were dating. Lance, a bank division head, said that Diana's work-load and benchmarks for being a loan officer would not change. To head off in advance a situation where someone might have a complaint or problem with Diana's work, Lance appointed another division head to handle such issues.

It turned out that there was no need for such precautions. Diana and Lance married two years later.

Tips for Office Romances and Affairs

Become mindful of your life situation. Are you too excited about the prospects of falling in love with a colleague? Are you accustomed to affairs as a way to manage unhappiness? What is going on in your life? Are you experiencing a crisis, for example?

Know your organization's rules about office romance. Don't flaunt the rules. You could lose your job.

Don't think that shared work interests automatically yield good love matches. Search for other important bonds such as shared life goals and values, compatible personality styles and good communication skills.

Acknowledge that intense work projects can create pseudo-intimacy. Wait until the project is finished to evaluate the depth of your attachment to a colleague.

Don't assume that work behavior and private behavior are similar. People often have dual selves.

If you do become an intimate couple, make sure you address key issues such as exit strategies if the relationship does not work. Also, consider the affects of your relationship on your colleagues. How will you handle their knowing about it?

Chapter 12

Work Dissatisfaction and Romantic Desperation

Many of the women in my groups expressed shock that their focus on career and freedom did not produce greater contentment. They had often overestimated their expectations of job satisfaction and underestimated the demanding workload, long hours and office politics. Changing careers or even seeking a job in related disciplines seemed unrealistic financially or insurmountable emotionally.

If you have spent many years completing your education, abandoning or modifying your career choice can be especially difficult. Lisa, an attorney, summed up these feelings: "Just the thought of going for another graduate degree exhausts me. Where's the time and money going to come from to work and go to school?"

The hidden fallout from such disillusionment is the toll it takes on your love life. To paraphrase the words of Sigmund Freud, the famous physician and psychoanalyst, happy adulthood hinges on gratification in both work and love. If your work turns out to be a serious disappointment, you might look for love to do more than fulfill you. You could find yourself unknowingly falling in love with a man in the hopes that he can take you far, far away, emotionally and financially, into a new world. The wish is that this opportunity will provide the meaning and value that is lacking in your job or career. The danger is that you will make an unwise relationship match out of desperation.[1]

Yes, love can give you many things, but it would have to work beyond its capacity in order to be the *sole* source of your happiness. This chapter will help you examine your work dissatisfaction and its consequences. There are no easy answers. And what works for one woman may not apply to your situation. You will always have to fashion—and refashion—the mix of work, love, family, goals, other activities and happiness. Look how Cookie manages her work burnout.

COOKIE SEES HER DATE AS A LIFE RAFT

Cookie is headed for trouble. She feels lonely and she is in rebound mode from a disappointing relationship. She doesn't dislike her job as a family attorney, but she isn't thrilled with it either. This date with a new co-worker seems like the best thing that could happen to her. She's already fantasizing about how she and Ron could start their own firm, become a famous husband-and-wife team, be nationally respected, go on television, even get their own show and...

Well, you can see how easy it is to let your unhappiness turbocharge your fantasies and take you down dangerous curves of difficulties. Romantic comedies frequently have scenes where the woman tries on almost every outfit in her closet until she finds the right one to—to what? Impress the man? Land him? Spur her new life?

The prospect of loving and being loved is truly exciting—and for good reason. However, become mindful of the intensity level of your excitement. It could signal deep hopes that this man will be the prince and you the rescued princess in your very own fairy tale.

Take an honest look at your current situation. Here are some questions that will help you become emotionally brave:

Facing Work Dissatisfaction and Its Consequences

Circle or underline the answer that best reflects your feelings and thoughts. There is no score or right or wrong answer. The purpose of these questions is to help you see your mindset more clearly. These questions came from my survey, focus groups and workshops.

1. I tend to work all day and most of the night.
    Almost Always   Mostly   Sometimes   Infrequently   Not Really

2. I make sure I laugh a lot.
    Almost Always   Mostly   Sometimes   Infrequently   Not Really

3. Outside of work, I really don't have any interests that excite me.
    Almost Always   Mostly   Sometimes   Infrequently   Not Really

4. After work I look forward to just going home and watching my favorite television shows.
    Almost Always   Mostly   Sometimes   Infrequently   Not Really

5. I take lots of work home.
    Almost Always   Mostly   Sometimes   Infrequently   Not Really

6. I'm seen as the go-to person when there is a problem to solve.
    Almost Always   Mostly   Sometimes   Infrequently   Not Really

7. Work concerns make me anxious.
    Almost Always   Mostly   Sometimes   Infrequently   Not Really

8. I don't feel as though I have a lot to come home to.
    Almost Always   Mostly   Sometimes   Infrequently   Not Really

9. If someone is having trouble at work with a task or issue, I take time out of my day to help them.
    Almost Always   Mostly   Sometimes   Infrequently   Not Really

10. My partner is really not good for me.
    Almost Always   Mostly   Sometimes   Infrequently   Not Really

11. If I were not so lonely, I would probably break up with my partner.
    Almost Always   Mostly   Sometimes   Infrequently   Not Really

12. My career choice has not turned out to be a good match for me.
    Almost Always   Mostly   Sometimes   Infrequently   Not Really

13. I fantasize about a new life but I don't know how to get it.
    Almost Always   Mostly   Sometimes   Infrequently   Not Really

14. I find myself having trouble managing food, alcohol,
    prescription or illegal drugs.
    Almost Always   Mostly   Sometimes   Infrequently   Not Really

Now let's see what your responses might indicate.

WHY AM I SO ANXIOUS?

Review your answers to items seven and fourteen. When the economy is weak and jobs or advancement are slim, it is normal to feel anxious about work. Unfortunately, as I've mentioned earlier, limited job markets can make you long for love with a wealthy—or at least a financially stable—man to serve as that ticket out of the rat race and its accompanying worries.

Anxiety breeds all kinds of deleterious behaviors. It can destroy a good night's sleep. Almost 50 percent of both the single and married women surveyed said that they had trouble sleeping. Over one third said that they woke up anxious.

Anxiety often accompanies depression. The Anxiety and Depression Association of America reports that the ratio of women who experience anxiety compared to men is two to one. Women are also more prone than men to experiencing depression along with the anxiety.[2] Suicide attempts have also increased in women, with a significant rise in suicide in women over age forty-five.[3]

In an article in the August 2010 issue of *Glamour Magazine*, various physicians in private practice and at major Unites States hospitals report that anxiety is one of the most common problems that makes women seek medical help.[4] Yet, ironically, anxiety is often under-diagnosed. The increase in the incidence of women's anxiety may be due to many factors such as women's brains being more susceptible to the increased stress in life today and hormonal fluctuations, as well as women's tendency to ruminate more.

Anxiety and depression can also diminish your capacity to control your use of alcohol, prescription or illegal drugs. If you don't experience these difficulties, then you might, instead, develop other addictions such as shopping too much or eating either too much or too little. One of the women with whom I spoke said that she became anorexic as "one way to feel in control and happy." She became obsessed with getting thin and she secretly hoped that being extraordinarily thin would make her more attractive to men.

WHY DO I FEEL SO BAD ABOUT MYSELF?

As your anxiety and depressed mood increase, your self-esteem and sense of self-worth decrease. If you answered item twelve with "almost always" or "mostly," then your dissatisfaction with your career choice can lead to mistrust in your judgment. You're left feeling that you are somehow flawed because you aren't in charge of your life. Having a sense of mastery over life is one of our basic needs. It makes us feel competent to handle life's ups and downs, even if we don't know specifically what they are.

When you get such an important decision as career choice wrong, it's easy to allow this misstep to cascade into all kinds of self-doubt. You question your knowledge of yourself and the world and you are left wondering if you are as smart and capable as you'd like—or need—to be. Rebecca announced in one of my focus groups, "If I had known how much I didn't like being a defense attorney, I would have gone in a totally different direction in college. I could have skipped law school, avoided debt and been happy. But I'm stuck and I don't have the energy to start over."

HOW CAN WORK UNHAPPINESS TAKE A TOLL ON MY ROMANTIC LIFE?

More than 50 percent of the women surveyed, especially ones with high-paying or high-status jobs, clung to relationships that they knew were unhealthy. Look at your answers to numbers ten and eleven. Over 20 percent of the women said that their fear of loneliness prevented them from breaking up with their partners.

Dissatisfaction with work can ramp up your need to feel alive and close to *someone*. Great sex, which makes you feel temporarily high, powerful, important and wanted, can become enough emotional glue to make you stay with a man who is wrong for you in other key areas. Slightly more than 10 percent of the women said that great sex was "like a blood supply"—even though they knew that sex was one of the few connections with their partners.

WHY DOESN'T WORKING HARDER MAKE ME HAPPIER?

Unhappiness in love can have a boomerang effect on both your work and love life. When love is gone from your life, it's likely that you'll throw yourself into your work, even when you find your job dissatisfying. In that situation, your job or career gives you most of your identity, sense of self-worth and an anchor—even if you have a partner or spouse. In my workshops, many women said, essentially, that they had pulled their hearts away from their existing and disappointing intimate relationships and put all their efforts into work.

For questions number one and three, over 40 percent of the women said they worked day and night, and more than a third said they had not developed any non-work-related interests.

Work can become such a vital source of feeling that you have accomplished and feel connected to *something*, that you actually thrive on being seen as the go-to person or rescuer.

Going home to an unhappy or empty house felt so emotionally draining that many women brought lots of work with them. Review your answers to numbers six and nine. Turning your house into a satellite office can numb you. Your home life could end up being such a potent mix of tedium, depression and loneliness that all you want to do is plunk down in front of the television and catch up on all the shows you taped. Look at your answer to number four.

Over time, however, your lackluster, limited life can take away more than it gives. Often, your stress levels increase. Life seems to close in on you and you realize that your over-commitment to work has left you frazzled and, ironically, less fulfilled.

For 20 percent of the women, work had dulled them so much that they hadn't laughed in a long time. Look at your answer to number two. Losing laughter can be unhealthy. Laughter reduces the stress hormone cortisol. Even gallows humor can make you feel that your burden is lighter. Going to a theater to see an outrageously comic and absurd movie can create a feeling of community. You feel less alone and therefore less likely to blame yourself for everything. Laughter also allows you to vent your anger and frustration in a less destructive way.

No wonder being all work and no play makes people dull boys and girls. If something goes wrong at work, such as not getting a promotion or recognition for your effort, then your life gets even smaller. By the time you realize that putting so much of you into work has not made you happy, you feel helpless to scramble out of your situation. Almost all the women struggled to strike work-life balances with multiple roles that provided various sources for self-worth.

Now, working to fill the dissatisfaction gaps has backfired and become one more source of unhappiness. It's at this point that you risk heading out to unwise love territory. You might pull completely away from your existing relationship, seek a divorce or start an affair. If you are single, you might just grab the next reasonable-enough choice of partner and settle.

With more women than men entering and staying in the workplace at jobs that allow for economic independence, it would seem that, like men before the 2008 recession, your economic success should allow you a *greater* range of decisions and choices of intimate partners. You could, for instance, seek a divorce more easily since you can support yourself.

Conversely, you could be happy with a man who doesn't make as much money or who is not as career-driven as you are. Some women do manage to forge mutually-satisfying partnerships with men who earn less, have less education or who do not have high-profile jobs and professions. But it is very difficult to bypass cultural norms and many men feel ill at ease about not being at least an equal breadwinner.

Women who succeeded in fostering mutual happiness with these partners often made sure to express appreciation for them and to include them equally in major decisions. These women did not feel they had to apologize for their men "only" being schoolteachers, for example. They genuinely respected their partners and spouses and they did not fall into the trap that whoever makes the most money makes the most and largest decisions.

If you decide to end your marriage or relationship, life can still feel empty rather than filled with relief or excitement. If you have children to raise, the thrill of freedom could recede quickly. The solution of involving yourself more in your work seems like a good way to feel better about yourself, but then you land right back in the stew of dullness, work disillusionment and limited life.

WHY CAN'T MY FRIENDS MAKE UP FOR MY UNHAPPINESS?

For the more than one third of the women in my survey who said they had not developed any non-work-related interests, their answers also included difficulties in maintaining and nurturing deep friendships and family connections. Look at your answers to numbers ten and eleven. Even though most women said they had good friends, these women realized that they often hid their unhappiness from their friends.

Almost all my talks, workshops and focus groups have included a town-hall-style meeting where participants could ask questions. In virtually every event I had the women write down their inquiries so that anonymity allowed them to pose honest and meaningful personal questions. One of the main issues was feeling distant and disconnected from their friends. Some women wrote, for example, that they felt that they "couldn't really tell" their friends about their inner turmoil. Most of the friend time was spent in groups and parties. As many women essentially said, "I have a social life, with friends who will be there for me in times of emergency, but it's the day-to-day, non-emergency unhappiness that I don't reveal or share." Over time, you still feel lonely and long for a richer life.

Don't let the difficulty and fear of changing your circumstances trap you in the quicksand of shallow friendships, love desperation, work dissatisfaction or reliance on work as your only source of identity and fulfillment. Many women in the study used the next recipe for too long.

Last Minute Meal for Work and Life Fulfillment

Add the following ingredients to a crock-pot:

1. Add one cup of an affair that excites, terrifies and drains you. If it's a work affair, put it in a blender on high speed so you can't see the difference between yourself and him.
2. Add half a cup of a divorce or break-up that makes you sadder and more frightened, angry, stressed, lonely, dulled and pessimistic.

3. Add a quart of latching onto a man who is just okay because you are lonely.

4. Add two quarts of falling for a man whose excitement, great sex and wealth also include insensitivity or even cruelty.

5. Sprinkle with the emotional crumbs you are tolerating. Let everything stew in the pot for a long time, even for years.

6. When it is finished, add a dollop of work burnout from being all work and no play, having no outside interests and having limited friendships.

WHAT CAN I DO TO FEEL HAPPIER ABOUT WORK AND LOVE?

Women who were so hurt by love that they swore off men tended to put all their energies and identities into work. When work disillusionment or a life catastrophe occurred, they often made the mistakes of having affairs or choosing men who were either barely acceptable or exciting but unkind. One of the things you will need in order to address your work dissatisfaction and your loneliness is emotional bravery.

Let's put your bravery in higher gear. Begin with planning your funeral and writing your own obituary. Most of us would like to think that we have made a difference in the world. Luckily, when you help one person, you help many. They pass on your teachings, guidance and model behavior to their children, friends, families and colleagues. Happiness, bravery, inner strength, goodness and success are contagious. No contribution is too small. If you doubt my words, think what would happen if everyone in the world thought that he or she had too little to offer others. Then there would be far less medical research, less charitable donations of time and money, fewer teachers, fewer nurses, etc.

I want you to imagine that you know when your life will end physically on this earth. What would you like your obituary to say? How do you envision your funeral? I know these questions sound morbid, but I want you to experience the feeling that life is indeed short and unpredictable.

You are going to get older. So, why not start things now that could make you happy about your work situation and its effect on your love life? So what if it takes time? As I said, you can't stop getting older.

Don't fall for the ruse that doing nothing and just leading your life, one foot in front of the other, is going to make an impact. One of my favorite stories as a child was the story about the emperor of ancient China and his chair.

The Emperor and His Chair

The emperor of China had a favorite chair. It was huge, much bigger than he was. The seat, back and arms were covered in red velvet so thick that it felt like moss. The wood around the arms, back and legs was painted a shiny gold, so bright that the servants could see rays of its reflected light pouring through the windows.

The emperor forbade anyone to sit on his chair or even touch it. He built a special viewing room for the chair so that once a year all the citizens of the land could walk by and pay homage to its magnificence. He wrote in the "Decree of the Empire of China and All Its Lands" that all his successors could not and would not touch or sit on his chair. Also, the chair was never to be removed from the viewing room.

In time, the emperor died, and then so did his son and his son after him and so on. All the emperors obeyed the decree. But after many, many years, no one from the empire wanted to view the chair. The red velvet fabric that felt like moss had frayed, the gold paint that shone through the windows had chipped and the legs and arms dried up and separated from the frame. Nothing stayed the same.

Remember the next lesson about inaction:

The Myth of Not Taking Action

There is no such thing as doing nothing about something and expecting it to change.

Over time, your disappointment and regret might fray you, and your energy and enthusiasm for life might lose its luster.

Now you are ready to write your obituary and plan your funeral.

MY OBITUARY

Think about these things:

- What are the top things that you want your obituary to say about you?
- What contributions to others have you made?
- How have you been a role model?
- How did you overcome your past?
- How did you become brave in facing your obstacles?

Here is an example that combines many responses from the women in the study.

OBITUARY OF SALLY ALLEY

This year, January 1, 2___, begins on what could be seen as a sad note. Sally Alley died this morning of _____ at the age of ____. She was from Tiny Townville, but more than just the population of that town will mourn her passing.

Sally was born into a humble household and, soon after her birth, her father deserted the family. Sally's mother was forced to work two and sometimes three jobs. When Sally was older, she had to work as a seamstress. Yet, she managed to put herself through state college undergraduate and law school. She worked for many years for the infamous Terrible Corporation of America as in-house counsel. At first, when she learned about the dastardly practices of the Terrible Corporation of

America, she stayed on. By then her salary was very high. She had a son to raise on her own.

Then, one day her son asked her to come to his school for career day to speak to his class about what she did for a living. A feeling of dread overwhelmed her. She knew she had to quit her job. She knew there was something else out there that could excite her and make her feel happy.

She decided to take continuing education courses at the local college. Sally discovered a whole new side to herself. She wanted to teach high school. She enrolled at the college, cut back on her expenses and established a neighborhood parenting group that took turns picking up the children from school and bringing them home.

Today, Sally will be remembered as the most inspiring and beloved history teacher and principal of Tiny Townville High School. She also showed others how to follow their dreams and take a chance on themselves. Her students published her sayings and the book has become a best seller. Sally will live on in all of us.

Write down your own thoughts.

THE OBITUARY OF: (WRITE YOUR NAME)

What do I really long to accomplish? What are my dreams? What do I want to impart to others?

Think about your funeral. Here is what Sally did. Use this as an exercise.

THE FUNERAL OF SALLY ALLEY

A Letter from Sally, presented by _____

Hello, everyone. Please don't shed tears of sadness for me. I will always be with you. Here is how you can be with me. For my funeral, I don't want people to cry or tell their favorite stories. Instead, I want you to sit down somewhere and use the pen and pad of paper provided to write answers to the following questions.

1. What would you like to change about your job or career?

2. Brainstorm ideas about how you can make these changes. Who can help you?

3. What other careers or jobs do you have in mind? Think of your interests and abilities.

4. What do you need to do to make these changes happen?

5. What holds you back from taking steps toward change?

6. What frightens you the most about making these changes?

7. What excuses do you make about not going forward?

8. What small steps will take you toward your goal?

I am not saying that making these changes is easy. It is normal to be afraid or to doubt yourself. Don't give up on yourself and the life you have remaining. Keep your eyes on the next step and don't allow the long journey to stop you. When I was in graduate school, I was surprised at how many fellow students had given up on their doctoral dissertations. Some quit their programs, others did not progress in writing their dissertations and still others were going on their eighth year or more of not finishing them.

After I completed my dissertation, I decided to help others write and finish theirs. But first I had to find out what got in their way. The number one issue was thinking about how big the task of writing the dissertation seemed to them. They were overwhelmed by the enormity of the project. I helped them see the process as a series of very small steps. You will need to do the same thing about changing your job or your career. You will also need to keep the satisfaction of accomplishing your end goal in mind. Especially think about Sally's last question in her letter at her funeral: What small steps will take you toward your goal?

You will probably feel burned out from time to time. You will think seriously about giving up. And you'll come up with very convincing excuses to quit. Here is the motivating exercise that grew from my workshops.

BE YOUR OWN FORTUNE COOKIE

Hopefully, you can see the dangers of giving up on your happiness at work. Life is not often fair or easy. But don't let that deter you from living fully and responsibly! Think about fortune cookies. Now is the time for you to write whatever will help you to avoid excuses and move forward. Create your own fortune cookie reminders. Print copies, cut out each one and put them in your handbag or around the house. Here are some examples:

> Good friends are good medicine. Tell them about your fears and problems. Only real connections offer real help.

> Ways of calm are everywhere. Massages and other treats are better medicine than hasty or addicting acts.

> Speed is for rabbits. Become the turtle and take your time with love and work. Zero to sixty is the wrong path.

> A smart woman follows smart goals and does not quit.

Now write your own fortunes.

Tips on Work Dissatisfaction and Romantic Desperation

Don't become all work and no play. Become mindful of allowing work to be your sole identity. Don't work until you are exhausted. Be aware of the danger of taking on too much work to fill your time and your life.

Make sure to develop other interests. Broaden and deepen your life. If work isn't your only outlet, you will avoid serious depression or hasty decisions.

Sustain meaningful contact with friends and family. Be open with them about your unhappiness. They can become a powerful back-up source so you won't feel so lonely or afraid of making changes.

Don't rely on romance to fix your life. Be mindful of fantasies of a man sweeping you away from your life and giving you a new one. And don't fill your work dissatisfaction with affairs or settling for a barely-okay man.

Value your life and your contribution to it. Face your fears. Recognize your excuses. Come up with a plan, even if it is long term, to change your life.

Part V

Recovery from Past Mistakes

Chapter 13

Smarter Assessments of Men and Smarter Questions to Ask Them

Sometimes dating can seem like an ongoing fishing expedition of catch and release. Throwing back a "fish," because it's unkind, controlling or afraid of life is smart. Make sure, however, that you're not releasing a good fish for the wrong reasons. Many of the women in my study passed up men because of physical characteristics such as being short or having a big nose. Some women wouldn't consider a man if he had children from a previous marriage or was financially comfortable rather than wealthy.

Women who made good love matches said dating was actually fun. They viewed the process as an ongoing course in improving their relationship skills. The cornerstone of reading a man rests on a mix of asking smart questions and observing his behavior in different settings.

Most of the single women in my study were surprised that their choices of men didn't turn out so well. They tried speed dating or interviewing men at the beginning of their dates. Many women, most especially busy career women, believed they'd already fallen in love through their e-mails and phone calls. E-mails and chats are not necessarily bad ways to learn about a man, but if you want to get solid information, you must ask the right questions, observe his behavior and be mindful of your emotional and physical reactions when you are together.

For most women, though, the purpose of dating is finding *Mr. Right*. Anyone who's been through speed dates, fix-ups, bar-hopping and match-up websites knows that searching for love makes you exhausted and anxious—feelings that can impair your ability to read men correctly. Identifying this perfect man often happens while you're under the pressure of your biological clock, aging and loneliness. It's too easy to make a poor choice. In the next cartoon, Cookie is reacting to her urgency about finding a man. She is in her therapist's office.

COOKIE IS IN A HURRY

Cookie is in danger of falling in love quickly while she's wearing blinders to her issues. Her heartstrings are vibrating to a song about the desperation from her loneliness, over-accommodating, aging and looking for *Mr. Right* while settling for Mr. Next Guy Who Comes Along.

This dilemma trapped many of the women in my study. To get out of this perplexing problem, remember this crucial tip:

Dating Goal

Change the goal of dating from finding *Mr. Right* to reading men accurately.

Sounds good, but you also need some tools to hone your people-reading skills.

HOW CAN I MAKE DATING, RELATING AND READING MEN EASIER AND QUICKER?

Unfortunately, first impressions—including wrong ones—can form very quickly. The neural wiring of the brain detects hundreds of cues from a man such as his posture, tone of voice and eye contact. If you are trained to pick up these signals, you can perceive them almost instantaneously and use the information to assess your date or partner. However, this assessment works best when you replace longing for *Mr. Right* with reading men accurately.

If you are not adept at detecting men's nonverbal and behavioral clues, then your impressions about the appropriateness of a man might not be correct. Rather than rely on the usual—and possibly inaccurate—associations of brain connections, use different methods of assessment. Fresh approaches require new neurological wiring that is less dependent on incorporating old associations and assumptions. These new neural networks strengthen with practice.

Once you're willing to change your dating goal, you'll be ready for these brain-cueing exercises about reading men. The best way to succeed is to make a mental game of testing and improving your people-reading skills while dating and relating. The next two exercises use visual images that add another method of gathering information.

Think of an Animal That Describes Your Man

1. **Think about what kind of animal comes to mind about your man.** Dogs are a good place to begin because they come in so many varieties, but almost any creature that comes to mind will help. You can also combine breeds. Think about animals you've seen in the zoo or on television.

2. **Imagine you are speaking or writing an e-mail to your best girlfriend about this man.** What would you say? For example, you tell her: "You know, Bob (or whatever his name is) really reminds me of..."

3. **Imagine your man in different settings such as when you want to talk to him about a problem, or when you are both with your family.** Keep your assessment of him on the back burner of your mind. Test it to see if your preliminary idea still holds or changes while you are with him.

MAN CREATURES

Rachelle described her husband as an alligator who seemed to disappear under the water at the first sign of trouble, only to emerge again with biting criticisms of her decisions.

Lindy said her men were prairie dogs that only popped out of the ground when they needed something.

Randi's husband reminded her of a mythic animal that was a cross between the daring of a St. Bernard dog and a steeple-jumping horse that managed to get over life's hurdles.

Suzette's first thought about her ex-husband was that he was a rattlesnake that liked to remain all coiled up until it sensed danger and then attacked.

Alyssa said her previous boyfriends reminded her of the doe-eyed little mutts at the Humane Society who were sweet and grateful for being picked but turned out to be extremely needy.

This next exercise requires a bigger stretch of your imagination. We are accustomed to thinking about men as animals—we even have expressions such as "He's a pig." However, we probably don't tend to think about our men as doors.

Practice Imagining Your Man as a Door

1. **Close your eyes.** Bring a particular man into view and think about him as a door. What comes to mind? The door could be open, closed, ajar, broken, locked, wooden, glass or steel.

2. **Concentrate on the lock.** It could be easy or difficult to open. Perhaps it's a trick lock that only turns the knob but does not release the bolt.

3. **Decide whether the door has windows.** Perhaps the door is all glass with barely a frame. Maybe it has tiny windows too high to see into. Maybe there aren't any windows.

4. **Choose a door material and knocker.** Your door could be a thick metal door with a skull and crossbones, or have the head of a growling lion for a knocker. Perhaps your door is made of flimsy wood with a koala bear or rainbow for a knocker. Maybe your door knocker is a tiger, but the door is made of cardboard.

> 5. **Review your choices to develop a preliminary reading
> of your man**. Imagine you have to give a talk about your
> man as a door. What would you say?

Cynthia used the door exercise when she went to a food-tasting fair. She made a beeline for the wine exhibit, because she knew it would attract men. She hung back, picked a man with rumpled hair and a T-shirt. She observed his actions and imagined him as a door. She evaluated him as a glass door that remained flung open. Instead of seeing a door knocker she saw a small pail that hung from the latch. Written on the pail was, "Door is open. Donations accepted."

When she examined her responses, Cynthia was appalled. Her dating history consisted of one man after another who owed her money and invited his buddies and brothers to hang out at her home. Cynthia was the chairperson of the English department at a private school and her good salary, status and level-headedness always attracted men who were irresponsible and underemployed but very charming and fun. In my workshop she vowed to find a different kind of door.

After a year and a half of dating many men, Cynthia found one whose door was made of wood, closed and locked but easily opened with just the right jiggle of the lever. The door had two windows at eye level. The door knocker consisted of a cluster of books, dogs, a gold star and a smile. Her new man was smart, discreet, gentle, welcoming and successful.

Practice your door skills when you are out with friends you already know. What materials are their doors—wood, paper, metal? How big or thick are they? Do they have door knockers? If so, what do they look like? Can you see inside? Are the windows big or small? Are the doors open? These assessment skills are your warm-up for the next step.

HOW CAN I SENSE MEN'S NONVERBAL CUES?

You must become a love detective to assess men more accurately. You need to identify key clues about a man's actions. No guide can include every hint of his conduct, but the following chart of the top ABCs of observations provides a method to sharpen your detection skills. I strongly recommend that you read Tonya Reiman's book *The Body Language of Dating* and that you heed this tip:

Staying Mindful

Keeping your "mind's eye" open is not the same as passing judgment on a man's right to be who he is. Instead, staying mindful is one of the chief tools in your dating and mating toolkit for being present and aware of your emotional and physical reactions, so you can detect whether a man is a good choice for you.

The goal is to develop an instinctual feedback system so that you can manage four tracks that run at the same time. The chart below keeps you focused on observing while you are in the present moment. It also alleviates your concerns that you are judging a man.

The Four Tracks of Being with a Man

1. **The present moment:** What are you doing or talking about?

2. **Your observations of him:** What do his body language and behavior tell you?

3. **Your emotional and physical reactions:** What are you experiencing, such as rapid heartbeat, upset stomach, nervous legs or hands, anger, fear, comfort?

4. **Your knowledge of your past dating and mating patterns:** What you've done before.

Over time, all four tracks kick in automatically. It just takes a commitment to remain mindful.

The next chart is your cheat sheet that describes the extreme ends of a continuum of men's behavior. There are two sets of descriptive words, one set at each end of a spectrum. For example, on one end of the scale about your conversations with a man is his *over-use* of the word "I." This behavior might signal to you that he is a braggart who is more interested in your view of him than he is in getting to know you.

At the opposite end of the same scale is a man's *under-use* of the word "I." A man who doesn't speak about himself might be secretive, untrustworthy or lacking in confidence. He might downplay his successful accomplishments or high-powered profession out of fear that you are just one more of the fame-seeking gold diggers he's trying to avoid. Your job is to assess correctly.

The list only names the extremes since the goal of this exercise is to help you develop a warning system rather than to worry about pinpointing your man's exact position along the spectrum. Exaggerated behaviors are, of course, easier to use as a benchmark. But people usually don't show behaviors that are at the extreme end. Most healthy people cluster somewhere around the middle and contain many variations of desirable attributes. Still, with practice, you will be able to detect little nuances that signal to you that the man may not be a good choice. The list is long, but soon you will be able to acquire the mental equivalent of a computer pop-up that demands attention.

ABCs of Observing Men: Learn the Extremes, Aim for the Middle and Accurate Assessments

Appearance and Actions		
Head, Neck and Shoulders		
Head, neck, shoulders bend down in self-doubt	or	Nose points up or down in superiority
Head does not face you during conversations	or	Neck swivels for other women
Eyes		
Looks away when he speaks to you	or	Stares at you in a condescending way
Dress		
Wears boys' clothes or sloppy, unmatched outfits	or	Flaunts designer labels, is a peacock

ABCs of Observing Men (continued)

Mouth		
Smiles too much	or	Scowls, smirks
Hands		
Fidgets and fusses as a sign of anxiety	or	Points, stabs food as sign of aggression
Touches you as sign of neediness	or	Touches you as sign of control and ownership
Taps heart to show sincerity	or	Rubs face as he lies
Legs		
Sits too quietly or mildly shakes legs as sign of anxiety, insecurity	or	Shakes legs vigorously as sign of impatience, dominance
Behavior		
Interpersonal Skills		
Asks more about you and says too little about himself	or	Can't listen, Uses "I" a lot
Is too agreeable	or	Is critical
Is passive	or	Is argumentative
Flatters too much to let you be in charge and like him	or	Flatters too much to bring you under his control
Lets you or waiter recommend	or	Orders for you for control and admiration
Borrows money or lets you pay	or	"Big Spender"
Doesn't return calls because of poor follow-through, insecurity	or	Doesn't return calls to keep you anxious
Calls too often to see if you still like him	or	Calls too often to control you
Is late out of anxiety and immaturity	or	Is late out of disrespect for you
Apologizes too much	or	Rarely apologizes
Is a loner or hangs out with buddies too much	or	Has only business friends

ABCs of Observing Men (continued)

Dates never include others	or	Dates include audiences
Seeks approval of your friends	or	Cuts you off from your friends
Is sexually clingy or cloyingly pleasing	or	Is aggressive, too demanding and selfish
Has sexual performance issues such as erectile dysfunction	or	Has sexual issues such as selfishness or cruelty
Career Attitude		
Has spotty work history	or	Is a "walking résumé"
Belittles self	or	Name-drops
Family Information		
Feels unloved and a failure	or	Feels superior to family
Is cut off from family or too tied to them	or	Is cut off from family or needs constant approval
Conclusions		
Is a pleaser	or	Is a taker
Is a "needer"	or	Is a hater
You tend to see *him* as insecure, small, not accomplished	or	Tends to make *you* feel insecure, small, not accomplished

HOW CAN I USE THIS CHART?

Many of the women in my workshops used this system with great success. Here are some stories of women who faced these dilemmas whose issues will help you use this chart.

Polina's Story

Whenever Polina and Steven met new people, he mentioned that he went to an Ivy League college. Polina initially beamed at Steven's accomplishment, but when Polina used the ABCs of observing men, she realized that Steven name-dropped that he went to an Ivy League school regardless of whether the topic fit the conversation.

Two weeks later, when Polina met Steven's family for the first time, his father explained to Polina that Steven was the black sheep of the family because he didn't get into his Ivy League college on his first try and only gained acceptance as a transfer student in his junior year. Now Polina understood better why Steven became a walking résumé to impress others. She looked at the ABC list and concluded that his bravado was an attempt to hide his low self-worth. He also took out his insecurity on her. When Polina won a scholarship to become a paralegal, he teased her mercilessly that the career was a far cry from being a lawyer. But it was just as well, he said, because she could never have gotten into the college he did. As soon as she finished her education, Polina left him.

Sarah's Story

Sarah relied on the list to help her eliminate Edward. When Edward first spotted Sarah at a coffee bar, he rushed over, pulled up a chair and said he really liked her red hair. Sarah was used to men commenting on the flame color, so she didn't regard Edward's pick-up line as unusual. Edward told her he was tired of being single. As he talked, Sarah noticed that he kept rubbing his nose and cheeks with the flat of his hand. Sarah remembered that the ABC list warned that when a man rubs his face, it might be a sign of lying.

Then Sarah felt a tingle in her stomach that signaled she was in danger. She learned to pay attention to that feeling. It's not called gut instinct for nothing, she thought, and she didn't give him her last name or phone number. Later, through the grapevine, Sarah heard that Edward was married.

Lindsay's Story

Lindsay's skills in reading men allowed her to make a good choice. At chamber of commerce meetings, Lindsay often saw the same tall, thin man in the crowd. He was always animated, his arms raised in the air whenever he spoke. There was something about him that intrigued her. She liked his confident walk and noticed that others sought him out, but Lindsay had made a mental note to pay attention to a man's hands and arms, and she worried whether his motions signaled anxiety or hyperactivity.

She walked over to him and learned that his name was Carl and he was an internationally known architect and urban developer. She was a realtor and they talked about home design. After two months of seeing each other at meetings, they went out for coffee afterward and they began dating. She concluded that his energy did not stem from nervousness but rather from the quickness of his mind and his eagerness to get going with his ideas—and she was right. On their second-year anniversary of dating, Lindsay and Carl became engaged and they were married eight months later.

Lindsay's excellent people-reading skills were not the only source of her success. Her willingness to give Carl a second look saved her from making a serious mistake. Carl's energy could have represented either anxiety or enthusiasm, but Lindsay spent time with him to resolve her observations.

Take a look at the next Cookie cartoon. Can you spot some warning signs that Cookie should heed on her first date?

If you guessed that her date would ruin and run over Cookie's life, you are correct. Notice that Cookie is wearing a turtleneck in the hopes that it will help her maintain self-control about falling head over heels and doing something stupid like going back to his place and risking a sexual and emotional disaster. Unfortunately, she could not stop her mind from falling back into her old pattern of allowing herself to be seduced by a man who knows how to charm.

Her date did three things that should have turned on those big, red flashing warning lights. The first thing he did was bring a gift on a first date—not necessarily a bad thing, but the gesture could suffer from being too grandiose.

The second thing that her date did was order everything for her. Having your man order for you can be an act of kindness and consideration when he knows what you like. If you happen to like everything, it can also be a sign that he wants you to enjoy the specialty of the house.

Cookie's behavior in this cartoon shows you that it was too early in the relationship for her to determine his true intentions. The third warning was that he assumed—almost commanded—that Cookie would go back with him to his place.

WHAT QUESTIONS SHOULD I ASK MY MEN?

Ask smart questions to get smart information. Many of the women in my study tried speed dating and were surprised that their choice of man didn't turn out so well. Since they fell for the myth that a woman knows within three seconds to three minutes whether a man is a good match, they thought speed dating was a great shortcut versus actual dating.

Similarly, women with partners often didn't know how to detect or read their men's moods and needs. The relating habits of many couples impede the ability to see the man clearly. In the beginning of getting to know a man, a typical date lands you in a romantic restaurant. Romance is great, but romance can't be created or built out of the flimsiness of an attraction or the appeal of a setting. Real, reliable romance happens later—and often in day-to-day life.

A better approach is to postpone the candlelight and the secluded table in the corner. Learn instead from seasoned job interviewers. If a candidate seems to be a potentially good match, many employers and department heads invite the candidate to dine with them. They observe the candidate's conversational skills and his or her table manners, including how he or she treats the waitstaff. When you spend time with your man, observe how he interacts with others, including people such as the bartender, waiters and maître d'.

How does the interviewer know that a candidate is worth this further evaluation time? Good interviewers first get behavioral information about prospective employees. They ask the interviewee, for example, to describe how she or he managed a difficult employee, or responded to negative feedback. The interviewer's goal is to get a *story* that shows the person in action at work. A man talking on the phone to you about himself can be as deceptive as itemizing résumé achievements. Anyone can shape his social presentation of himself or tweak a résumé. The best employment interviewers ask for detailed stories that demonstrate leadership and decision-making. Don't get facts—get information from your dates or partner. But just how do you do that?

You need to use similar techniques to get a better sense of your man in relationships. For instance, you should ask him to tell you about why he divorced his wife. Books and Internet sites tell you not to talk about your exes. Complaining about your ex is not a good idea. But asking your date to tell you a story about what he learned from his past relationships gives you a living picture of your man and his values rather than sound bites or complaints. Women with partners and spouses also learned to ask smart questions to learn about their men's moods and situations.

Your ability to get these answers depends, in part, on your conversational skills. But if you are equipped with good questions, you can weave them into your conversation. You may not be able to ask every question that you want on your first few dates, but eventually you will assess your man better. You'll need to experiment. It's okay to feel awkward.

Here are questions and topics to get you started on constructing a living view of your man. Explain that you are on an uncritical learning mission and that you would not ask anything that you wouldn't answer about yourself. You don't have to fire questions at him. For instance, you can ask your man to guess what he thinks your family or past partners were like. Tell him he will have the same chance to ask you questions. As the man speaks, think of him as playing himself in a movie about his life. Roll that film in your mind as he describes the story or circumstances.

When your existing partner is struggling with something, test your preliminary understanding of him by asking him if he is worried about a certain issue. If you are wrong about your guess, then ask him to tell you what's going on. You will learn about your partner and be better able to help him next time.

Running that Movie

Ask your man to tell you a *story* about these topics:

- What women or his ex have disliked the most about him
- What he dislikes the most about his ex or women
- The top things he learned about himself in relationships
- What he would like to change about himself or the way he handles problems
- How he would like you to act when he is stressed
- How he spends a typical week, weeknight, weekend, holiday or vacation
- Key incidents that depict his family and how they affect him
- How he differs from his family
- What others would be surprised to know about him
- How he would describe his temperament on a frustration continuum
- How he would describe his attitude toward any or all of these topics: religion, money, children, neatness, fitness, food, alcohol
- His inner strength in what he has overcome
- His life goals and plans
- An honest description of his bedroom and family room (you are finding out where he falls on the continuum from disgustingly sloppy to neat-freak)
- Examples of deal-breakers from past relationships

Be careful about your own deal-breakers. Many women misidentify them. Make sure that you know the difference between real deal-breakers and mere likes or dislikes that may not be a significant factor in establishing a healthy love life in new or existing relationships.

The goal is to get smarter—not pickier. You need to be more flexible and to differentiate between important and unimportant issues. Here is an example about getting smart information.

Loretta's Story

Loretta wanted to know why William broke up with his previous partner. Rather than ask him outright, she told him about her past boyfriend and what she learned from being with him. She made William feel comfortable enough to describe his experiences. As William spoke, Loretta ran the imaginary movie in her mind.

William explained that he underestimated his previous girlfriend's anger and mistrust of men. The smallest misunderstanding triggered a tirade—once she even cut up his clothes and keyed the side of his car. During dinner on what turned out to be the last night of their relationship, William's girlfriend answered the phone and heard the voice of an unknown woman asking for William. When the girlfriend asked her name and inquired about the nature of the call, the woman said that her name was Patty and that William knew why she was contacting him. William's girlfriend smashed the phone against the wall and accused William of having an affair. She grabbed the dinner plates and hurled them to the floor. She was screaming and swearing so loudly that she couldn't hear William explain that Patty was the new temporary secretary and was calling about a meeting change with a client whose name she didn't want to reveal.

The incident was William's wake-up call. He said he had managed his father's frequent rages by rationalizing that all men get angry. His acceptance of the abuse made him vulnerable to tolerating hot-tempered women.

Over time William and Loretta ran more movies of each other. William asked her what she had learned about herself from her family. She told the story about when she came home from school and realized her mother was on the phone with the school principal. As soon as Loretta walked into the living room, her mother belted her across the mouth. "What's that for?" Loretta asked. Her mother said, "It's Principal Green, and he says a girl who looks like you was caught stealing a test from the Spanish teacher."

Later, Loretta's mother learned the principal had identified the wrong girl, but the emotional damage was done. Loretta's mother never apologized. Yet, for years Loretta minimized her mother's abusiveness. Loretta and William promised to help each other speak up in their new relationship. Within a year, they got engaged and moved in together.

Although Loretta and William had romantic dinners, they continued to learn about each other by doing activities together. They went to outdoor art exhibits and auto shows, and walked around scenic areas. She even dragged William along with her to run errands such as food shopping.

Their time together was not necessarily spent in attending events but rather in hanging out instead. They met up with each other's friends for Sunday brunch and then walked around downtown. Loretta was learning how William acted when he had to stand in line, had to wait for her to decide between peaches and blueberries and had to socialize with their friends.

Keep this tip from Loretta in mind:

Dating and Reality

The more your time together resembles real life, the more real information you will get about him. Hang out instead of going on a date. If you have a partner, aim for variety in your time together. True romance is grown—not made.

If you are unsure about your reading of your man, use this potent exercise:

Ice Cube or Iceberg?

It's very difficult to know how to apply the clues you are sensing about a man. You don't know whether you are seeing hints about something inconsequential about him or something important that might indicate he is not a good choice for you. In other words, is his behavior a sign of an ice cube floating down the river or the tip of an iceberg of problems? You may not know for sure, but here are some steps to take that might help you.

1. **Note a specific behavior**—especially if it creates an emotional and physical reaction in you or falls on the extreme ends of the ABCs of observing men. For example, is he taking command of the dinner? Has he gone silent when he's with your friends?

2. **Now *exaggerate* the behavior** and drag it into the future movie you are rolling about him. Is he running your life and not letting you be independent of him? Or, is he impossible to reach emotionally?

You probably also want to know how he would respond to learning about your past and to handling your making relationship mistakes. The following tips can help you assess your man's character and his empathy.

HOW DO I TELL MY DATE OR NEW PARTNER ABOUT PAINFUL THINGS IN MY PAST?

Referring to your past in *general terms* can teach your new man about *your* supportive nature. You could make general statements such as saying that "people can overcome their past" or that you "didn't have great parents but managed to transcend their limitations." Sweeping comments like these are especially useful in the very beginning of getting to know someone. They present you in an empathic light, prevent you from getting labeled as a problem and alert the man that your past was hardly perfect. It's as though you made a movie trailer of a slice of your life and essentially said "there is more to come if we are right for each other" and "I don't expect perfection."

At this point, the man often tells you more about *his* past. He senses your compassion for yourself, and he feels more comfortable telling you his story. Men often don't talk to other men about their past and inner struggles. It can be quite a relief for your man to tell you about himself. You learn about his strengths and weaknesses and his potential for accepting yours. This approach also works with existing partners.

If you decide to continue to date the man, reveal some items from the *bottom* of your most private list to see his reaction. Alternatively, like some women in my study, you might risk telling him the most important and emotionally difficult information early so you can see his reaction and rule him either in or out.

Be cautious about buying into one of the trends in our culture that promotes baring your soul by telling right away all or the most painful details of your life. It may seem that cleansing yourself with your date is more honest and authentic, but you run a big risk of a man pigeon-holing you as a difficult person and denying your strength to overcome obstacles. You rob him of the chance to experience a new and stronger you and form a positive impression.

Most women, however, believed waiting for the relationship to develop was wiser than revealing the most painful details too soon. They reasoned that once a man has feelings for you, he is *more* likely to accept your past. It is not a good idea to hold back telling him *every little thing* that is not perfect about you.

You should allow your man to experience some of your quirks and shortcomings. Be yourself. Otherwise, how else are you going to know if he is tolerant, loving and realistic about love? Dating is not a time to present an emotionally airbrushed version of yourself. Paradoxically, revealing a few of your issues is a good way to test your man's capacity for empathy. Here are two examples of women facing this dilemma.

NINA DROPS HER GUARD

When Nina went out on a second date with Charlie, she said she "dropped her guard" and let him see that she didn't like sitting with her back to the aisle in restaurants. "Ever since a waiter spilled hot coffee down my back, I feel sort of anxious if I can't see what's going on." Nina said she waited for a reaction, but then she was happy when Charlie didn't seem to have any problem re-arranging the chairs. "I discovered something about men," Nina said. "They like to feel important and needed."

CRYSTAL TESTS LOVE'S WATERS

Crystal faced a different problem—how to tell Ralph about a serious issue. Almost the moment Crystal met Ralph, she was excited. *Too* excited. She had never met a man like him before. He was educated, had a great job in marketing and, like her, he liked bird-watching. She said, "I mean, really, what are my chances of meeting someone who likes doing *that*?" Crystal owned a travel company and she loved traveling to far-off locales to watch exotic birds.

The women in my workshop cautioned her about fantasizing about a life with this man so quickly. They reminded her that falling head over heels for a man because of one trait or interest was not wise. Luckily, Crystal took their advice. Her biggest fear was that he would not react well when he learned that she had once had a problem with alcohol.

Instead of coming right out with it, she talked to him about a news item about a famous actor who was having problems controlling his drug habit. The actor was very close to going to prison for his behavior. Crystal said she felt sorry for the man. "He's so talented. Something must have gotten to him early in life," she told Ralph. He said that he "had no patience for people with problems like that and didn't trust anyone who had."

Crystal was devastated. She was "inches" away, as she said, from telling him her life story. Crystal had found an inventive way to test the love waters.

HOW DO I INTRODUCE MY MAN TO MY CHILDREN?

In Steve Harvey's book *Act Like a Lady, Think Like a Man*, he's clear on answering this question: introduce the children right away. The women in my study discovered that this advice was both good and bad. Certainly mention early in the dating phase that you have children. Some women told the man right away, others waited one or two more dates. There are no rules and you will have to trust your instincts. Some women waited until they felt a connection that might override any of the men's misgivings.

The other issue is when should everyone meet? Introducing your new man to your children right away isn't necessarily wise. Would you want the children to meet *every* man? Children like to know what's going on and who's who in their lives. There's no point in confusing them about whether they should care about this man—even if you say to your children that this man is your "friend." Kids are wise these days. If you introduce a man too soon, your children might behave *too well* to please you—or act like little monsters.

A reasonable guide is to determine first whether this man is a potential match for you. After you've told him that you have children, tell him that you would like everyone to meet. Prepare your children by telling them you'd like to include a man you like in a brief activity together such as going out for ice cream. Your children still might act too well or too impossibly. As your relationship grows, include your children for longer or more frequent times. Don't be surprised, though, if your children misbehave or ask lots of personal questions as their fears increase. They will be looking to you for support and assurance about this man. They will also want to know if this man is more important than they are.

WHY IS IT NECESSARY TO KNOW A MAN IN BOTH GOOD AND BAD TIMES?

A smart woman wants to know her man in both good times and bad. Some men, for example, reach out to a woman in time of need. When Brian lost his job as an advertising executive due to a merger, he felt especially vulnerable. He welcomed Debra's attention and warmth. Debra was the director of a prestigious early childhood program, and Brian loved her warm and caring nature. Then when he found another good position, he broke up with her. Later, Debra learned he was dating a woman who liked the fast lane and adrenaline rush of deadlines and stylish clients. "I wasn't what he really wanted," Debra said.

If possible, get a long view of your man through good and bad times—both yours and his. It's a great way to see your partner's coping skills, strengths and weaknesses. But since you can't invent a crisis, rely instead on asking smart questions. Ask him to tell you a story about how he got through trials and successes. Ask him how both good and bad life experiences changed what he needed in a relationship.

When smart and brave women found they had not assessed a man correctly, the secure women were more able to end the relationship quickly. Recovery from making a wrong choice in men did not derail their sense of trust in themselves, the world or men. Instead, they examined their experiences with the man and looked for the warning signs that they missed. Some women kept mental notes while others wrote their observations and predictions in journals and reviewed what they wrote.

By now you should be not only smarter about dating but braver as well. These steps have been your dating training wheels to steady you while you learn to read men and yourself better.

Tips for Smarter Assessments of Men

Observe his nonverbal behavior and actions with others. Pay special attention to his eyes, hands and posture. Watch how he treats others. Does he listen or talk mostly about himself?

Observe your own emotional and physical reactions. Is your heart pounding or your stomach churning? When have you felt that way before? Do you feel suddenly diminished or disrespected? Stay in tune with your body. If necessary, go to the ladies' room and ask yourself how you are feeling and reacting.

Be wary of men who rush a positive impression of themselves. Does your man order for you without knowing your preferences or buy you expensive gifts on the first date? This charming behavior can charm you right out of your mind.

Hang out with your new man. Make your time together resemble ordinary life as much as possible. Observe how your date deals with errands, waitstaff, traffic jams and your friends.

Aim to know your partner during good times and bad. Life has ups and downs. Know what your man is like during both periods.

Exaggerate his behavior. It's always difficult to know whether you are seeing the tip of the iceberg of problems or just a little ice cube floating down the river. One possible way to distinguish the extent of his behavior is to exaggerate it. If he's shy, imagine his not being open and emotionally available. If he is courtly, imagine him always needing to be in charge.

Chapter 14

Bravery in Mastering Fear of Change

If, every time you were unhappy about your love situation, you could figure out what the problem was and make changes, you might resolve issues more easily. For example, you might wait and see if the hints that your man is cheating are true or just a mirage rather than confront him. Making an immediate decision is a terrible bargain because you believe that you only have two unpleasant choices—stay or leave.

Leaving seems scary because you're unsure what life will hold for you. You might become lonely, worse off financially or make another bad love choice. Living with such anguish erodes your sense of being in charge of your life. You may long for improvement, but the intensity of your emotional pain from your situation immobilizes your ability to change.

Because of your unfulfilling love life, your fears have hijacked your common sense and you wonder what it will take to be happy. I hope this chapter will acquaint you with techniques for the bravery and psychological self-examination you will need to change your situation. If you utilize them, you'll be able to open your eyes to your problems, manage your anxiety about resolving them and face some of the underlying forces that prevent you from taking action.

COOKIE CLOSES HER EYES TO HER PROBLEMS AND TO CHANGE

This morning Cookie thought she saw a sign. A bird with a red plume landed where the path split, and it made Cookie and the man coming toward her stop in the middle of the fork in the road. His T-shirt said *Legal Beagle*; it had to be a sign—she was an attorney, too—so she smiled at him. But when he adjusted his earbuds, she saw the glint from his wedding band.

As she neared the corner of the courthouse, she had an urge to get a cup of coffee at the local café. That had to be the real sign. She almost always got coffee from the office cart. She dashed across the street and in front of her in line were two guys discussing a divorce settlement. Yes—that urge was the correct sign—two handsome guys talking about her legal specialty. One smiled. It would make a good story years later. She could hear herself explaining it to her mom and friends. "Well, for some reason I ran over to the café—you know, you get this feeling—and right there in front of me was this guy..."

Just as Cookie was about to speak up to the two guys, she saw they were holding hands. Running into them wasn't a sign at all. Her therapist was right—don't rely on love happening when you're not looking. Then again, the same therapist said to explore the connection between her parents' divorce and her habit of hiding out from meeting men. Well, Cookie thought, that divorce was a long time ago. Besides, Cookie was over it. She didn't go back to that therapist. A girlfriend gave Cookie the name of a person who was a better fit for her—someone who "makes you feel good about yourself." Now *that* was a sign. The next cartoon shows Cookie's new "therapist."

AlmostSMART COOKIE ™

WHY IS CHANGE SO DIFFICULT?

Like Cookie, even if you are very unhappy about your situation, your efforts to deal with it may—like hers—take you in the wrong direction. Imagine a winter's day where the sidewalks and streets are covered in snow. You go outside and notice that your footprints from the night before are still in the snow. You extend your leg as far as it can go; you've got to make it to that first footprint where you'll be safe. You got it. Walking is easy, but your trail doesn't lead you to the sidewalk. You remember that last night you stepped into the yard to get a closer look at a bird. Now it seems you have no choice but to step into the untouched snow. Ice has formed, your feet make a crunching sound and the hardness of the snow throws you off balance. You retreat to your footprints from the night before. It's the long way, it takes you into the next yard, but you don't care. It feels better to stay on your usual path.

True, there's nothing wrong with stepping in those footprints of life sometimes. But the key word is *sometimes*. When you're unhappy and not getting the results you want, you need to step outside your comfort zone into untried territory.

Your comfort with your "discomfort zone" kicks in, that is, you are by now used to and have actually become comfortable with tolerating the unpleasant aspects of your relationship. To change means giving up something that has safeguarded you from feeling anxious, insecure or confused. This something that you give up is unique to you. In fact, you often can't identify it. Whatever it is, it serves as an anchor that impedes your ability to change. So now you've looped right back into your previous footprints of unhappiness where the unknown is (almost) worse than your current situation.

In Cookie's situation, she is afraid to make the same mistakes as her mother did. She saw her mother crying too many times over men who disappointed her. Yet, Cookie wanted to please her mother by making a good marriage. Cookie's childhood experience of divorce taints her hopes and it leaves her torn between her desire for love and her fear of getting hurt. This explanation is clear but Cookie doesn't buy into it.

Nighttime is the worst for Cookie. Her heart races, a feeling of terror takes over and she fears that she might have missed her chance at love. She recalls scenes of her mother dating one man after another. In the morning, there would be a different man in pajama bottoms and no shirt sitting in the kitchen. Cookie would feel a sense of dread come over her, and she wondered if she would grow up to be as desperate as her mom. Was Cookie feeling that anxiety about her love life? But, no, that couldn't be it, she assures herself. It's just a bad patch of luck right now. She's nothing like her mom.

Despite Cookie's toughness as an attorney, she can't handle her own truth about her insecurities. Now you're seeing how hard it is to change. The chart which follows shows you the interaction between longing for change and fear of taking a chance.

The Seesaw of Pain and Fear

1. Fear of change weighs more than emotional pain.

EMOTIONAL PAIN

FEAR OF CHANGE
(Weighs more, so seat is low.)

2. Battle of pain and fear goes up and down equally, and the stalemate causes greatest anguish.

EMOTIONAL PAIN   FEAR OF CHANGE

3. Emotional pain weighs more than fear of change.

FEAR OF CHANGE

EMOTIONAL PAIN
(Now this weighs more, so you risk change.)

Your emotions go up and down as though you are on a seesaw. This battle between wanting to make changes and avoiding them creates high anxiety. You can't decide and soon you get to a stalemate where your fear and desire for change are almost evenly matched. The lack of resolution and the ups and downs cause great anguish.

When the pain from your present situation intensifies, your fear of the unknown lessens. Soon, the pain of not dealing with your relationship problems is greater than your fear of making changes.

Usually, you're more likely to seek professional help when your pain and fear of change balance equally or when your pain is far greater than your fear.

An odd thing happens sometimes, though, if you take action when your pain is highest. You would think that such intense pain would make you hit bottom, and motivate you at last to change your dating and mating situation. Because you are addicted to your comfort with your discomfort zone, you don't change. Oh, you might make an appointment with a therapist or a divorce attorney. You might even pack your bags or break up.

Yet, as soon as the pain subsides, so does your resolve to change your love life. The crisis almost always passes because you have unknowingly made a pact with your fears. The pact goes something like this:

Secret and Unwise Fear Pact

I am a human being, so I know I like peace and pleasure. So I'll let myself get all worked up just in case I should really contemplate changing. But, most of the time, I'll let the pain be intense but brief so I can go back to my old ways and avoid having to risk rocking the boat.

Soon, you and your partner make up, realize that changing the situation is harder than you thought and return to your old pattern or situation. Usually, you return within days or months, but some of the women in my study resumed a previous and unhealthy relationship after more than a year.

Think of a snow globe and imagine that all those flakes of snow represent your emotional pain. When you are in high crisis mode, your pain gets shaken up, just like the flakes inside a snow globe when you shake it. But when you stop shaking the globe, those snowflakes fall right back down to the ground and the scene returns to its old ways.

You will more likely settle back into your relationship unless you are able to sustain the intensity of the emotional pain long enough to take effective action that includes serious self-reckoning. For example, your partner could say cruel words or hit you. Yet, even if you argue, cry or take shelter at a friend's house, you might resume your old ways until you can overcome your fear of change, self-truth and anxiety.

HOW CAN I PUSH MYSELF TO FACE MY FEAR?

It's very difficult to push yourself to do something on your own without being motivated by the urgency of deadlines or personal crises. The women in my study who found good love partners or who improved their existing relationships were able to radically change their realizations and behaviors. For many of us, life is lived in third gear where you just cruise along without having to speed up or stop too much.

Motivating yourself to create a new path requires a long-term commitment to being your personal best and high levels of emotional bravery. Anxiety is not your enemy—but getting anxious about being anxious is. You have to be willing to feel your unpleasant feelings without necessarily acting on them. Here are some tips and exercises that have been very helpful to my research participants.

REALIZE THE IMPORTANCE OF YOU

We are all little specks on this earth and we might not matter very much to very many. But don't use this negative thinking as your excuse to trudge along and do nothing. Treat your life with respect—especially your love life. Be wary of falling into the trap of believing that you are born, you live for a while and then die. Life is precious. When you act as though you matter to yourself, you will also increase your chances of mattering to others and acting with love.

Joanne, one woman with whom I spoke, was overweight and in an unhappy job and marriage. Her husband wasn't a bad man—he was just equally resigned to trudging along. The turning point came for Joanne when their twin daughters married and moved far away. Now she felt the impact of the staleness of her life. Her friends tried to coax her out of her funk by asking her to help out with a charity event for developmentally impaired children. Joanne loved to draw and she discovered that art was a great way to help these children. She found a purpose and passion.

Her happiness was contagious. Soon, her husband decided to revive his hobby of refinishing boats. As their sense of self-worth increased, they began to tackle harder problems such as their weight. "One day, my husband came home and cleaned out all the junk food in the house. He said he needed to get healthier if he wanted to do the heavy work of remodeling his clients' boats." A domino effect of happiness created a cascade of change. They went for walks together, had sex more often and actually enjoyed being with each other. "I realize that earlier I had given up," Joanne said. "Everything just seemed too hard."

My Importance

Answer the following questions:

Who would miss me if aliens suddenly abducted me?

Who relies on me?

Who cares about me?

Why do people like me? What do I have to offer them?

What would I like to offer others?

PRACTICE REGRET MANAGEMENT

On Eileen's fortieth birthday, she felt a flood of regret. Most of her friends were married with children. She'd devoted the past twenty years to her career as a district manager for a big box store. Her birthday was filled with remorse about the chances at love that she didn't take.

Regretting what you did or didn't do can eat away at self-worth. Many of the women in my study berated themselves for passing up men whom they now saw as viable partners. The women realized that their fears of being hurt had prevented them from being emotionally available. Don't choose the short-term goal of guarding against these feelings. Instead, take a long-term perspective of protecting yourself from regret.

Include regret management as part of your life plan. Your best motivator is the march of time. Heed that alarm clock.

Think about what you want to accomplish before you die. You don't have to think big. Don't fall into that trap. It's just another excuse for not taking action.

Melanie's Story

One of the married women in the study, Melanie, longed to learn how to knit and do needlework. Every week she'd go to the farmer's market and craft shows to examine the handiwork of others, even though she thought it was stupid that women would waste their time on such trivial things. She even belittled her husband's interests in saving wildlife.

In truth, she envied her husband's interests. They had always lived like two peas in a pod. Now she felt abandoned and lonely whenever her husband went on excursions with local wildlife clubs. Her job as a school principal felt routine and she didn't know how to add joy to her life.

Her parents were movers and shakers in Melanie's hometown, and she always felt inadequate compared to them. Even though she was the only one of her four sisters to get a college education, as well as a graduate degree, she felt like the ugly duckling. "My sisters were gorgeous and married well. I was always the one my parents picked on. And in their eyes my husband was 'just a teacher.' My parents were horrified that I was the major breadwinner."

Then one day, when she criticized her husband for working so hard on saving turtles, he said that he wasn't going to be the whipping post for her problems. A light bulb went off. Melanie realized that she had been the scapegoat for her parents' unhappiness with each other. "It was a wake-up call. I could just be me. I didn't have to set the world on fire—and neither did my husband," she said. For the first time Melanie felt lucky to have an interest in something that was beautiful and that gave her joy.

Melanie said her greatest accomplishment was overcoming her family's belief that she didn't matter. What do you want to overcome? What words would you write on your tombstone? What would be your last—and lasting words? You certainly don't want these:

*HERE LIES A WOMAN AFRAID TO FACE HER FEARFULNESS
WHO LIVED HER LIFE WITHOUT HAPPINESS*

Write down the things you would like to include in your life. You might choose another education degree, children, travel, a home or love. Think about the relationship fears you'd like to master and triumph over. Now come up with your own words for your tombstone.

My Last and Lasting Words

Think about what you would like to teach others, and what kinds of memories and inspiration you'd like to impart to them. These thoughts might be part of your *last and lasting words*. If you aren't sure, search the Internet for famous quotes about life and see what clicks with you. Now write your own lasting words.

MAKE A HAPPINESS PACT

Now you're ready to make a pact to seek a healthy love future. Here is a composite of pacts that the women in my study used to motivate and calm themselves. Add your own ideas.

My Personal Pact with Love Happiness

- I will get emotionally brave enough to withstand the ups and downs of my commitment.

- I know that I will have to battle the same fear many times. I expect to slide back into old habits.

- I will not beat myself up when I do mess up—but I will get back on track.

- I will seek professional help when my efforts aren't working.

ACCEPT THE PATH OF FEAR—AND TOUGH IT OUT

Earlier in this section, we discussed how your biggest foe was your reaction to your fear. It's okay to be anxious about letting down your guard and getting close to someone. You can walk around with your anxiety. It is not lethal. The more comfortable you are with feeling frightened without taking self-destructive action, the faster you will be able to become brave enough for love.

Think about those model ships encapsulated in a bottle. Some of those boats are built with decks and sails that collapse. The person who is building the boat inserts some compressed items through the bottleneck, positions the ship in the center and then pulls a network of strings that opens up the decks and sails. Imagine your fears are those collapsed sails and decks of the boat. As you enter the bottle, your fears intensify for a short time because all your fears are bunched up at once. It's a tight and scary squeeze through the bottle's neck, but if you keep forging ahead, you will open up your sails of bravery that will propel you toward many opportunities for love and loving behavior.

Monica had many similar fears. Monica's fear of choosing the wrong man and ending up in a hostile marriage like her parents almost prevented her from dating. Her unhappiness motivated her to persevere. She was still frightened of making mistakes, but in her struggles Monica discovered an important lesson:

About Decisions

Since most important decisions in life are made with incomplete information, experiencing anxiety is actually a normal response.

Monica avoided getting anxious about getting anxious and she was able to observe her men better. Her clearheadedness allowed her to make a good mate selection. At the age of forty-one, she married and gave birth to a baby boy a year later.

Classic children's stories and movies are frequently about bravery and independence. Believing that you can take care of yourself with less parental supervision is one of the tasks of growing up. When you are a child, the thought of being on your own is so scary that some children like to rehearse and triumph over this fear by watching and reading tales about finding safety and security after being orphaned or lost.

We never totally get rid of this fear of abandonment and the failure to cope with whatever life tosses at us. We feel more confident about mastering this fear when we face our circumstances and take effective action. We end up *liking and respecting* ourselves for not needing to obscure, deny or minimize our issues. Complete the following sentence quickly.

Becoming More Emotionally Brave

If I were emotionally brave in love and wanted to be my best self, I would...

Many of the women surprised themselves by writing responses such as: Leave my husband. Go back to school. See a therapist. Not be so critical next time I meet a guy or deal with my partner. Renew relationships with my family. Change my job. Go to church more often.

Which of your responses surprised you? What would you add? Think about what it would take to overcome your fears so that you could be brave and kind to yourself and others.

WHAT CAN I DO TO GET USED TO LIVING WITH MY FEARS?

Being emotionally vulnerable is not easy. Sometimes you have to tend to it daily. Once you value your life and make happiness in love your goal, you need to become more mindful of your feelings and your management of them.

READ BOOKS ABOUT OVERCOMING YOUR FEARS

Use the Internet to search for books, articles and CDs about overcoming your fears. I especially like the products of Louise L. Hay, who addresses in-depth fear management. Some of my research participants also felt the book *Feel the Fear and Do It Anyway* by Susan Jeffer was very helpful. Getting educated is a less intense step and many of the women in my study began to accept change by first reading about it.

KEEP A FEELING JOURNAL

Some women found that keeping a journal of their feelings, reactions and improvement was very useful. Other women dashed off notes to themselves on scraps of paper, laptops or even their cell phones. There is no one right way. You need to get into the mindset of observing and expressing yourself. Most of the women in my study discovered that journaling was a powerful tool for revealing thoughts and understanding them. They realized, over time, that life was a story with several recurring themes.

Marie, one of the women in my study, discovered that even though she had won awards as a highly-respected financial advisor, she wasn't winning any prizes in the love department. "I was used to being in charge, so I kept marrying men who let me."

Marie resented that each of her husbands couldn't pull his weight financially or emotionally. Then one night when she felt very low, she wrote in her journal: "Hate unhappy endings. My parents got divorced and then fought with the next spouses and the next. I bossed my husbands, criticized and made snide remarks. Not very nice. Hated them. Now I hate me for being so mean. I am really that same little scared girl. Control is not the way for me to feel safe." Her words and feelings startled her.

Eventually, Marie learned to observe her own reactions and to chart her progress at curbing her critical nature. "It was all out of fear," she said. "I thought if I jabbed enough at my husbands, they would shape up. It was me and my bad choices of men that needed changing."

Once you can connect the dots of your life story, you can measure your progress by observing improvement in three areas. Pay attention to the *duration, intensity and frequency* of your fear, negative thoughts and ineffective behavior. Don't worry about what to write. Just get started and your themes will emerge. Now let's put some of your resolve into action.

CREATE YOUR OWN EMOTIONAL FEARS BOOT CAMP

Put yourself on a training course that will help you build a more resilient and positive self. Begin by taking small steps in areas that make you feel scared. When you challenge yourself in one area, you often gain enough emotional bravery to take on challenges in other parts.

The boot camp programs that help teenagers face their fears are based on this concept of increasing self-worth through the accomplishment of a series of frightening physical tasks. When these teens scale mountains or survive for days in the woods, they are weakening their previous self-view of being a person who fails. They gain enough inner strength to face their emotional problems because they have created a *new self-definition* of being someone who tries hard, against many odds, and succeeds.

<hr>

Connie's Story

My client Connie said she was scared to try new things. Her fear was so great that it made her stop dating. She was sure that once men got to know her, they would see her flaws. "So, I just told myself that there weren't any good men in my town," she said.

Connie's parents had given her up for adoption when she was eight. Connie was a willful child and she believed if she had behaved better, her parents would never have sent her away. She strove for perfection, in the hope that perhaps someone would love her. Later, she spent all her time on her career as a marine biologist and preferred keeping her head underwater rather than venturing onto land to find love.

In her few relationships, Connie was adept at defending herself against getting hurt or criticized, so men told her she was as tough as one of her marine clams. She micro-managed employees' projects and was only happy when she approved their every little step. Small disagreements provoked the same reaction as large ones—a chink in her armor felt like a mortal blow to her self-worth and control.

<hr>

In my workshop, I suggested that Connie do something that frightened her but was unrelated to dating. Since Connie had always wanted to learn to water ski, she decided to build her bravery with ski lessons.

On the first few days of classes, when she fell off the skis she made excuses and blamed her falls on the screaming kids. Soon, however, she gave up her façade of being perfect. She let the skis pop up from under her and slammed into the water repeatedly. Connie learned to water ski—but she also learned to be more comfortable about feeling vulnerable or wrong. When Connie returned to the workshop, she announced—with pride—that she had accepted a blind date. Now it's your turn to attend boot camp.

My Emotional Fears Boot Camp

1. Make a list of things you'd like to try—but are too afraid to attempt. You don't have to think big. It might be something as simple as trying a new cuisine or going to the movies alone. Or it could be learning to tango, bungee jump or travel alone.

2. Write down what is so frightening about taking action.

3. What self-talk can you use to push yourself forward?

4. Make a vow that you will act on this idea.

5. Tell your friends about it.

6. Do it. Repeat the same action. You might see that it was not so difficult.

7. Now repeat these steps for another frightening action.

Tips for Beating Your Fears

Learn about the balancing act between your fears and your desires. Accept that you will often go back and forth in making change. Keep a feeling journal to track and learn from your fears.

Value yourself as a person. You do matter and you are the one who can look out for yourself.

Use regret management to motivate yourself to live your life fully. Get the big picture of your life. Don't let fears paralyze you emotionally.

Accept that all change is scary. Most major decisions are accompanied by anxiety.

Do things that frighten you so you can get accustomed to feeling anxious. Know your fears. Experience them so you can lessen their impact.

Chapter 15

Recovery from Past Hurts, Mistakes, Meltdowns and Suicide Attempts

Some women persist in hanging a sign around their hearts that says "No Solicitors." All of us make mistakes, but not all of us have as great a fear of making them as a majority of the women in my study. Love's disappointments made them close down their hearts to relationships—even if they were already in one.

They also found all kinds of rationalizations that were the equivalent of "men are dogs" to convince themselves that smart women don't have time for love. These women were often highly wary of even kissing with one eye open because the risk of getting hurt was too high. Many women clung to the liferaft that men were the problem. The women couldn't see that their own fears contributed to getting an F in love.

HOW DO I KNOW IF I HAVE THESE FEARS?

To give love the best chance, you first have to face your fear of making mistakes in general. It's probably of little comfort to know that everyone makes mistakes—big and small. Somehow, your love mistakes *feel* bigger and more potent. Even worse is your fear of feeling afraid of feeling afraid. Your seemingly-obvious cure is to hide your heart from your existing partner or to avoid dating or falling in love.

To assess your fears, answer the following key questions that I asked women in my lectures and workshops or whom I surveyed. There is no scoring, since the goal of this exercise is to make you aware of your fears and past behaviors.

Circle or underline the choice that best describes your agreement or disagreement with the statement.

Fear Assessment

I really have trouble getting over past hurts.

Almost Always	Often	Sometimes	Rarely	Never

I really can't stand making mistakes.

Almost Always	Often	Sometimes	Rarely	Never

It takes a very long time for me to drop my guard.

Almost Always	Often	Sometimes	Rarely	Never

More than half of the women whom I surveyed said that they couldn't stand making mistakes and that it took a very long time for them to drop their guard. Almost 60 percent said that they had real trouble getting over past hurts in love.

In my workshops, the numbers were slightly but not significantly lower, because as the women heard other participants speak about their experiences, they modified their true answers from the survey with adjectives such as "mostly" or "frequently." But the overall conclusion was that women saw love mistakes such as break-ups, emotional hurts and unhappiness as dangers to avoid rather than opportunities to learn.

They managed this often unacknowledged fear by pulling back their hearts from their existing partners, avoiding or severely limiting dating. In the next cartoon you can see how Cookie handles being hurt in love.

COOKIE BURIES HER HEAD

Cookie is reeling from a romantic relationship with a colleague. She was so sure that Ron was right for her. For starters, unlike her previous boy-friend Tim, Ron had a great education and a good job. Cookie thought that she had hit the jackpot with Ron. She and Ron were both attor-neys, close in age, both single, with average weight and normal facial features—slim requirements for sure, but seemingly enough. Well, enough if you are feeling desperate, lonely, old and plagued by family messages to "settle down." Cookie put her heart into this relationship, so wasn't she entitled to bury her head under the covers and not come up until...well, until when?

Most of us have had painful emotional punches from a break-up. Many of us manage not only to survive but to learn and thrive in love. Yet, for many of the women in my study, recovery from hurt was not so easy. Several divorced women had not dated for more than a decade. They never got hurt again, but they secretly wondered if there was something wrong with them.

The problem is that if you don't put yourself in the love ring where you very well might get hurt, then you won't be able to find love. The secret is that you have to believe that you can survive the blows. Several of the women in one of my workshops said that they'd be happy living in a castle with a double moat—and possibly with a man who doted on them. Keep that image in mind.

Consider the castle again. No one can really ever get to you. Your walls are thick, and access to your true inside is very limited. Even when you fall in love, you choose a man beneath your exalted position as owner of the castle.

WHY AM I SO AFRAID OF MAKING MISTAKES?

Making a mistake is not an enjoyable experience. You feel foolish at best; lost, confused and hurt at worst. Soon that adage about learning from mistakes kicks in and you tend to feel wiser and not as sad. Yet, the adage is only true if you understand and can correct the sources of the misstep. Identifying those factors, however, hinges on the emotional bravery necessary to withstand self-examination. When you put all these items together, you end up with a very tall order. Here is a list and discussion of the top issues that contribute to your fear of mistakes.

UNDERSTANDING YOUR FEAR OF MAKING MISTAKES IN LOVE

YOU LACK TRUST IN YOUR JUDGMENT

If you've been burned in relationships, putting your heart out there can feel so frightening that you raise your protective wall high enough that even if you date or remain with your partner, you can't be reached emotionally.

Negativity becomes a major component of your self. Soon your pessimistic view of men and love feels justified and accurate. You believe men can't be trusted, that they hide things and often have a false exterior that they show the world. Many of the women in my research hung out with male friends and saw the underbelly of their lives. As one of the women said, "They cheat, lie and use hookers."

Fleeing into male company with men whom you deem not to be "relationship material" is a common pattern. Seeing an unvarnished—and often tarnished—view of men convinces you to wall up your heart and feel smart and lucky that you don't have to go through what your friends endure. Your negativity is actually a thin veneer that covers your lack of trust in your own judgment to choose men wisely.

YOU HAVE A MELTDOWN AND FEAR THAT YOU CAN'T SURVIVE THE HURT.

Sometimes the hurt from relationships is so great that you have an emotional meltdown. You might get very depressed and find it difficult to do your daily tasks and routines. You drag yourself to work, put on a happy face and come home to cry, eat, sleep and just generally feel as though the world has turned upside down. For many women, it has.

Some of the worst situations involved phony investment schemes, embezzlement, theft, sexual abuse of children, lies about marital status and cheating. The intensity of the betrayal disrupts your sense of trust, your judgment and your sense of value, as well as your faith in the world and people.

Recovery or even survival seems almost impossible. The destruction of all the things that you took for granted feels traumatic because it *is* a trauma—an experience that feels as if life as you know it has disappeared. Women discovered, for instance, that their partners were cheating on them or had abused their children.

The hurt was so excruciating that some of the women attempted suicide. The shame of their lives was so enormous and they felt so powerless that they didn't see suicide as something shameful. They thought about the wake-up call their deaths would be to their families, about their men or situations. These suicide attempts were often the result of a last-straw incident with their partners.

Ten percent of women in my study said that in the past they had attempted suicide over love and relationship issues. For a newer, more comprehensive accounting of suicide risks, the 2007 findings of the Centers for Disease Control and Prevention revealed that women *attempted* suicide three times more than men.[1] Similarly, www.suicide .org's 2001 statistics found that there were 750,000 *attempted* suicides per year. Women had three attempts for each male attempt.[2]

The Centers for Disease Control and Prevention also discovered that the number of women's suicides peaked to almost nine for every 100,000 women between the ages of forty-five and fifty-four and the rate reflected a steady climb from the age of thirty-five.[3] The reasons for this increase were complex, but a 2008 article in *The New York Times* speculated that hormonal changes and illness were contributing factors.[4] I would add problems with their intimate partners.

This disturbing trend in women's suicide attempts is evident in capable women who over-accommodate and accept emotional crumbs from a man of authority.

Twentieth-century American poet Sylvia Plath—who committed suicide—captured this tendency of women to acclimatize to men's mistreatment in her poem "Daddy." Plath says in her poem that women "...adore...The boot in the face..."[5] She is talking about her own father and, figuratively, about women in relationships with powerful men.

Let's look at Ingrid's reaction to her situation, which may be extreme but highlights the potency of betrayal and other serious emotional relationship hurts.

Ingrid's Story

Ingrid had been unhappy in her marriage for a long time, and she felt horribly guilty about it. It would have been so much easier to end the marriage if Craig had been a mean and rotten husband and father. But he wasn't. He was a decent man, but he was a quitter. He didn't finish college or his medical technology training. After their twin sons were born, he stayed home and tried to start a computer consulting business. However, he undercut his fees and referred to other professionals if the problem got too big. "Why don't you go for more training?" she'd ask him. Craig's answer was always a defiant, "I can teach myself."

She never thought their relationship would turn out so badly. They were so excited to find each other in college. They were both studying engineering and they loved going to hear the latest indie bands. When Craig had a chance to fill in for the bass player for a start-up band, he dropped out of school and traveled with them. Ingrid admired his ability to take off and go with the flow. She was so organized.

They shocked everyone by getting married as soon as Craig came back from his tour with the band. Ingrid graduated with a degree in metallurgical engineering and got a job in Peru. She loved that her husband was adventurous and willing to go to Peru with her. He bought a pistol and taught her how to use it for protection while in Peru. But it turned out that living without a plan or stability was the only thing at which Craig was adept. Establishing a routine or finishing anything was not for him. When Ingrid discovered she was pregnant with twin boys, Craig was thrilled. He had visions of the three of them forming a band.

That was eight years ago and now, back in the United States, Ingrid, who had begun drinking too much at times, worked for a major engineering firm while Craig stayed home to cook, clean and pick up after the boys—and once in a while dabble with his next career idea.

Ingrid had had enough. She couldn't believe she had ever felt safe with this man, but she once had. Then she met Ryan at her office Christmas party.

He was the husband of Jenna, whose home-based graphic design business provided the company with the artwork and layouts for brochures. Ryan and Ingrid developed an instant rapport. As usual, Jenna got drunk at the office party and Ryan had to take her home.

Ryan was a nutritionist and was starting up a consulting business for hospitals and restaurants. His wife, Jenna, came from a wealthy family and really didn't have to work, but she loved staying home and drawing. Ryan said she could wall herself up in the study with music blasting and just doodle all night.

It was after the Fourth of July office party that Ingrid and Ryan began their affair. "It just crept up on me," Ingrid said. "We were having another one of our soul-to-soul talks about our lives. He told me how unhappy he was with Jenna, how there wasn't any sex and hadn't been for years. And then we just kissed. It was the beginning of the most amazing relationship I'd ever had."

After a year, Ingrid was exhausted from sneaking around and lying to Craig. One night, after dinner and lovemaking in her office with Ryan, Ingrid brought up the issue of both of them divorcing their partners and then getting married. "He was so sweet," Ingrid said. "He said he just wanted to wait until his new business venture was more solid. He didn't want me to be the main breadwinner. It was so refreshing to hear a man stick with something and make it work."

And then it happened. Ryan's wife Jenna came to the office to present her new graphic designs, and everyone was crowding around her. Ingrid wondered what all the commotion was about. She left her desk and came into the main hall. "What's going on?" she asked. The receptionist's words felt like a punch to the stomach: "Oh, poor Jenna," the receptionist said. "On her way to the printer to pick up these brochures for us"—the receptionist held up a stack—"she saw her husband come out of one of those Route 7 motels with a call girl and…'"

Jenna interrupted her and said, "You couldn't mistake her for any other kind of woman. She had on a skintight red corset and five-inch heels." Jenna held up her fingers to show the height of the shoe. "So I pulled up alongside his car just in time to hear her say, 'Next week I'll bring along our baby. Wait till you see his two front teeth.'" Jenna hid her head in her hands. "A baby? What am I going to do?"

Ingrid ran back to her office. Ryan had told her there was no one but her. Everything he said had been untrue. The whole past year was a big fat lie. Her hopes and plans and dreams—all one enormous lie. She had nothing— nothing. Ingrid grabbed her handbag and ran out the door for home.

She wasn't thinking. There were no thoughts in her mind at all. Just this urgency to end the pain of the betrayal. As soon as she arrived home, she ran up the steps, took out the Peruvian pistol and shot herself in the head. The bullet grazed her temple and there was a lot of blood. When Craig found her, he called 911 and Ingrid's life was saved.

Ingrid got divorced, but Ryan didn't. He needed his wife's money to support his new business. "Looking back, I can't believe that I tried to kill myself," Ingrid said. She also said she would never trust any man again. "I'll never survive another hurt like that."

YOU DON'T HAVE A PERSPECTIVE ON THE DEGREE OF THE EMOTIONAL HURT

Not all hurts are as "all or nothing" as Ingrid's. Yet, many of the women said they had trouble gauging the depth of emotional hurts from their partner or date. Sometimes, you might find yourself ruminating over whether you really were hurt. You wonder if you are just too sensitive. Or, maybe you are too hard on your partner.

You struggle to get a perspective and a reality check. Perhaps you are experiencing a non-suicidal meltdown, a deep psychological wound or a possible deal-breaker. You can't imagine how couples manage to stay happily together for a long time.

As we've discussed earlier, marital researcher John N. Gottman's various studies in long-term, mutually-satisfying marriages revealed that even happy couples went through tough times, including incidents where they were dissatisfied with their partners. One of the factors that got them through the rough patches was their faith in the solidity of the marriages. My research findings add two more factors about managing emotional hurts.

Success in Recovering from Hurts and Mistakes

Hurt recovery requires at least:

1. The ability to gauge and rebound from setbacks, disappointment and hurt.
2. The ability not to let any hurt, criticism, error or slight *define* you or your relationship. One slip-up does not mean that all of yourself—or all of your relationship— is a walking slip-up.

The satisfied women in my study said that happiness with their partner required knowing how to pick their battles and how to assess the degree of their own hurt and their spouses' transgressions.

In my workshops and lectures, I asked women to keep an image in mind of a continuum between a feather and a brick. The next time you experience hurt, disappointment or any other unpleasant situation with your partner or date, use the continuum below to evaluate him, yourself and the relationship. Ask yourself these questions and add your own questions or points on the continuum.

Assessment of Hurts and Problems

Can our ongoing relationship survive this upset?

Forget about it   Needs discussion   Needs time   Needs counseling   Break up

Can I give my new partner or date a second—or even a third—chance?

Forget about it   Needs discussion   Needs time   Needs counseling   Break up

Can I survive this rejection, hurt, disrespect, devastation or criticism?

Forget about it   Needs discussion   Needs time   Needs counseling   Break up

*YOU FEAR REJECTION, ABANDONMENT, HURT
AND DISAPPOINTMENT BECAUSE YOU FEEL
FUNDAMENTALLY TOO FLAWED OR UNLOVABLE*

If you dread being wrong or being hurt, it's likely that deep inside you are afraid to face your shame about *feeling so imperfect that you believe you are flawed.* This fear makes you doubt that someone could love "the real you." You also don't believe you are strong enough to recover. Here are some of the top reasons that made women in my study feel too flawed to risk being loved. Check the ones that describe you. Add your own.

What's Wrong with Me?

There is something wrong with me. If I could pinpoint it, it would include:

- ❏ Too fat
- ❏ Not pretty enough
- ❏ Have a physical flaw
- ❏ Too old
- ❏ Don't come from the "right" kind of family or background
- ❏ Am a disappointment to my parents
- ❏ Had an abusive family
- ❏ Not rich or accomplished enough
- ❏ Don't have enough education
- ❏ Didn't go to the "right school"
- ❏ Not outgoing enough
- ❏ Not fun
- ❏ Too much of an egghead
- ❏ Don't like lots of things
- ❏ Picky
- ❏ Have health problems
- ❏ Have a temper
- ❏ Difficult to live with
- ❏ Don't speak up enough
- ❏ Have a history of substance abuse, divorce or financial problems
- ❏ Have children

If you recognized things on this list, you might fear that even just one of these things is so terrible that few men would find you appealing. It's as though you've somehow fallen overboard from a boat and no one is coming to help you. You reason that the shore is too far away, the boat is moving too quickly and even if there was a liferaft, the boat isn't stopping for you because you are so flawed that you're not worth the boat's changing course to rescue you.

This next exercise will help you acknowledge and de-fang your underlying feelings of being flawed or unlovable.

A VISIT FROM YOUR FAIRY GODMOTHER

Cinderella was a lucky young lady. She had a fairy godmother to look out for her and correct her feelings of not being good enough. Well, you are lucky, too. Your fairy godmother has decided to visit you and take away what you think is wrong with you. She touches you with her wand, you see beautiful sparkles in the air and then in an instant you actually *feel* better about yourself. Those things that you checked off in the last exercise are gone.

Now answer the following questions:

1. Now that there is nothing wrong with me, what will I now do about men, relationships and love?
2. What behaviors will I stop? What new ones will I begin?
3. What will I no longer feel or believe? What new feelings and beliefs can I add?

YOU OVER-CORRECT YOUR FEARS BY AVOIDING LOVE OR BY LOOKING FOR THE PERFECT MAN

All of your beliefs about yourself activate your basic fear of abandonment, and they lead you to assume that the only way to avoid hurt is to find that one man who meets every item on your impossible-to-fill checklist.

To help you see the self-deception of holding this belief, read the following dialogues:

THE PERFECT MAN QUEST

THE HUNT FOR A PURPLE MAN

You: I'm looking for a purple man.

Me: Are there many purple men where you live?

You: No.

Me: Where are they?

You: Oh, closer to Berryville.

Me: Have you thought of going to or moving to Berryville? Or searching on the Internet for men in that location?

You: No. I want a purple man who lives where I do.

Me: But you said there weren't any purple men where you live.

THE HUNT FOR A MAN INTERESTED IN FLYING SAUCERS

You: I'm really interested in flying saucers so I want a man who is interested in them, too.

Me: Does your town or area have any flying saucer clubs?

You: Yes.

Me: So why don't you go to those clubs' meetings?

You: I don't like those clubs. They're not my kind of setting.

Me: But you're not going for the setting.

You: Well, there are too many men who like flying saucers who still are not my type.

Me: Then why restrict yourself to just men who like flying saucers? Do you have any other interests or qualities that you are looking for?

You: No. I want a man who is interested in flying saucers.

Do you see how your fears keep you running all by yourself in circles? Don't *volunteer* to close doors. There are enough things that happen every day in life that say no to you and prevent you from doing what you want. Luck, timing and connections are not always part of your resources. So don't lessen your chances at success by saying no ahead of time and adding to life's already existing nos.

YOU ARE MARRIED TO YOUR FEARS, DEFENSES AND UNHAPPINESS

The distance between who you are and who you think you are can seem as much as a light year. Most of us struggle to see ourselves honestly. Sometimes, we discover aspects that are painful to experience and admit. If you have built a solid foundation of self-worth, you search for that black cloud inside you because you know that facing it is the only way to master it, change it and create happiness.

If you have created a false sense of strength that is held together with the sticks of bravado and the glue of anger, resentment and self-righteousness, then you will reframe these maladaptive defenses against being hurt by naming them as strength and wisdom.

One of my favorite stories is *The Emperor's New Clothes*. There are variations on the tale, but essentially the emperor is running around his kingdom with nothing on except his underwear. No one from the town says anything and the emperor doesn't seem to notice it either. It takes a young child's simple view of the world that allows the child to shout out that the emperor isn't wearing any clothes. It is at that moment that the townspeople and the emperor finally realize that the emperor is almost naked.

Fearful, well-defended women rarely see themselves as barely wearing any clothes. They are married to their fears and they wear a flimsy and false front of defenses as though that gives them strength and wisdom.

Think of an image of yourself wearing a dress inside out with the zipper in the back. You have control of using that zipper tab to close or open the zipper, depending on how strong and secure you feel about letting in the outside world. It seems like the ideal arrangement of being in control of unexpected hurts. But, oops, you didn't realize the degree of difficulty in reaching that zipper tab that is against your back. Eventually, you don't try to unzip the dress.

Even if your love life makes you miserable and lonely, you cling to wearing your dress inside out and to maintaining your defenses and definition of yourself *because it does not yet frighten or hurt you to be that way.* I add the word "yet" because often, as I discussed earlier, some external event such as illness, aging or job loss happens. The event is powerful enough to burst through your defensive self-view. The more you see yourself as flawed, and the more you feel that you cannot survive hurt, the longer you stay married to your self-lies. But this marriage will not aid you in becoming your best self.

YOU DEFEND AND PROTECT YOUR
EMOTIONAL INVESTMENT IN A RELATIONSHIP—
EVEN IF IT IS NOT A HEALTHY RELATIONSHIP

It's very easy to hide your fear of risking a healthy relationship by clinging to the one you are in. Here is a list of the top reasons why you might be trying to convince yourself that you should stay. Mark the ones that apply to you. Add your own.

I WILL STAY WITH OR PURSUE MY CURRENT MAN BECAUSE:

- ❑ I've logged in years and effort with my partner.
- ❑ I am not getting any younger or prettier.
- ❑ I have children and don't want them to be from a broken home.
- ❑ I want to avoid another hurt or loss.
- ❑ I don't believe there will be anyone else for me.
- ❑ I don't know what happy-in-love looks like.
- ❑ There's enough good to hang in there—even if my top needs aren't met.
- ❑ I'm not sure I want to do all the things you need to do to be happy.

It's too easy to construct an alternate reality that lets in some things and keeps out others. Hurt recovery depends on risk and a sense of self-worth. Keep this triangle in mind about how you deceive yourself about love by activating the three corners of the triangle.

Traps that Prevent Me from Achieving Emotional Bravery, Hurt Recovery and Happiness

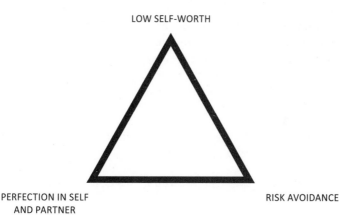

LOW SELF-WORTH

PERFECTION IN SELF
AND PARTNER

RISK AVOIDANCE

HOW DO I KNOW WHAT I NEED IN A MAN?

Knowing your specific core needs is one of the best safeguards against falling for a man who can't accept, acknowledge or fulfill many of your top ones. When I asked women in my study what they needed in a man, I was amazed at how many women answered with descriptions of physical characteristics. Sometimes they mentioned that he had to have a good job, but for the most part they didn't mention those qualities in a man that would fulfill their most important, unique emotional needs.

It is often difficult to pinpoint these needs. You might be closed off to them because you don't see yourself as someone who should have needs for things such as to be taken care of. So rather than start with identifying your needs, think instead about your previous love relationships.

What *character* qualities did you like or dislike in your men? Read the next list and underline or circle the qualities that you have discovered you like. Add your own categories and choices.

Personalized List of Most Important Qualities in a Man

Personality: quiet, easygoing, shy, calm, thinker, go- getter, sensitive, negotiator, leader, honest, positive, cooperative, outgoing, secure, rational, decisive, team player, warm, likes luxury, worldly, street smart, communicator, man of few but important words, risk taker, skeptical, spiritual, patient, persistent

Appearance: takes care of himself, weight proportionate with height, not taken with himself

Interests: outdoors, sports, cultural events, politics, travel, business, charities, science

Values: family, religious faith, friends, commitment, marriage, political and community involvement

Profession: career-oriented, economic security, creative maverick, values education

Relationship Behavior: caregiver, accepting, in command, influential, secure, predictable, lets me make decisions, likes lots of time on his own, likes doing things together, affectionate and sexual, not sexual

---

Look at the selections you made. Do the items also describe your needs? Which ones would you delete or add?

Now pretend that you have one chance to run a personal advertisement in the newspaper for your kind of man. What would your ad say? Remember, want ads are not long. Take a look at them in your newspaper. Can you fit your top requests in a typical space? Veronica wrote this ad:

VERONICA'S AD

> ## Smart Woman Looking for a Very Good Man
>
> **Experience necessary. Minimum emotional requirements are:**
>
> No smokers. Social drinking OK. Weight according to height. Even-tempered. Caring. Open-minded. Affectionate. Manageable debts. Likes outdoor activities. Attends church. Has profession and disposable income. Age 29-40.

Now write an ad of your own. Revisit your ad occasionally and see what you add or drop.

> ## Good Man Wanted Now
>
> **Experience necessary. Minimum emotional requirements are:**
>
> _____
>
> _____
>
> _____
>
> _____ .

The next section will focus on how to expand your ability to combine your knowledge of your fears and needs with emotional bravery.

HOW CAN I REDUCE MY FEARS OF MAKING A MISTAKE IN LOVE?

Begin by reviewing the last exercises. They are your training wheels for knowing what you need, building emotional bravery and withstanding self-examination. The goal is to get mistake inoculation by acknowledging your fears and needs, being emotionally available and honest with yourself, and seeing your self-defeating behaviors as friends who warn you when you are about to become your own worst enemy. The following exercises will put you on the path to taking greater risks in love. They will help you tease out your very personal, deep-seated fears of opening your heart to love someone.

Worst Case Relationship Scenario

Complete these sentences:

I'm afraid that if I drop my guard, I'll...

My biggest fears about love are...

I have these fears because...

My best guess about my fears is that some of them are because in my family...

Some of the women in my study wrote that if they dropped their guards, they would never recover from the hurtful experiences that they assumed would occur with their partners. Many were afraid that their partners would lie or be insensitive.

Surprisingly, despite the career and education accomplishments of many of the women surveyed, they said that one of their biggest fears was that they wouldn't be good enough for their men or accepted by them. Review the sentences you completed. What are you learning about yourself?

Many of the women used their success journals to remind them of their achievement in managing a similar problem or fear in the past. After all, if you can do something once, you can do it twice, thrice and more. Here is a format that might be helpful:

Success Journal

1. Problem:
2. How I usually handled this fear or problem:
3. The reason I usually fell back on this ineffective approach:
4. What I did to handle this issue successfully:
5. What I did to become emotionally brave enough to manage this success:
6. How I can use this bravery to address the problem now:
7. What specifically I will do, not do or say:

Reread your journal to remind you of your successful ways of handling problems.

Use this boot camp exercise to do something that makes you look dumb. When you do something that you are not good at, the experience activates your sense of being flawed, unloved, unacceptable and not as defended as you think you need to be. As you do the task, you will not only become mindful of your fears, thoughts and defenses, but you will become accustomed to tolerating your fears so you don't have to erect self-defeating walls against feeling them.

Boot Camp Tasks to Reduce Feeling Flawed

1. Write down something you'd like to try but have felt too embarrassed or frightened to do, because you don't want to look incompetent. For example, you might want to learn to sing, paint or ice skate.
2. Do the activity with friends who care about you. Tell them why you are doing it.
3. Do the same or a different activity alone where no one knows you.

Many of the women I surveyed also felt emotionally naked when they were the ones who made a bad mistake with their partners. Embarrassing situations included getting a little too drunk, criticizing or misunderstanding the man, raising a sensitive topic with his family or having a disagreement in public.

These women worried that they had committed a deal-breaker. Ask yourself, "How would I want my man to manage his misstep if he acted as I did?" Wouldn't you expect him to offer an apology?

Don't protect your man from accepting you, rolling with the punches and managing your gaffes and emotional hurts. Wouldn't you want to know if your man has the capacity to forgive? Don't shield him from demonstrating to you whether he is good relationship material. One of the workshop exercises that could help is issuing a product recall.

ISSUE A PRODUCT RECALL.

Manufacturers sometimes issue recalls for cars, toys, medicine or food. The public often panics, but this reaction is usually short lived and soon consumers are buying goods from the same supermarket or toy store. Try issuing a product recall about yourself if you have stumbled in a relationship by overreacting or not presenting your best self. A product recall can be humorous but should be very serious and honest as well. You have a lot to lose by not gaining a deeper understanding of your man's character, by not trying to alter his incorrect assumption about you. Even first impressions can be changed.

Here is Cecily's product recall about saying something unsupportive to her boyfriend, Thomas. She e-mailed the message to him. Use it to help you write your own.

Important Notice of Cecily's New Product Recall

Cecily announces the recall of a previous conversation that made you wary of frequenting the Cecily product, issued on May 1, 2012. This conversation was produced in the Mind Factory of Cecily during a time of transition from an old facility with outdated equipment of fear and defensiveness to the newer facility with state-of-the-art equipment of emotional bravery and best-self behavior. This unkind and

---

immature Cecily product was an extremely rare event and she apologizes for the pain and inconvenience that her hurtful words in the previous conversation caused. She invites you with open arms and an open heart to spend time with her again since you are her most important consumer.

It worked. Cecily's recall accelerated her knowledge of Thomas's character. He offered more information about himself. "He felt safe that I was able to make mistakes—and then apologize. In a strange way, it made him trust me and see me as somebody who would accept him," she said. Think of a product recall you'd like to issue and write it.

Now you are ready to take a more educated—and braver—look at what you think are the flaws that prevent you from taking chances and recovering from mistakes. Do the following exercise to learn more about your self-assessment.

GO BEFORE THE LOVE JUDGE

Pretend that you live in an imaginary time in the future where the population has dwindled dramatically due to some cataclysmic event. Survival depends on forming intimate partnerships and family groups. The great judges of the new land have decreed that partners and family groups must be established, and that these partners must be able to solve their own problems with care and wisdom. Cases where positive and caring solutions cannot be resolved must go before one of the love judges. A judge will hear your story and provide a remedy so you can become your best self and benefit from the survival decree. Failure to take the love judge's advice could result in your banishment.

Imagine that your previous partner has hurt your feelings and that you cannot recover. You have avoided forming an intimate partnership. The word of your situation has been told to others and now you must go before the love judge to plead that you should be exempt from the decree of having to form an intimate partnership. You are standing in the high courtroom, and you tell the judge:

"Your Honor, I wish to be granted permission to be exempt from the partnership decree, and be allowed not to try any longer to search for and accept a partner, because there is something wrong with me. You are a caring judge, so I know you will exempt me when you learn my flaws, fears and reactions. Here is my list:"

If you need a refresher, look back at the list of things you selected in the box *What's Wrong with Me?* on page 268.

The judge has decided *not* to exempt you. He found good things in you. And he gave you good advice about how to overcome your issues. What advice and feedback do you think the judge gave you? Write down your ideas.

These exercises provide ways for you to increase your access to positive thoughts about yourself. But you probably aren't going to do all these exercises in the middle of your busy day. A good idea is to consult your success journal. This last exercise about facing and managing your fears is one that will help further develop your bravery and best self. Write it down and keep a copy in your drawer at work or in your handbag.

Walk and Talk with Your Fears

1. Make a list of events from your past that are crucial for a man to know about you—eventually. Imagine that you have to tell a new man or your existing partner about them.

2. Read your list *out loud* to yourself to experience which ones cause the most anxiety. Explain to yourself why these items cause you emotional pain.

3. Imagine the worst-case scenario of your man's responses. For example, envision what you are afraid he'll do or say when you tell him you have a history of depression or substance abuse. Change your brain's hard-wired emotions by practicing the discussion with him several times when you are by yourself. Each time you feel afraid, say out loud: "I can handle this. I am not my past."

4. Make a list of your good qualities and progress in bravery.

---

5. Make a list of the things you've helped your partner with, like managing his shortcomings and fears.

6. Tell your partner that you value him and want to be closer to him. Tell him you need his help in aiding your ability to face your struggles. Ask him to use the same approach that you used to help him.

7. Now, with your new knowledge and bravery, discuss the things that scare you the most to reveal.

Tips for Recovery from Mistakes, Hurts and Fears

Recognize your fear behavior and your attitude about making mistakes. Are you guarding your heart too much or avoiding dating? What self-defeating behaviors do you use to protect yourself? Have you fooled yourself by trying to believe that all men are high risks?

Understand your fears. Where do your fears come from? What have you generalized from your past experiences in love?

Build belief in your ability to recover. You want to trust in your judgment, but you can't always be right. Focus on fortifying belief in your inner strength to recover from all kinds of setbacks and betrayals.

Get a perspective on your fears and mistakes. Not all mistakes in love are mortal wounds. Learn to examine and rate your missteps so you can strengthen your capacity to open your heart to love.

Know your emotional needs in a relationship. Looking for a perfect man is a sure way to make sure that you never find anyone. Get realistic and become aware of your unique needs. There are no right or wrong personal needs.

Use your success journal. Remind yourself of how you managed to survive and triumph over emotional disasters.

Become brave enough to get divorced from your defenses. Give up your false view of yourself, so you won't live in fear and excuses all your life.

Closing Thoughts

I hope reading this book has been helpful and that you have become smarter about work, life and love. I want to leave you with some quick tips from the core ideas and advice that grew from my workshops, focus groups and lectures with so many brave women. Use them as a refresher to keep you on the track of being mindful of your reactions, choices, decisions and solutions to finding and maintaining a fulfilling love relationship.

Increase your tolerance of emotional self-examination. There is no way around this. Withstanding the temporarily acute pain of self-reckoning is worth the reward of happiness, inner strength and coping skills such as mindfulness. Get brave because you are worth it.

Develop emotional management regulation. Don't become afraid of feeling afraid. Feelings, in and of themselves, can't hurt you. Learn to act in spite of your feelings, especially when you are tempted to rely solely and early in a relationship on chemistry. Take time to observe your man in many settings. Postpone your urge to connect too quickly sexually.

Keep dating and relating. Don't wall your heart up because you've been hurt. Get back into life so you can learn about yourself and become stronger and braver emotionally. Don't become all work and no play.

Respect yourself. Develop a best self policy in relationships. Make sure you like who you are with men. Don't accept emotional crumbs and experience "death by a thousand accommodations."

Keep a success journal. Life will always be a challenge. When you find yourself falling back on old habits, read your journal. Refresh your memory of the skills, strengths and actions that helped you triumph.

Learn from your past. Examine your previous relationship patterns. Understand your family's influence and power without blaming them—or airbrushing them. Build bravery in comprehending your emotional family role, loyalty and comfort zone. Keep in mind that your parents' beliefs, lessons and reactions to you often say more about them than about you.

Know that you can improve and be happy. Bad childhoods are not like DNA—you can make some realistic changes. It's not where you come from but where you finish. You may not accomplish all your goals and you may not break through every love problem in your love ceiling, but it's important for you to know that you are working earnestly and honestly toward them.

You are not at the end. Well, technically, yes, you are. But this book is about keeping your eyes and heart open to yourself and your experiences. Happiness in life requires many trials and errors. The goal is always to learn from them. Rather than berate yourself emotionally for your missteps, get brave enough to study them, apply revisions and be proud that you picked yourself up and faced life and love again in honest and productive ways. And for that, you get an A in love.

Acknowledgements

There are so many people to thank. Most of all, I want to thank all the women who were truly generous and brave in telling me about their lives. It's not easy to look at yourself honestly. It's even harder to let someone else know about what you discovered about yourself.

I am grateful for my husband's ongoing support and cheering for me. I couldn't have taken all the hours away from our time together without his belief in me.

My friends, too, have listened to my thoughts and helped me clarify and challenge my ideas. I am especially appreciative of my dear, departed friend Erilda Waters as a source of inspiration and determination when I felt like just watching a classic movie on television instead of working.

The Women's Resource Center of Sarasota, Florida, has always given me the opportunity to conduct research and workshops. They are an amazing group of women.

This book would not be in your hands if it weren't for the guidance and professionalism of my talented team at www.radianttribes.com, the generosity and genius of Octavio Perez of the Ringling College of Art and Design and the staff of New Horizon Press.

Thank you all,
LB Wish

Notes

Chapter 5: Your Parents' Relationship

1. John M. Gottman, *The Seven Principles for Making Marriage Work*, (New York: Three Rivers Press, 2000).

Chapter 6: Mothers, Fathers and Family Loyalty

1. Martha Saxton, *Louisa May Alcott*, (New York: The Noonday Press, 1995).

Chapter 7: Myths, Facts, Cultural Messages and Affairs

1. Tom W. Smith, Peter V. Marsden and Michael Hout. General Social Survey, 1972-2010 [Cumulative File]. ICPSR31521-v1. Storrs, CT: Roper Center for Public Opinion Research, University of Connecticut/Ann Arbor, MI: Inter-university Consortium for Political and Social Research [distributors], 2011-08-05. doi:10.3886/ICPSR31521.v1, http://www.icpsr.umich .edu/icpsrweb/ICPSR/studies/31521?q=inidence+of+extramarital +affairs&permit[0]=AVAILABLE.
2. U.S. Divorce Rates and Statistics, "Divorce By The Statistics: It Doesn't Add Up," http://www.divorcesource.com/ds/main/u-s-divorce-rates-and -statistics-1037.shtml.
3. Robin Fretwell Wilson, "Keeping Women in Business (and Family)." Washington & Lee Legal Studies Paper No. 2008-34. http://papers.ssrn .com/sol3/papers.cfm?abstract_id=1115468.

4. Betsey Stevenson and Adam Isen, "Who's Getting Married? Education and Marriage Today and in the Past: A Briefing Paper Prepared for the Council on Contemporary Families," January 26, 2010, http://www.contemporaryfamilies.org/marriage-partnership-divorce/marriagemyths.html.

5. D'Vera Cohn, Jeffrey Passel, Wendy Wang and Gretchen Livingston, "Barely Half of U.S. Adults Are Married – A Record Low: New Marriages Down 5% from 2009 to 2010," December 14, 2011, http://www.pewsocialtrends.org/2011/12/14/barely-half-of-u-s-adults-are-married-a-record-low/.

6. Rose M. Kreider and Renee Ellis, "Number, Timing, and Duration of Marriages and Divorces: 2009" U.S. Department of Commerce, Economics and Statistics Administration, Household Economic Studies, May 2011, http://www.census.gov/prod/2011pubs/p70-125.pdf; Boy Scouts of America, "American Households and Populations," Environmental Scan 2012, http://www.scouting.org/filestore/media/ES_American_Households.pdf.

7. Wan He, Manisha Sengupta, Victoria A. Velkoff and Kimberly A. DeBarros, "65+ in the United States: 2005," U.S. Census Bureau, Current Population Reports, P23-209, (U.S. Government Printing Office, Washington, DC: 2005) http://www.census.gov/prod/2006pubs/p23-209.pdf.

8. Pew Research Center, "The Decline of Marriage And the Rise of New Families," November 18, 2010, http://www.pewsocialtrends.org/2010/11/18/the-decline-of-marriage-and-rise-of-new-families/2/.

Chapter 9: Your Body's Messages

1. "Happiness stats: The numbers behind anxiety and depression in women, from a survey by SELF and Discovery Health," http://www.self.com/health/2010/05/stats-for-anxiety-and-depression-in-women-slideshow#slide=1.

2. Jon Kabat-Zinn, *Full Catastrophe Living*, 15th ed. (New York: Delta, 2009).

3. Ibid.

4. Ibid.

Chapter 10: Cultural Messages about Women and Work

1. United States Census Bureau, "More Working Women Than Men Have College Degrees, Census Bureau Reports," http://www.census.gov/newsroom/releases/archives/education/cb11-72.html.

2. Current Population Survey, Bureau of Labor Statistics, "Table 11: Employed Persons by Detailed Occupation, Sex, Race, and Hispanic or Latino Ethnicity," Annual Averages 2012 (2013), http://www.catalyst.org/knowledge/women-medicine.

3. Philip Cohen, "More Women Are Doctors and Lawyers Than Ever—but Progress Is Stalling," The Atlantic (December 11, 2012), http://www.theatlantic.com/sexes/archive/2012/12/more-women-are-doctors-and-lawyers-than-ever-but-progress-is-stalling/266115/.

4. United States Census Bureau, "Census Bureau Releases 2010 American Community Survey Single Year Estimates," http://www.census.gov/newsroom/releases/archives/american_community_survey_acs/cb11-158.html; Robin Fretwell Wilson, "Keeping Women in Business (and Family)," Washington & Lee Legal Studies Paper No. 2008-34. Available at SSRN: http://ssrn.com/abstract=1115468.

5. State of Our Unions, "Executive Summary," http://stateofourunions.org/2010/SOOU2010.php.

6. The Center for Work-Life Policy, "Generation X: Overlooked and Hugely Important finds New Study from the Center for Work-Life Policy," https://www.worklifepolicy.org/documents/X%20Factor%20Press%20Release%20final.pdf.

7. Anne-Marie Slaughter, "Why Women Still Can't Have It All," The Atlantic Magazine (July/August 2012), http://www.theatlantic.com/magazine/archive/2012/07/why-women-still-cant-have-it-all/309020/.

8. Robert Frost, "Desert Spaces," http://www.poemhunter.com/poem/desert-places/.

Chapter 12: Work Dissatisfaction and Romantic Desperation

1. Gordon Marino, "Freud as Philosopher," The New York Times (October 9, 2011), http://opinionator.blogs.nytimes.com/2011/10/09/freud-as-philosopher/.

2. The Anxiety and Depression Association of America, http://www.adaa.org/about-adaa/press-room/facts-statistics.

3. "Suicide Facts at a Glance," http://www.cdc.gov/violenceprevention/pdf/suicide-datasheet-a.PDF.

4. Shaun Dreisbach, "Anxiety: The New Young Women's Health Crisis," Glamour Magazine (August 11, 2010), http://www.glamour.com/health-fitness/2010/08/anxiety-the-new-young-womens-health-crisis.

Chapter 15: Recovery from Past Hurts, Mistakes, Meltdowns and Suicide Attempts

1. Centers for Disease Control and Prevention. Web-based Injury Statistics Query and Reporting System (WISQARS) [Online]. (2010). National Center for Injury Prevention and Control, Centers for Disease Control and Prevention (producer). (June 23 2010), www.cdc.gov/injury/wisqars/index.html.; EG Krug, LL Dahlberg, JA Mercy, AB Zwi and R Lozano, editors. "World report on violence and health," May 2004, cited August 9,

2009, www.who.int/violence_injury_prevention/violence/world_report/wrvh1/en.

2. U.S. Suicide Statistics (2001), http://www.suicide.org/suicide-statistics.html.

3. "Suicide Facts at a Glance," http://www.cdc.gov/violenceprevention/pdf/suicide-datasheet-a.PDF.

4. Patricia Cohen, "Midlife Suicide Rises, Puzzling Researchers," *The New York Times* (February 19, 2008), http://www.nytimes.com/2008/02/19/us/19suicide.html?_r=0.

5. Sylvia Plath, "Daddy" from *Collected Poems*. Ed. Ted Hughes. (Harper-Collins: 1992), http://www.poetryfoundation.org/poem/178960.

Bibliography and Suggested Reading

Bowen, Murray. *Family Therapy in Clinical Practice*. New York: Jason Aronson, 1978.

Bowlby, John. *Attachment and Loss, Vol. 1: Attachment*. New York: Basic Books, 1982.

———, *Separation: anxiety and anger*. New York: Basic Books, 1973.

Gilbert, Daniel. *Stumbling on Happiness*. New York: Knopf, 2006.

Greenberger, Dennis, and Christine Padesky. *Mind Over Mood*. New York: Guilford Press, 1995.

Gottman, John M., and Nan Silver. *The Seven Principles for Making Marriage Work*. New York: Three Rivers Press, 2000.

Harvey, Steve. *Act Like a Lady, Think Like a Man*. New York: Amistad, 2009.

Kabat-Zinn, Jon. *Full Catastrophe Living*. New York: Delta, 1991.

Kantor, Elizabeth. *The Jane Austen Guide to Happily Ever After*. Washington, D.C.: Regnery, 2012.

Leman, Kevin. *The Birth Order Book*. Michigan: Revell, 2009.

McGraw, Phillip C. *Relationship Rescue*. New York: Hyperion, 2000.

Reiman, Tonya. *The Body Language of Dating*. New York: Gallery Books, 2012.

Seligman, Martin. *Learned Optimism*. New York: Vintage, 2006, reprint.

Shimoff, Marci. *Love for No Reason*. New York: Free Press, 2010.

Toman, Walter. *Family Constellation*. New York: Springer, 1976.